Wrestling Year B

Connecting Sunday Readings with Lived Experience

Wesley White

in medias res

In Medias Res, LLC
Publisher
Onalaska, WI

Wrestling Year B
Connecting Sunday Readings with Lived Experience

In Medias Res, LLC
imr.publisher@gmail.com

ISBN 978-0-9911005-2-1

White, Wesley
Wrestling Year B: Connecting Sunday Readings with Lived Experience / Wesley White

1. RELIGION / Biblical Meditations / Spirituality
2. Christian Rituals & Practice / Worship & Liturgy
3. Revised Common Lectionary

Dedicated to
Brenda Smith White
who listens people into being
who they intend to be
and much more

Foreword

On the heels of a year focused on the mystery of God, Wesley White now offers a volume that cracks open the scriptures with the challenge of bringing G*D's mercy to our daily living.

I've been a long-time visitor to Wesley's weekly lectionary blog, first to edify my personal engagement with the weekly texts and then, often, I bring Wesley's wrestling insight to the living realities of the community I serve from the pulpit.

Wesley's care-filled ordering, in this volume, gives colleagues and preaching aspirers a double-gifted resource— one that makes one squirm or smile personally and one that elevates the preacher/teacher's ability to bring the sacred to the street; both gifts are offered through the lens of justice that calls all of us into accountability.

This second bound volume offers a balanced and reflective theology of both head and heart that illumines the edges of our self-imposed and institutional boundaries and exposes the space for the merciful heart of God to beat through the work of the preacher/teacher/minister/servant.

In my early years of preaching I struggled to find resources that moved my heart and my mind. Then I found Wesley's lectionary blog! There, wrestling with God and Lectionary is grounded in common, real language anchored in justice, inclusion, and love with a vigorous (almost annoying – sorry Wesley) consistency that keeps me accountable to the heart of God and the gospel rather than safe in my own comfort zone.

Wrestling Year A and now *Year B* are my go-to resources as preaching guides and personal study resources for the work of pastoral ministry and daily discipleship.

Wesley White first caught my attention with his use of the * asterisk in his naming of G*D – expanding the meaning and potential right off the page and into my own experience and understanding. In *Wrestling Year A*, Wesley applied this visual and symbolic expansion to the definition of neighb*r. Brilliant! Faithful! Awesome! Praise be to God for the creative and co-creating work of Rev. Wesley White with gratitude for his willingness to engage in this endeavor. May he be blessed as we are blessed through its use to the glory of God in the celebration of ALL of God's creation.

Wesley, your words give me (us) courage to stand, to speak and to live the faith-filled way the Gospel (Jesus) points me (us) toward as I (we) strive to be fiercely hospitable to ALL.

Thank you for questions, for the prompts and new names; for the poems, prose and links and for the deep theological "pining". You bring us to the mat of justice and love as we wrestle with these year-long lections that point us toward God's incredible mercy.

Rev. Kelly R. Fowler
Ministering with the people of the
Reconciling Congregation of Bay View UMC
Milwaukee, WI

Preface

Every time through an established cycle brings new insight. Our experiences change and prepare us with renewed courage to practice what we are now seeing. This is a place of Joy that doesn't regret "being too late smart", but knows it is for "such a time as this" that we are now ready to make a journey to a next level or stage of life. Others were gifted with responsibility in the past to call out, "Danger! This way!" and others will be so gifted tomorrow. Today, though, this is our year.

As this commentary was being put together from writings of the past, it became evident that this is a year to emphasize Mercy. The blog comments selected or newly written to complete this cycle contained numerous references to mercy, which appear to have been aspirational, and the word "mercy" was used as a matter of course. Mercy is a wonderfully religious word that has covered over the necessity to actually be merciful in everyday living. May Mercy ring out this year.

Last year emphasized the mystery of G*D and how much more there is than can be put into a word. In fact, making G*D into a proper noun (God) constrains said God to the cultural and religious norms of the day—we get to define God rather than enter into a living partnership with a living G*D.

My use of "G*D" follows an idea from Rustrum Roy in his 1979 Hibbert Lectures, *Experimenting with Truth*. Roy uses an unfamiliar cloud-of-dots symbol 🏵 to represent "God". I use an asterisk (*) between a "G" and a "D" rather than a random pattern of dots, but the intent is the same—to blur or thin the boundaries within which G*D has been trapped by language. An asterisk stands for "more can be found elsewhere, so look in another place for what is not here".

Later, I added "Neighb*r" to help me remember how easily I limit neighbor to those I am comfortable with. May these shocks to the eye slow down your reading to consider what we know about what we say.

There is more to G*D than God, more to Neighb*r than neighbor, and a greater degree of humility in our language is in order.

This volume is inconsistent in the use of capital letters and *. This represents my own growing into a new way that always seems to come with fits and starts. May you find the absence of an * as fruitful a place to wonder about your partnerships as an * pushing its agenda of pushing boundaries.

This book continues references to alternative names for the days and seasons of a Church Year. By our names we are known and, currently, there is simply too much baggage with the received names for feast days and seasons. If they do not carry meaning beyond the religious realm, they have lost half their power. My renamings are only a draft and await your edit and use in everyday life.

One significant reason the church has plateaued is that we talk and pronounce outside the realm of everyday reality. In book language, publishing without marketing is an exercise in futility. In biblical language, we become hearers of a new word but stop short of doing or being a new word. In life language, I have found wrestling with a received text to be life-giving.

What began as an exercise in participatory education has become an exercise in disclose(t)ing what my bottom-line affirmation of life is and a willingness to let it lead me to divest from a loyalty based on habit and reinvest in affirming actions, even if this disrupts my life and the lives of those around and about.

My engagement with these four websites gives evidence of this growth:

> *Wisconsin United Methodist Federation for Social
>   Action* (wumfsa.org)
>   continuing the tradition of Peace and Justice within
>   The United Methodist Church
>
> *Kairos CoMotion* (kairoscomotion.org)
>   bringing liberal religious education to Wisconsin
>   United Methodists
>
> *Love on Trial* (loveontrial.org)
>   being on the defense team for Rev. Amy DeLong
>   when the Wisconsin United Methodist Church
>   tried her for officiating at a Holy Union and
>   being a "self-avowed practicing homosexual"
>   (a terrible, institutional, depersonalizing phrase)
>
> *Love Prevails* (loveprevailsumc.com)
>   advocating direct action to change The United
>   Methodist policies regarding LGBTQQIAA persons

Being able to wrestle with the texts of the Revised Common Lectionary has brought me deeper into the direct action of Love and Justice as expressions of a larger Mercy. Here is another way of putting this: If faith, Hope, and Love do not result in Mercy, a false Faith, Hope, and/or Love has crept into my life.

What is offered here are thoughts I blogged to help me see where there may be a crack in our usual way of reading the Christian scrip-

tures to touch again some primal energy from Annunciation (a Creation of the World) to the present. These thoughts, along with experience within a congregation, began the sermon preparation process I
used while an appointed pastor.

One of the readers of the first of this series of lectionary comments (*Year A*) spoke with me about the inordinate number of questions that are present here. They noted that this is a different approach
than the usual meditational material they read for their own spiritual
growth. This conversation reminded me that I expect more of a resource than something to assent to. At their best, these offerings invite
another look at one portion of our spiritual grounding, a wrestling
with scripture.

Notes on Format: Even though there are usually four scriptures
designated for each Sunday of the church year, they are presented
here in book order rather than calendar order. While tempted to use
the Jewish order for the Hebrew readings, I will stick with a traditional
Protestant Christian ordering. This allows reading the over-arching
story as a devotional book while also providing a relatively easy way
to find the four readings. If there is a question about what the peri-
copes for a given date are, go to lectionary.library.vanderbilt.edu/ for
the chapter and verse and to www.textweek.com/ for all manner of
resources regarding the readings.

An Appendix contains a chart of the seasonal variants used in this
book. I look forward to hearing how you have improved on these alternative names of the Sundays of a Church Year. In this and other
ways, we encourage one another to engage and modify tradition
through current experience.

What some have called poetry, because of a visual presentation of
phrasal fragments strung together, is a modified Cut Up process used
by William Burroughs. I simply call these Fragments.

Mercy and Joy abound
take plenty
and some to pass around

Wesley White . . . October 2014 and 2025

For the greatest benefit,
remember to read the Biblical text
immediately before proceeding to the comment.

Genesis 1:1–5
Guiding Gift [1] — Beloved

These five verses set an important tone of blessing: an assurance that care has been given and will be given. A case can be made for these being the most important five verses in the Bible. Come back and visit them regularly

Let's listen in to Everett Fox from *The Five Books of Moses* as we first find ourselves *in medias res*, between evening and morning.

> *At the beginning of God's creating*
> *of the heavens and the earth,*
> *when the earth was wild and waste,*
> *darkness over the face of Ocean,*
> *rushing-spirit of God hovering over the face of the waters—*
>
> *God said: Let there be light! And there was light.*
> *God saw the light: that it was good.*
> *God separated the light from the darkness.*
> *God called the light: Day! and the darkness he called: Night!*
> *There was setting, there was dawning: one day.*

G*D brings order out of an empty darkness of chaos.

G*D is like "an eagle protecting its young" (Fox footnote)—Ruah hovers.

The eagle speaks, "You are my beloved. Let there be light! Let me see you."

Order comes – separation – setting/dawning

Later, Baptism comes to parallel Creation – separation – repentance/forgiveness

- Who are "your young" that you will protect?
- Who is not "your young" that you will let fall back into chaos?
- Who are you? In whose image are you living?

Can you separate cultural from rushing-spirit values? Can you live in an empty darkness between the setting of civic religion and the dawning of rushing-spirit with an appreciation of ambiguity, without being crushed?

In the setting and dawning of this day, a blessing begins and continues to bloom. Join it.

Genesis 1:1–2:4a
Hopeless Hope Vigil — Live Together

An important threesome can be helpfully related to a reflection on a "trinity" – Environment, Humans, Sabbath – a Theology of Blessing.

> The creation narrative is a statement about the blessing God has ordained into the processes of human life. Three times the term "blessing" is used: of living creatures (v. 22), of human creatures (v. 28), and of the sabbath (2:3). God's action is sometimes regarded as extrinsic to life, essentially alien to it, and even in some tension with it. There is a tendency in some theological traditions to articulate a deep gulf between the goodness of God and the unhealthiness of the world. Sometimes the "otherness" of God is linked to the depravity of the world. Curiously, this is articulated both in some forms of Reformation thought and in Gnostic traditions. But here that gulf is denied. The world itself is a vehicle for the blessings God has ordained in it as an abiding characteristic.

> [*Genesis* by Walter Bruggemann in the Interpretation series]

Imagine with Bruggemann, Matthew Fox, and others, ancient and contemporary, who describe a theology of blessing. Is there any better way of beginning a story? "Once upon a time" means we have grown from that time to this. A blessing of opportunity sets the stage for our current reflection on and appreciation of life in its glorious particularity and diversity. A blessing grows from "Once upon a time".

A whole series of once-upon-a-times have built us to this time and place and community. For now, it may be enough to remember that this moment will become a later once-upon-a-time starting point for a blessing realized. After a bit more practice with blessing-it-forward, we will better appreciate Native Peoples' insight that we do best when we anticipate seven generations of echoes of our decisions.

In what might be described as a Year of Blessing, this starting point will continue to resonate. Listen for it.

Genesis 2:18–24
Proper 22 (27)

"Deep sleep" connects to creation time when darkness hovered over the face of the deep.

In a sense, creation keeps going and going, just like that pink bunny. It comes out of the deep and the dark. Then comes a word, an act, and a spark of light—a mere glimmer sometimes—to awaken a weary world to new hope.

This month, two congregations here will be doing an online study of an older resource, *The Wounded Healer* by Henri Nouwen. From a deep and dark night of the soul comes a glimpse of being bound together when it feels like everything is being torn and ripped open in preparation for abandonment and death.

In the wound is the healing; in the deep sleep is the awakening.

The deep sleep of Eden and flood and slavery and captivity and crucifixion and the dark ages and the present age is intended to awaken us to a new day, a new earth, and a new heaven.

In *Thy Nature and Thy Name is Love: Wesleyan and Process Theologies in Dialogue*, Michael E. Lodahl's chapter, we hear:

> ...there is a somewhat insidious implication of *creatio ex nihilo* that should be brought to light and expunged: The doctrine often seems to imply that God works like a magician who pronounces "Presto" and pulls a rabbit (i.e., the world) out of his or her top hat (i.e., nothing). In this picture, the creation of the universe appears perfunctory and arbitrary with little, if any, real investment or care on the Creator's part—a picture that lends itself to a devaluing of the world and our lives in it. It is safe to say that this is not, and cannot be, what Christians (or Jews or Muslims) mean by creation out of nothing. The particularly Christian conviction that God has created by the Word—the Word that became flesh in the person of Jesus of Nazareth—belies any hint of arbitrariness or caprice in God's act of creation, suggesting instead that creation is the deliberate expression of divine love revealed at Gethsemane and Golgotha. In this case, perhaps *creatio ex nihilo* might be well-complemented by: God creates out of (and as an expression of) self-giving, creative love....

What in you has been created by love? Is that enough? What of you is creating out of love? Is that enough?

Sleep deep. Awaken refreshed, a new creation.

Genesis 3:8–15
Proper 5 (10)

Who is in and who is outside of family? Likewise, what is in and what is out?

In politics, we have desired a leader who will lead us into war unending and more taxes for the poor. Patriotism is the measure of family?

In relationships, we have internal secrets that heighten our fear, so one lie leads to a next. Your lie justifies my lie and mine, yours. Co-conspiracy is the measure of family?

In religion, we are determined to have G*D's love both steadfast (enduring forever) and doubtful (do not forsake me). We cry to be heard, even if all we have to say is confession, appealing for forgiveness with a claim it is for G*D's glory rather than our benefit. Justification is the measure of family?

In identity, we continue to be who and what we are. If not in this world, we will claim it in eternity—never letting go. Pride and greed are measures of family?

In biology, we are to protect our genes, blood being thicker than water. Genetics is the measure of family?

And then the questions get deeper. Who is my family beyond all our usual measures? Those who do not give up on hope of better than we have! This cuts across all political, religious, personal, and racial/cultural lines. Here we can find common cause in the widest of families: openness to new learning.

I give thanks with all my heart
strung out with commitments
to you and you and you

voluntarily enslaved to you
my heart knows liberation
because of other commitments

so many families I already have
rubbing each other the wrong way
dividing and falling

so many families I dream of holding
creating dancing imagining
fertilizing each other as well

pray may our frictions
not bring burning heretics
but pentecost wonder sharing

my village of families
invites your village
to an easy evening

kings and slaves dissolve
creator and creation resolve
division questions salved

Genesis 7:1–5, 11–18; 8:6–18; 9:8–13
Hopeless Hope Vigil

Signs of a new covenant are not present before the covenant is in place. There is no predicting that the building of an ark and loading it with a potential new earth will actually bear fruit.

Noah is not so much righteous as preternaturally anxious—should a flood come, how would we deal with that? This vision of an ark was made for Noah, and he for it. The others involved all had their own reasons for dealing with Noah's compulsive response to his question. And so we journey with Noah and his wife Emzara, Shem and Sedeqetelebab, Ham and Ne'elatama'uk, and Japheth and 'Adataneses. [Note: These names are from the *Book of Jubilees*. While recognizing different traditions have different names for the wives—we again ask, "What's with the patriarchy?"]

We could spend hours with the imponderables of who was on the ark and why. Even putting all the various tales together wouldn't get us any closer to the surprise of a new covenant.

We all know we are trapped in an expectation that the future will be more of the present. To expect more or different is just foolishness. We got on the ark to escape death, not to arrive at a new and different life. We even expect that plants will survive even if animals don't because we didn't bring seeds to plant, just as food for the interim.

Repeating this or any of the other creation or re-creation stories leaves us on a wheel moving of its own accord or resurrecting the old to go through it again. A vigil question is how to be open for yet another sign beyond that of a 7th Day/Sabbath or Eden East or Rainbow or Passover or Jericho or Cross or Empty Tomb. What sign today will lead us past our debilitating angst?

Genesis 9:8–17
Conviction [1]

Covenants change. This is a blessing.

A prior covenant had folks being vegetarians. Here, the covenant shifts to that of our being omnivorous (vs 3). This leads to a trick covenant. God covenants with all living things not to drown them out again (maybe a fire next time, but not a flood). Instead, we can do one another in. Humans can eat enough chickens that it becomes a commercial enterprise with only a bottom line to care for, not the care of chickens. So what that their legs aren't strong enough to hold them up before they are slaughtered. Chickens are slyer than they look. They can't battle themselves out of cages, but they can sneak a bird flu through the bars to do in their tormenters. The next generation of chickens may well be truly free-range.

When was the last time you connected the rainbow with Mother Gaia setting things right, providing justice for chickens?

Rainbows take a moment of light in the presence of suspended water and diffract such light into many lights. From one comes many. When we have our rainbow lenses in place, we find our own life and that of others to be scattering many-hued evidences of opportunity. When we have our reverse-rainbow lenses on, we try, ultimately unsuccessfully, to bring all those colors back to one (our own), as though life does not advance into the joy of greater complexity.

A rainbow is a covenant to fast from flooding. Made in G*D's image, we, too, are to fast from flooding others out when they don't measure up to our desires. What is a positive corollary to the rainbow? What are we fasting toward here? Has the prettiness/form of the rainbow obscured its result of watering down a prior covenant? Is this an early example of fooling us with forms/titles like Healthy Forests, so old-growth forests can be cut, Clear Skies to allow more pollution of the air, and Iraqi Freedom to preemptively destroy the infrastructure of another nation?

What disingenuous language is going on in your congregation, and how might it be brought to light and healing?

Genesis 17:1–7,15–16
Conviction 2

Anytime we get into conditional covenants (the proof of the covenant is in some improbable future), we find ourselves conflicted. How long do we stay with hope? How soon do we fall on our face laughing that we ever considered being a party to this farce?

Of course, we can always fall back on the equally difficult to prove issues of testing (we are just being tested, so never think twice) and plans (God has a plan in mind that will come to pass simply because it is God's plan and God is all-powerful and unchanging). Of the two, testing is the easier concept, but neither is very satisfactory and requires an inordinate amount of denial of experience.

Abram and Sarai did pretty well, all things considered, with hanging in well past any reasonable time frame to see a promised result. There was a little side-track through Hagar (but how can we honestly dismiss Hagar and Ishmael so?—only if we are so captured by some storyline that what happens to people doesn't matter as long as G*D comes out of it smelling like a rose).

Here then is a covenantal conflict—between our love of G*D and our love of self/neighbor/tribe.

A covenant without a present blessing every bit as significant as some future promise is simply a contract.

Genesis 22:1–18
Hopeless Hope Vigil

There's a song popularized by the Mills Brothers:

You always hurt the one you love
The one you shouldn't hurt at all
You always take the sweetest rose
And crush it till the petals fall

You always break the kindest heart
With a hasty word you can't recall
So If I broke your heart last night
It's because I love you most of all

words: Allan Roberts
music: Doris Fisher

What strange things we project onto love. Can you really love sinners without really simply loving sinners? Can you love G*D and then go all the way to hurting a loved one in your heart (if not in deed —stopping one ram short of sacrifice)?

"Love me more (and more and more and more)" is an appeal to betrayal of other loves.

In an Edenic garden, no slack was given; G*D sacrificed G*D's own image. At the beginning of this story, still no slack is given; Abraham is to sacrifice his own image. This is either profoundly counterintuitive or just dumb. What have you found about losing your life for the sake of another? What have you found about the cost of not losing your life?

What we are looking for here is a shifting point that moves from "prove your love to me by betraying another love" to "Stop that!"

Exodus 12:1–4, (5–10), 11–14
Courage Thursday

This is to be the first month of the rest of your life.
    Did you know that?
This is the day the Lord has made.
    Did you know that?
This moment is to echo on.
    Did you know that?
There is no other time for freedom than now.
    Did you know that?

Yes, there have been previous acceptable years of jubilee, and months, days, moments. They have played their part in bringing us to this time. Each has been a blessing in its time.

In anticipating and remembering, we are bold to be in a hurry to set things right. Are you doing what you can in conversation and action?

Yes, we have had our hopes raised and dashed before, but a part of who we are is found in the meaning of never giving up on freedom.

A part of our freedom is to pray for the rear-guard of days gone by. Someday, we will measure people by "the content of their character" not color, gender-preference, labor-status, class, or any other cultural boundary. That someday is already assured, and we will speed its arrival with our boldly living as if someday were today.

So, workers of the world, unite! We have nothing to lose but our chains!

This old, but venerable chant begun by prophets of old, reshaped by Karl Marx and Friedrich Engels, and used by the Wobblies, needs to be heard again and again wherever people are in cultural and religious bondage (yes, the two do go hand in hand).

Exodus 14:10–31; 15:20–21
Hopeless Hope Vigil

An act of liberation has more than one moment of desperation. There is an easy movement toward termination with extreme prejudice: "We are going to die". This is also true before personal transformations: "I'm going to die".

We go through all manner of last-minute bargains. Almost any humiliation will be considered. Here, it is a bargain to return to slavery rather than die.

Before too easily taking off our shoes to walk on the mystery of resurrection of a people or ourself, it is important to vigil deeply enough to experience this sense of being trapped before generating a spark in the dark in hope of a wick.

It is not enough to read the despair of old without facing the fear of today and a lack of vision for tomorrow.

Before coming in from the cold and dark, speak as clearly as possible where your hope has run up against a vast nothing, such as that in the writings of Michael Ende (*The Neverending Story* and *Momo*).

Until this boundary is acknowledged and re-experienced, any light shed our way becomes an impediment. Avoiding "Nothing" as a category of life leads us to a false understanding of where lies our blockage to full life.

No chaos, no creation. No chaos, no resurrection. No chaos, no dancing.

Exodus 15:1b–13, 17–18
Hopeless Hope Vigil

Do you remember the biggest moral equivalent of a "roadside bomb"? — G*D and Moses and the Red Sea!

How did you first react to this passage? With joy because you identified with trapped Israelites? With sorrow because of the insanity of persecution?

Have you kept to your first reading, or have you found another perspective from which to view such events?

Miriam dances her response. How would you use your body to demonstrate your response?

Was it for such a time as this that cloud and fire had led the Israelites? Are we again proving a G*D's need for praise, demonstrating the essential weakness of a chosen people needing saving, time after time?

This praise doesn't last all that long. Moses, who used a staff to beat water into rock, will soon be baited into beating a rock into water. Neither of these grand actions move the story along; we are kept in a retributive and reactive mode.

When there is no Truth and Reconciliation process, forgiveness is not forthcoming. New life is held in abeyance. So threats continue to be made, lacking any wisdom or different model. In response, a defensive action becomes offensive. And we are set up for further conflict, both internal (golden calves and rampaging death) and external (seeing giants and committing genocide).

Imagine a vigil that represents a loss of hope from being trapped between an army and a sea. What would that look like in the moment, not what would it look like from the other side of the sea?

This is the same tension we have with an Easter Vigil. It is difficult to sufficiently be days into death and still wait for a visitation. This is a tension we have with every difficulty come through. We all too easily become the hero of the story after a resurrection, and our sense of desperation at the time fades.

In whatever trap you sense yourself currently engaged, may you have the blessing of a hopeless hope to see you through.

Exodus 16:2–4, 9–15
Proper 13 (18)

What we experience as freedom, others experience as great discomfort. Images and experience of a G*D beyond theism, seeing creation as a flowing river rather than a series of start-up points, and placing a culture of welcoming hospitality over the rules of time-specific doctrine, all allow differing responses of freedom and discomfort.

To yank people into a desert of reliance upon experience rather than regularity of structure does cause discomfort for them beyond their previous discomfort. It is no wonder that complaints come. In fact, this response might be expected.

One of the questions here is whether the experience of meat and potatoes (quail and manna—"¿What is it?") came as a prediction or an interpretation.

Our tendency is to want a prediction, but the words are crafted to assist folks to see in a new way so they can move from discomfort to comfort by taking small steps toward freedom. This can be seen as a story moving on a continuum between comfort and freedom.

One of the reasons I am attracted to the "freedom" end of life is that the stated purpose of the quail and ¿manna? is to assure people that G*D is G*D and is on their side. Obviously, this result doesn't come about in any lasting way. Any evidence that G*D is on our side slips and slides away and is open to misuse. [Later, the people will choose the known desert with its ¿manna? over going into a land overflowing with milk and honey—people don't know how to easily separate their experience of G*D with them from the particulars of an event and choose to keep the details rather than experience G*D with new options.]

A part of the work of an apologist has to do with what Moses did: define what is already in front of people—their experience—as the presence of G*D.

In the midst of the ¿manna? of life, may you experience G*D and aid others in experiencing G*D in the midst of the ¿manna? of their life.

Exodus 20:1–17
Conviction [3]

So, how would you redact this version of 10 commanding words?

Are the many more words about idolatry and Sabbath than the other commands needed because these are necessarily more complex and subtle than the rest? Can we really simplify these, or do they need more said about them because of the little ways they can be subverted?

Wherever you come out on that matter, the harder questions are those beyond commands. Are you comforted by Moses' response, urging us to have no fear because this is only a test to see how fearful (awe-full) we can get? I suspect that our rejoinder to Moses may well have been, "O, right! There's no reason for us to be afraid; it's only a test we can't pass. How could we have been so foolish – Not! We're still afraid!"

This response seems to be implicit because of the way the story proceeds, and THE LORD goes on to give law upon law. And now the Israelites are corroborated in their fear—"Who, now, can do anything without going down in flames? Ten we could deal with, but hundreds?!"

During these days of Lent, it might be good to remember the principle of a Selichot Prayer and its revelation of mercy before, after, and during a test.

In light of steadfast love and mercy, failure can be borne.

Thank goodness for the comfort of steadfast love that hedges us round and mercy readily applied.

Woe for thinking any number of commands will suffice for adequately participating in the messiness of life. Woe for choosing more and more comfort over enough and reality.

––––––––––––––

Now, in light of this passage, a pop-quiz:

1) If you were to name your place of safety that allows your prophetic side to take the risks it needs, what would you name?

2) If you were to name your place of imposed boundary, from the outside or inside, that keeps you from maturing, what would you name?

Numbers 6:22–27
Naming Day

When people think of you, what characteristics are attached to your name? One intention we might have is to have our gravestone etched with our best blessing, whether or not our name is also there.

If that is a desired end, we need to be attending to that blessing while we live.

Aaron and his sons receive a secondary word from G*D about how they are to bless the people. These are G*D's words, but we know them as Aaron's. Likewise, it is possible for folks to hear additional blessings and have them be connected with our name.

> *You are blessed and blessings are anticipated from you!*
> *The light of creation shines on you with everyday grace!*
> *Kindness and Peace attend your way as you attend to them!*

With or without a LORD's name attached, there is blessing aplenty for all who receive such a blessing and begin to practice its presence.

Consider your name, your breathing, your visage is to be a blessing for you have been blessed. This paradigm articulated during Abram's time is to be carried on. It may or may not change your name, but it won't change your blessing.

Here are two blessings I have used over the years:

> *take care*
> *dream strong*
> *smile gentle*
> *and so go well*

> *Mercy and Joy abound*
> *take plenty*
> *and some to pass around*

Write your current blessing here.

Numbers 11:4–6, 10–16, 24–29
Proper 21 (26)

We have, all of us, been sold. We have sold ourselves and those dear to us. Pottage is that cheap. We have sold our children into the hands of boredom and violence. Our willingness to sell is that great. We have sold our enemies to death and hurried them on their way that we might get our bargain.

In our buying and selling of self and others, we lose track of where deeds of power reside—outside of market economies. When we see a deed of power beyond our control, we get jealous and covetous. It is so easy to forget that whoever is not against us is for us, and when a deed of power is accomplished—no matter to whom it is directed or through whom it comes—all are benefited.

---

anyone sick
anyone anyone
it's time for a day off
we will wander
and it will save our soul
a multitude of sins
will be blessed
and grown from

[*With thanks to Ferris Bueller*]

Numbers 21:4–9
Conviction [4]

The poisonous language of complaint usually ends up in a community that bites each other. Any way one turns, there is a complaint ready to strike. Everyone is a heel to be struck and a heel who strikes.

In a poisonous context, working from the inside is no longer an option for healing. Healing will come from the outside. A discipline or methodology needs to be designed and followed, for poison is too strong to fight against on one's own, and poison breeds poison—that which we abhor, we do; that which we intend, we don't.

Look clearly at the result—a complaint becomes a snake. Look clearly at this connection. Perhaps by turning it around and seeing the snake on its way (still on a pole, but ready to descend to bite me instead of you), we might yet change our complaining ways.

Can such clarity stop a consequence simply by seeing it? Here, clarity is prayer. Prayer for a larger context. Prayer of thanks. Prayer for mercy. Prayer for deeds of light.

In this Lenten season, prayer is not just duty, but a lens through which we might yet see more clearly. Or, as St. Richard of Chichester prayed in the 13th century and the Shrine of St. Jude modified for use as a midday prayer in the 21st:

> Merciful Friend, Brother and Redeemer
> May I know you more clearly
> Love you more dearly
> And follow you more nearly
> Day by day.

[May this prayer be more, this day, than a pious covering of crusade preaching (complaint) against another faith; Richard did have his limits and blind-spots, as do we all.]

> a serpent is raised as a question mark
> "is this what you want to become"
> that question twines itself around our lives
>
> a messiah is raised as an exclamation mark
> "come on in life is fine"
> that call echoes within and through our lives
>
> a singular you is raised to take them both
> and demonstrate that steadfast love endures
> that good works are . . . our way of life

Numbers 21:4b–9
Relic Day

These words from Everett Fox in *The Five Books of Moses*:

> The strange events surrounding the "viper of copper" … provide a reminder, even amid the progress of the march and military successes, of the Israelites' usual waywardness. As usual, the problem is food; several things, however, make this brief story unusual amid the rebellion narratives. For one, the punishment is unique; for another, the people call upon Moshe to remove the plague—in a manner that is more reminiscent of Pharaoh of Egypt, with the Plagues, than of previous Israelite behavior. Finally, there is the Bible's record of what happened to the copper object: it was preserved in the cult and worshiped by the people, until it was smashed during the large-scale religious reform under King Hezekiah of Judah….

On this day, when relics are at the forefront, we would note that the cross developed over time as a cultic object for Christians to signify their claimed unity. It has been worshiped for longer than was the bronze or copper snake.

At question is how much longer the cross will hold as an institutional sign before a reform occurs to demote it to optional use and eventually to non-use. This will probably take a revision of the sacrificial atonement theology that has sprung up around it.

Before a cross became "the" sign of a follower of Jesus, there were fish and trees. Our expectation is that some circular form will be used in days to come. The Yin-Yang and Ouroboros have been taken, but some form of the potential of emptiness will be needed as we corporately move on to a next integral level. How we image the dynamics of emptiness is a worthy endeavor. Yes, holding an image and empty together is a paradox too far. Nonetheless, here is the image from Love Prevails that frees them to deal creatively with the Church Institutional:

to see it in color go to LovePrevailsUMC.com

Deuteronomy 4:1–2, 6–9
Proper 17 (22)

Listen, give heed to the rules and regulations that life may improve tomorrow as we live them today.

It is important that more than hearing was asked—the practice of doing what is heard. Listening, as an operative word, suggests a desire for understanding. Understanding means paying attention to the dynamic of the rule. Now, given our particular starting point, if we put what we have heard into practice, what is the intended result?

When the dynamic is listened to, and not just the rule stated, it becomes possible to live according to the spirit of the law and make needed adjustments as the circumstances of a journey to a desired outcome change and are clarified.

When this dynamic is set aside and we have only words heard, it becomes required to hold to the letter of the law, no matter what. When a creed takes over, it doesn't matter what we have learned along the way or how different the circumstances now are in which the words are to be active. Without practice, it isn't long before the current helpful words become inappropriate and counter-productive in a next setting.

To extend verse 9, we may hear:

> Be careful to not forget these things that you have seen with your own eyes and heard with your own ears. May they always be with you. Teach them and, in teaching them, have your eyes and ears open for what you are about to see and hear. Passing on both past and present to your children and children's children will aid them in engaging your tomorrow, their new day.

Listen, give heed, you may even begin to learn from changed circumstances and find yourself saying, "You have heard me say it, but now...."

Deuteronomy 5:12–15
Guiding Gift [9] — Proper 4 (9)

It is one thing to acknowledge the value of a period of rest in the midst of a never-ending creation. It is quite another to insist that others come to the same insight.

Coercion of behavior appears to be important for the survival of young ones. Their ability to travel life without the accumulated wisdom of the ages is greatly reduced without cultural norms. While constraint long enough to encode behavior found to be helpful has value, there comes a time when it ceases to benefit and becomes a constraint that reduces both the individual and the tribe to what has been.

Every system of child rearing begins to erode into the grandest of peer pressures—Thou shalt see it as the emperor sees it. This is not a negative, but a positive constraint; the hardest to avoid.

This is revealed in the lines about servants who are to rest because the master rests. This seems a good thing, but reveals the hard-and-fast rule of what is to be a natural rhythm.

What would it mean to learn our different bio-rhythms and seasons so well that we would listen to them? A hard-and-fast Sabbath insulates, isolates, and immunizes us to both our own rhythm and that of others.

Should we come to learn our rhythm, it wouldn't be long before we would need to recognize that simply leaving it to everyone to decide their own Sabbath runs as great a risk as only having a corporate Sabbath.

Eventually, we would not want to set these at odds with one another but affirm both our own rhythm and that of the group. Sometimes these would be in sync, and sometimes not. In either case, we would take our time of renewal alone and our time of renewal together as complements of one another, not competitors.

Imagine two Sabbaths a week; mine and yours.

Imagine two Sabbaths a week; yours and ours.

We may even begin to imagine unenslaving and sharing service.

Deuteronomy 6:1–9
Proper 26 (31)

The command for Israel to love God becomes one of Deuteronomy's most distinctive doctrines, acting as an important corrective to the emphasis upon awe and fear in worship.

(*New Interpreter's Study Bible* note on verse 5)

This is something worth telling to our kids and friends and others: *Love trumps Fear*.

In recent days, we have not done so well with this affirmation. Its latest iteration comes at it from around the corner of "No Fear". I'll be glad when we can get back to the Love language as an affirmation rather than the more brittle entrenchment of, "Don't Fear".

Deuteronomy 18:15–20
Guiding Gift [4]

A distinction between prophet and false-prophet is whether or not they say only what is known. To go beyond what is known is to begin to please one party or another. To begin to please the privileged powerful is to lay oneself open to not be able to call them to account. This is prophetic idolatry.

One of the hardest struggles is to not say more than one knows. The temptation is always to look good in someone's eyes by adding just a little bit until finally life is simply, as Gallagher would have it, about "style". Behind this is some form of manipulation of others through information enhancement.

Can you imagine going through a day saying only what you know —no little extras added to a storyline, no explaining G*D, no elaborations? In such a way, we more clearly reveal the world. *Being There* by Jerzy Kosinski, gives a literary example of not saying more than you know. No matter how simple, there is great authority garnered by not making up what isn't known.

I sometimes propose this as an antidote for the sense of entitlement that leads to each of the seven deadly sins. By simply slightly-inflating the situations of life, we lose touch with the presence of G*D.

It seems court prophets, looking out for their own profit, have proliferated over time. There is no shortage of pundits (today's spelling of prophet). Would that they understood the importance of speaking carefully, lest they be considered heedless and cast away.

Most true prophets end up getting heartburn as they live between a compulsion to speak and a fear to speak beyond what they know. Most false prophets end up prospering under whatever political system they are currently working.

Just know that the next prophet is coming from the people, just like you. And it may well be you. Enjoy the ride.

Joshua 24:1–2a, 14–18
Proper 16 (21)

One issue at hand is how much we build our relationship with G*D on past events. In Joshua's recounting of the Israelite history and the people's shorter version, we hear some of the highlights of past relationships. This leads to the middle of verse 18 and that powerful word, "therefore".

We get caught in a lot of therefores, on the horns of various dilemmas. We also get caught without a therefore when we remember when we were very, very good and, at the same time, fail to remember when we were horrid.

This may be part of the choice Joshua talks about. Choose to remember and move on. Choose to remember and not repeat. Choose to remember how surprising the past was and choose to be ready to be surprised again.

When we can remember the marvel of the many moments of coming through and not just the fact of coming through, we are able to shift into an active anticipation of a future and a willingness to be present in the present. This is a very different orientation than remembering and therefore-ing.

In light of another conversation from Ephesians 5, we may need to also look at the word "serve" in this verse. What does it mean to submit to, to serve, to mutually love and respect G*D's next encounter with us when we so easily get caught in only justifying our obedience, service, etc., on the basis of what we have so far encountered?

How does this play with John 6:56–69 about difficult teachings and choosing to leave or affirm? What does the congregation or friendship circle where you are need to wrestle with? Past therefores or present service or future surprises or ...?

Ruth 1:1–18
Proper 26 (31)

When looking at the rest of the Hebrew scriptures, we find Moabites at odds with Israelites. When looking at this particular tale, there is no such tension.

In the midst of bumper-sticker and 10-second sound-bite politics, the harangues of pundits of every stripe provide classic examples of stereotyping, straw arguments, excluded middles, and so much more. Pick a logical fallacy, and you'll find it in their enthusiasm to be right. The blessing we yet hear and know as still possible is that, on the personal level, two disparate people can still find one another as beloveds.

When the discouragement of "news" and rumors/realities of war gets you down, remember Mahlon and Orpah, Orpah and Naomi, Chilion and Ruth, Ruth and Naomi, and Ruth and Boaz. Love in the midst of other differences makes all the difference. This story shows how poorly conceived are tribal differences. As the laws against miscegenation fell, one-by-one and altogether, so we find hope that the laws against same-gender relationships shall fall.

We can even cast our hope wider so it is not just individuals, but whole nations, that can pledge *hesed* (loyalty) to one another by way of a larger picture where everyone benefits more through peace than our *status quo*. A recent paper looks at the UN in this light:

> In short, what is required is a complete revolution in our values and ways of living. It is not at all surprising to me that the UN and its initiatives spark controversy and fear among many in our society. The thought of a world in which all people live happily and contentedly is, on the surface, a very nice idea, but in practice a hugely difficult thing to achieve for those of us who are accustomed to live with privilege. And yet, if we are willing to revise our vision, we will see that giving up that privilege, if it leads to a more peaceful world, might just be worth it. On this UN Sunday, I would encourage us to follow the model of Eleanor Roosevelt, roll up our sleeves and support the radical work of the UN. [*Imagining a Safe and Dignified Life for All* by Dr. Deborah Buffton — wumfsa.org/reflections/ un_2009.html]

Instead of putting the roles of Ruth and Naomi off on Eleanor, how might little ol' you pay attention to both the personal and public parts of your life? In part, it is a choice of loyalties—more expansive and expanding love or continued privilege (personal and social).

Ruth 3:1–5; 4:13–17
Proper 27 (32)

When called to put all we have into life, it is helpful to have little. We don't have to sort through tough decisions about what to save when a fire is bearing down on us or flood waters are rising. When it is very clear that we only have this cup of flour or these two coins, we might as well offer them now rather than wait—sort of like going all in when short-stacked—it is the only reasonable decision in an uncertain world.

Our senses are heightened when everything is on the line and, at the same time, there is a blessed quietness. This combination of choice and non-choice leads to the type of living that will force action. When in this space we are open to doors we never would have considered and, if nothing else, we are a blessing to any who observe our response to a dilemma as we invest our reputation, resources, and hope where we can.

———————————

a house is being built
a habitat for humanity
rises from random materials
a foundation here
a stud there
insulation blown or blanket
paint all around

a house is being built
a model of participation
sweat equity
partnering with G*D
and one another
pick up your skill set
and use it well

a house is being built
its transformation
to a home
is in vain
without today's risk
sleeping with Boaz
cooking for Elijah

a house is being built
that requires
everyone's hands
to raise it up
not even G*D
does this alone
without a widow's help

1 Samuel 1:4–20
Proper 28 (33)

The "house of the LORD" [by extension the Temple, the Sanctuary] is a place of hope and prayer, a place to make vows, and a place of satisfaction.

This very same "house" continues hurtful premises such as "children are the measure of a woman" or "gender orientation is a measure of purity". In this regard, Church is also a place of last resort rather than first thought and a place where leaders can't tell the difference between drunkenness and desperate prayer.

If you were to make one change in the holy space sensibilities of our present time, what would it be?

On a different tack, what, in your experience, is "closed" and needs to be "opened"? An online study by two local congregations of Henri Nouwen's *Wounded Healer* suggests the closed reality in our lives is that of "loneliness" and the ministry area this opens/creates is that of "hospitality". How do you connect Samuel and Nouwen? Is open hospitality the issue of this and every day?

One of the biggest blocks to moving ahead is our perception that day follows day, year follows year. Eventually, we are reduced to tears. We lose track of what we have (a loving Elkanah) and can't see that we will have to give up that which we have yearned for (a potential Samuel).

Do apply the stages of grief to this short story.

After doing so, don't confuse getting through a grief with a particular result. Finally going in peace with a promise of fulfillment is not the same as arriving at some "due time" that is your due. Playing the grim-determination-of-the-soul game is no guarantee of getting what you desire. While rejoicing in a Samuel, I can still refrain from buying into Hannah's process of wanting something she promises to leave behind if only her want can be fulfilled.

Do apply the placebo effect to this short story.

After doing so, don't confuse effect with cause.

1 Samuel 2:1–10
Proper 8 (13) — Elizabeth and Mary Meet

Is a reversal of fortunes the best we can dream?

Victory songs of the oppressed that turn things on their ear so the oppressed becomes oppressor are a dime a dozen. This dualistic alteration of bottom to top to bottom to top to bottom is part of a cycle that turns out to be war to war to war with nary a moment of peace to consider an alternative pattern.

Admittedly, when in an oppressed position, there seems to be nothing but a hoped-for grand reversal to hang on to. Every other option feels like a shorter or longer suicide.

One smidgeon of hope here is the last part of verse 9, "no one succeeds by their own strength".

Multiple generations of privilege and its resources multiply the power one can bring to bear to subjugate others, either softly or aggressively. Oppression is also helped by the teachings of religion and economics that there is a direct cause and effect between our personal worth and our societal worth. Control of others also succeeds by keeping others weak long enough that they believe it.

May we see a dynamic of resistance that can lead to more than mere reversal. A desired success needs an enlargement of currently invisible understandings of common-good if it is to last past a next reversal.

When success is not mine alone, it becomes possible to include more and more folks into processes of greater common-success.

See where idealism can lead. Such an idea is currently ludicrous, but it gives a possible focus to escape the fate of one reversal after another.

Given mutuality as a model, religious institutions might be able to move from a limited Magnificat model to a more realistic model of G*D not succeeding without a creation and I/we not succeeding without G*D and Neighb*r.

1 Samuel 3:1–10, (11–20)
Guiding Gift ² – Proper 4 (9)

The prophetic tradition raises up people who are very sensitive to wrong-doings of the decision-makers of a nation, even if such leaders are still able to mostly cover up or get away with their silliness in the short-run.

This awareness is not just something one is born with. Paying attention to the discrepancy between what is said and the consequences of following that which is said is a skill that can be learned.

Prophets are not cynical in looking for the flaw in everything, but they are alert to projected consequences. When we talk about war as though it had no consequences, it doesn't take a full-fledged prophet to see and speak about how silly our talk is. It only takes a girl or boy who can see the nakedness of the emperor to be a prophet.

In fact, where prophets are usually seen as dour old men always coming around with bad news that no one wants to hear, we can play prophet from a position positive and progressive.

Knowing how much we do learn through play, this would probably be a good educational tool for us to use more often than we do. Anyone out there adept at creating a board game called *Prophesy This*? The cards would be scenes from real life, as contemporary as possible, and after reading a scenario, the player would have to note a consequence that would come, how soon it would come, and how it would draw us closer or push us farther away from one another. So there would be both prophecy that would be a forerunner of blessings as well as prophecy of disaster because of faulty thinkings and feelings.

What would it be like to play prophet with a youth group? They come with both the cultural baggage ingrained in them and yet an ability to see the flaws. This would be a great way to begin to nurture more prophets. So, play away.

1 Samuel 8:4–11, (12–15), 16–20, (11:14–15)
Proper 5 (10)

And the crowd says:
>Samuel, you are doing it wrong.
>Jesus, you are doing it wrong.
>(<u>your name here</u>), you are doing it wrong.

In all times and all places, you will be accused of doing it wrong, of being crazy.

This is a test. You might be crazy and doing it wrong. You might be the only sane voice in a hubbub of same-think.

There is no sure-fire guarantee that you are simply off-base or on-target. In this uncertainty, consider how the world would be different if we didn't follow the temptation to uniformity and empire. To follow in this direction is about as close as we can come to testing our participation in creation's growth.

Election days mark what the crowd will advocate for—power and riches over common-wealth (Saul) or people banding together to care for themselves and one another (alternative family members).

Election day is today. It is time we practice what we preach.

1 Samuel 15:34 – 16:13
Proper 6 (11)

Here we can play between the unexpected leadership of the youngest and the rooting of a cedar's growth tip.

In the first instance, every institution desires to clone itself at its maturation level and to develop the kind of leaders that are currently present. To turn things on its head is to move back to the movement level, pre-institution. Here creation of a next day is clearer. This is a case of evening and morning, in that sequence. Here we reprise beginnings, with all the attendant uncertainty and subsequent errors, to focus simply on the unexpectedness of a new beginning.

In the second instance, we note information about a Cedar from the website *Vegetative Reproduction*, "Cuttings may be rooted with relative ease. A recommended practice is to use cuttings from tips of major branches from the lower crown of young trees, taken from December to February.... Most reproduction, however, is from seed".

Again, there is the unexpected process. Instead of propagation from a typical planting of seed, we have growth through cutting. A branch tip is transformed from being a vulnerable part of a tree, with no strength of years ringed around it, to a central spot of strength around which new years of growth circle and widen.

This calls into question all forms that posit a once-for-all G*D setting things in motion and hiding secret doctrine deep within nature or an institution. When we look at the sweep of scripture, however, we find a cutting process of growth to go on and on and on—new beginnings from old institutions go on and on and on.

A call to us, still, is to find new leadership for a new way [are you willing for that to be you?] and to rely upon a tip of new growth rather than the accumulation of rigid doctrine good for documenting growth rings, but beyond that is static until death [are you willing to be moved beyond that which birthed you?].

Ramah – Where Samuel was conceived
Ramah – Samuel persuaded to anoint a king (Saul)
Ramah – Refuge from a last view of Saul
Ramah – Refuge after anointing David
Ramah – Samuel's burial place
Ramah – a high place
Ramah – a place of illicit worship
Ramah – a sanctuary city

Sometimes, a place weaves together a number of different life strands. What place keeps cropping up in your life?

1 Samuel 17:(1a, 4–11, 19–23), 32–49
1 Samuel 17:57–18:5, 18:10–16
Proper 7 (12)

What to do in the face of assured destruction? We are not talking here about mutual assured destruction (MAD), which was the basis of the Cold War arms race, just assured destruction. When the world is after your head and there is no way out—what to do?

We hear here about five smooth stones. Not the jagged ones that would slow down on their way to their target, but smooth ones that fly straight and dive deep. One image of these smooth stones is to consider them as the deep questions that cause a pause and a change of thought, of heart.

Liberation forces have never tried to best their adversary on the same level. There needs to be some soul-judo that goes on where an opponent's strength is turned back on them.

Goliath had assurance to the max. He was right. He had might. He would rule.

Going against Goliath's assurance is not a winning tactic. He'll probably win and feel more righteous. The same holds for Goliath's might. What is left is the issue of being right. This is an entry point for the smooth stones to go to the heart of Goliath's operating system. To raise a question dampens enthusiasm and brings a moment of hesitation in execution.

Imagine coming to someone in the name of the LORD OF QUESTIONS. What would that do to your interaction with someone constrained enough in their behavior that they think doing away with you would answer some important question? What would that do to your image of G*D? How would it change your relationship with whatever "Goliath" you are facing?

David put his head to the matter, took out a question, asked it, and struck Goliath on his assumption of right; Goliath took a question to the head and he began to change. (Acknowledgement: This is not a magic formula. You may remember the enormous and multiple pains incurred during the Salt March in India and the Civil Rights Marches in the United States of America—many were injured and killed, but questions were piled as high as their sacrifice.)

What would you ask Goliath?

1) Will a superiority of equipment or a widening of some privilege-gap assure your happiness?

2) If you met your match and were defeated, would you still have worth?

3) How many people must die before you, too, will know that too many people have died?

4) What color are my eyes that see productivity, not destruction, still alive in you?

5) What harm would come if we shared our dreams before you murder me? Why don't you go first.

Now, facing your particular "Goliath", what five smooth questions would you ask of both your "Goliath" and yourself?

The Revised Common Lectionary goes on here with a follow-up that has David not just killing Goliath, but tens of thousands. And now those five smooth-stone questions need to be asked of David rather than by him.

In our context, these smooth-stone questions also need to be asked of a "common defense" we put so many resources into that our "general welfare" suffers—and, in so doing, ultimately weakens our uncommonly strong defense. These are the questions that Buffy Saint Marie asks in her sad song, *The Universal Soldier*. This may be the day of the year when we need to revisit what is meant by "common defense" and connect it with this pericope.

Is there any other reason to keep on killing both softly and quietly as well as openly and brutally, than to keep a power we mistake and substitute for love flowing our way?

Is there any reason to continue believing that G*D wants blood and more blood so all the world can be chosen? Wasn't it G*D who sent diversity in Creation and Babel? Blessings on wrestling your way through these difficulties.

2 Samuel 1:1, 17–27
Proper 8 (13)

Methinks David doth protest too much. How the mighty have fallen, indeed. It's as if David hasn't been at odds with Saul. All this mighty talk simply says is that David has done extraordinarily well to have survived against someone so mighty. Praise of Saul redounds to David's benefit.

This dirge is neither religious (not about G*D) nor national (not about Israel). It does reflect on how courage does not keep one from their "fate". Considering that laments usually end with some word of hope or praise, the closing words here are: "The weapons of war perished!" But this is more realistically a question mark, not an exclamation mark. We are still looking for courage-in-action to do away with weapons of war, not just opportunities to bemoan them or protest against them.

In what is a very personal response to the loss of anointed and known leaders, there comes a word of prophecy: living with a sword turns everything into violence, like having only a hammer turns everything into a nail. This applies to Saul falling on his sword, harakiri-like, wherein violence toward others ends up being self-negation.

There might be a sense of this happening institutionally to the Christian church. After generations of power (ruling politically and militarily, enforced conversions, and the like) there is a question whether it can only be meaningful as top gun; 2,000 years of history may be no more than 3 days in Ziklag—waiting and surprised when Saul finally goes down and Godot shows up with a new identification card in another name, with another face.

———————

For an interesting read, try the elided section in conjunction with 1 Samuel 31:4. Now, try to sort through which story rings true for you today. This may be a more fruitful preaching place to tie in with than the Markan passage for the day (Mark 5:21–43).

2 Samuel 5:1–5, 9–10
Proper 9 (14)

Israel and Judah are both ruled by David, and yet they remain Israel and Judah. There is one Davidic kingdom, and yet they remain Israel and Judah. For 33 years, David rules over Israel and Judah, and always they are Israel and Judah.

Is this an intractable divide or an acknowledgment of individuation within a larger system? Can we claim this is simply the way life is and that those who follow another coming from David's city will continue to remain Orthodox and Roman, Roman and Protestant of various orders and denominations?

Yet we have this drive to be seen as having the best response to the "Ah, sweet mysteries of life". Though I might be willing to acknowledge another if they first allowed my identity, there is this reverse expectation that if I acknowledge their right to be, then they will, in turn, acknowledge mine. When this doesn't happen, I am doubly frustrated with not being affirmed simply for being and not being responded to when, for a moment, I have the good grace to accept another.

Ah, Israel and Judah, there is so much still to learn about being a new creation.

While we are in a learning mode, consider that David became greater and greater, for the LORD, God of hosts, was with him. Contrast that with the gospel lesson, Mark 6:1–13, where Jesus became less and less. It was the disciples who were growing greater.

2 Samuel 6:1–5,12b–19
Proper 10 (15)

In temporary lives in a temporary universe, we find it comforting to point at some eternals. An Ark-of-G*D is invested with such an eternal characteristic. A new cart (technology) may be constructed, but it is for the carrying of an old god. In the end, this is not any better than trying to put new wine into an old wineskin. Eventually, the Ark is misplaced, forgotten, again. And again.

For now, there is blood aplenty. There is Uzzah's death for touching the ark and knowing it to be acacia wood (temporary, not eternal). There is the death of an ox and a fatling (or 7 as per 1 Chronicles 15:26 or 70 or 100s), unnamed and temporary, in anticipation of placating further G*D-anger against even David (also temporary).

Bringing an Ark to Jerusalem has the feel of later rulers playing the bread and circus card to distract folks from an unmediated experience of radical temporariness that has about it a universal quality and thus an eternal quality.

Most ironic, this moving Ark o' G*D, intended to be with the people on their way, is now safely ensconced in Jerusalem—and "the people went back to their homes" rather than continue on a larger journey. They settled for temporary in the presence of eternity. How does that speak to the church of today? To you?

With what dignity, fear, and élan are you bringing your experience of the universe into the specific and temporary time and space where you are?

2 Samuel 7:1–11, 16
Needed Change [4]

It is still a good question—Is G*D localizable?

That does seem to be our experience—we take what has happened to us in a particular instance and universalize it. G*D becomes our particular writ large.

Hopefully, we are more than our experience.

Hopefully, we are not simply an extension of the experience of others.

All that being said—here is our experience writ large and beyond our understanding—even when wrong, we are never without love. What a difference this can make to our common life when we not only receive it for ourselves but pass it on to others. (Of course, this comes from the deleted part [verses 14–15], but it seems too good to pass over, and it is of a different quality than the reported part that glorifies the nation state. It is worth reading anyway.)

Have you ever made an announcement that you were sure about and then found out you had to take it back? We do have a tendency to approach announcements with surety. We may not be right, but we are sure. Appearing decisive and resolute is all the rage.

Participating in announcements puts us at risk for getting it wrong. At its best, this calls us to practice humility. If we've not had time before we announce something, it is prudent to check as soon as we can to see if we got it right. It is always easier, in the long run, to fess up to an error early on. The longer we put off making a correction, the more "sure" we get, and when we wait until we can't avoid coming clean, it is too late to reclaim our integrity.

Here, Nathan announces his understanding that David is in-like-Flynn with G*D. "Go for it, David, you're the man!" Then, that night, correction comes. The next day, the correction goes forth. Nathan's integrity holds. He shifts announcements as new information comes in. This will hold him in good stead several chapters down the way when he will need to again bring a word of correction to David, this time regarding Uriah and Bathsheba.

How goes your announcement integrity? Hopefully, you are not waiting until everything is clear to make an announcement because that will be some twelfth-of-never. Say what you mean and mean what you say until you have additional information, and then, like shampoo, repeat the process to remain clean.

2 Samuel 7:1–14a
Proper 11 (16)

Apparently, G*D doesn't experience being over-the-hill. "Ain't no son-o-mine gonna build me a house and settle me down. I'll do the building here!"

This business of housing is an intriguing one as it comes in both physical and metaphoric man(sion)ifestations. If we free-associated that just a bit to man-scion, we could have a good playtime.

Mansions have their heir-itage. Are you an ark-of-the-covenant as you wander around? Do you carry the presence of G*D with you? Why would you consider limiting that to a poustinia, meditation space, or a sanctuary? G*D's space has many mansions, and ours only one. And still we think we can constrain G*D's multitude into one way—ours!

May we hear G*D speaking to us as a gathered community, "You (plural) are the house of G*D". As you (singular) build your life, you weave the presence of G*D into the life/house of others. May you be well-built. May others notice. May they soon be surprised to find themselves part of the house of G*D.

Here are some community houses of the presence/justice of G*D:

Metropolitan Organizing Strategy Enabling Strength (MOSES)
The JEREMIAH Project
Northeast Organization Allied for Hope (NOAH)
Residents United Through Hope (RUTH)
The Ezekiel Project
Interfaith Strategy for Advocacy and Action in the Community (ISAAC)
Aurora Area Religious Organized Network (AARON)
Joliet Area Churches Organized Body (JACOB)
Hope Offered Through Shared Ecumenical Action (HOSEA)
Milwaukee Innercity Congregations Allied for Hope (MICAH)
Equality, Solidarity, Truth, Hope, Empowerment, Reform (ESTHER)
Justice Overcoming Borders (JOB)
Advocating, Mobilizing, Organizing in Solidarity (AMOS)

Do you know of a community organizing organization that intentionally follows NATHAN in telling truth to power? Perhaps you might begin a quiet organization for change in the heritage of Nathan—not flashy, but honest.

2 Samuel 11:26 – 12:13a
Proper 13 (18)

We can all see David's betrayal of his army by staying home and breaking an adultery commandment. No higher-purpose here opposes his desires.

It is not so easy to see Uriah's betrayal of his commander-in-chief. He gets a pass because of his dedication to his army buddies, as though one faithfulness outweighs one betrayal. Presuming loyalty to his king is at least as important as loyalty to his troops, why not go home to a spouse?

Bathsheba has often been exonerated as an innocent and as powerless. A question is—how conniving she is here. Consider the end of David's life and, coming in on Abishag warming David, Bathsheba proceeds to further a plot to have Solomon, her son, ascend to the throne. Does that end require this beginning? Does this remind you of Rebekah and Jacob and the various betrayals there?

Perhaps the trickiest question has to do with your betrayal and mine. We wrap them in such wonderful justification of loyalty to some higher good and to further our favorites. We seem to be no better than our ancestors.

Can we apply to ourselves the same high standard we expect of others? This is tough stuff, being conscious about our own lives as we are conscious of the lives of others. This is part of our work of progressing in our own lives as well as doing what we can to assist the society and culture around us to progress.

2 Samuel 18:5–9, 15, 31–33
Proper 14 (19)

This is a scene to pull at our heartstrings—David mourning the death of his rebellious son Absalom.

Had David shown the same level of involvement with his daughter's rape by another of his sons, we may never have come to this moment of grief.

So, whose misdeeds are you ignoring or protecting through your silence? What will you announce to be a larger consequence that will come from ignoring the pain of one?

This gerrymandered pericope is fair warning to look beyond the moment or particular piece of scripture. Since this is a continuation of the prior story from chapter 13, it will be important to do some contexualizing. If we just let it go with this part of the story, we will get into the same bind the church has gotten into with particular verses justifying slavery or condemning women in leadership and miss the larger picture. This kind of narrow-vision approach has also caused us to reap the whirlwind regarding additional gifts of sexuality (LGBTQQIAA...). The larger picture reminds us there is no racial difference between Gentile and Jew, no gender difference between female and male, no loving difference between homosexual and heterosexual, etc.

Let's back up a bit to 14:25–26. "No one in all Israel was so admired for his beauty as Absalom; from the sole of his foot to the crown of his head, he was without blemish. When he cut his hair—he had to have it cut every year, for it grew too heavy for him—the hair of his head weighed two hundred shekels by the royal weight."

Absalom's outer beauty went to his head. From the time David did not punish Amnon for raping Tamar (Absalom's sister), Absalom plots revenge upon both Amnon and David—"I'll be a real king." Absalom succeeds in killing Amnon but is finally killed in a revolt against David, caught by his own beautiful and bountiful hair.

David would not discipline Amnon and did not grieve with Tamar. Now he weeps for Absalom. Remember when he wept for his dying son (offspring from his adultery with Bathsheba) and then simply went on without weeping when that son actually died.

We are such a mass/mess of contradictions! Do David's genes seem to be in you as well? Privileged by G*D and yet unable to build upon that? May we be given the gift of seeing more of the consequences of our own behavior and engaging in the difficult parts of life regarding them now, rather than mourning them later.

2 Samuel 23:1–7
Evaluation Day

In looking back, David cuts through the good and absence of good to summarize a road better taken, even though it is not descriptive of his own journey. As you look back over your life, what do you distill from it? Would someone who knows you well recognize you in the maxims you claim as critical or foundational? Even if your distillation of wisdom doesn't exactly fit your own life, is it generally true over a longer time than your life and in a context of a series of cultures?

It is very tricky to divine meaning from specific journey points in a life. We keep getting caught in what appears to be immediate cause and effect. How do you discern fair governance in David's relationship to Bathsheba and Solomon? Are these details extraneous to some larger picture?

To sharpen your thinking about psychohistory, browse again or read for the first time, Isaac Azimov's *Foundation* series from 50 years ago. The always intriguing *Wikipedia* has gathered disparate responses to the series, which leaves room for yours. They note psychologist Martin Seligman identifies the *Foundation* series as influential in his professional life, because of the possibility of predictive sociology based on psychological principles, and Paul Krugman, winner of the 2008 Nobel Memorial Prize in Economic Sciences, credits the *Foundation* series with turning his mind to economics.

How do you see actions in your personal life and the lives of individuals around you limiting the duration of a coming "dark age", to be a sun rising on a foggy day?

---

where did I come from
alpha
where am I going
omega

  right now I am between
  mu and nu
  I am glad to be here
  me and you

for this I was born
for this I will die
in the meantime
we enjoy between times

we are and were
and are yet were-ing
to a new witness
all are loved free

look up and down
jump and kneel
remember and anticipate
amen and amen

1 Kings 2:10–12,; 3:3–14
Proper 15 (20)

Leaving out verses 2:13–3:2 dramatically changes the nature of this passage. What we miss is all the very practical political consolidation work Solomon did upon becoming King in Israel. Do read these details because the question coming to Solomon about what he desires takes on a different tone than if we just read the high-minded request for wisdom without this important context.

It is evident from the elided material that Solomon is a very accomplished accumulator of power, and that takes a kind of wisdom, a conniving. Solomon knows very well how to "go out or come in", to move around the political realities of his time.

Without the historical references, "wisdom" is some ethereal, spiritual state unconnected to the real world. With them, we see how Solomon plays G*D for a sucker in the same way he does his rivals. There is nothing like sucking-up to G*D or Jesus or Spirit or Nation or Boss or Family or my bad habits to get them off my case.

It won't be long, however, before even sagacious old Solomon comes up against death and G*D and dissolution of power. So read this pericope with a big grain of salt. If you read it as currently cut and pasted, there is real danger that one's preaching will be superficial and one's listeners lied to.

---

wisdom connects
far better
with departing
from evil[1]
and doing good[2]

when wisdom
gets mixed up
with riches and honor
there is going to be
hell to pay

to keep wisdom
increasing in stature
attention to G*D's presence[3]
even more than any list
becomes our joy and focus

[1, 2, 3] are references to The General Rules of The United Methodist Church.

1 Kings 8:(1, 6, 10–11), 22–30, 41–43
Proper 16 (21)

While I am glad the committee putting this camel of a lectionary together tried to give a bit of context for Solomon's ego-centric prayer beginning at verse 22 (prayed in the presence of all the people), it is revealing that the parts they left in only spoke of the leaders and priests of Israel. Overlooked was verse 2, which begins, "All the people of Israel assembled. . . ." Once again, the people are an invisible background against which the history of power and privilege plays.[1]

It is noted in verse 11 that the priests become ineffective when G*D's presence needs no mediation. In the midst of a rule-giving prayer, there are signs of something larger breaking through. If a foreigner comes and prays, their prayer is to be heard. This is to show G*D's glory all the more—even foreigners will find their way to honoring our god. Deeper than glory is the process of the last coming first and a learning that will be needed all too soon in the annals of history—it is the Israelites who will be strangers in a foreign land, and it will be their prayers, as foreigners, that will then be heard.

To hear these little hints ahead of time helps us remember all the people and not just the leaders and priests. Strangers build a groundwork for hearing important information that we will later need. May you remember the presence of the foreigner, know your own foreignness, and give direction to G*D as only a foreigner can.

---

[1] Become familiar with resources such as *A People's History of the United States* by Howard Zinn.

1 Kings 17:8–16
Proper 27 (32)

Nain? Zarephath? There are widows and soon-to-be widows all over the place—even in the place you are. A part of our work is to not narrow a definition of widow beyond that of the root of "widow" in Hebrew (*'alam*), "one unable to speak" and, by extension, unable to be spoken for.

In this larger role of being silenced, we can get beyond our usual picture of a widow—"a woman who has lost her husband by death and usually has not remarried."

Who is being silenced these days? Where is widowhood today?

Of interest is the possibility of there having been an *Order of Widows* in the early Church—see references in 1 Timothy 5:9–16, through to the 3rd century *Didascalia Apostolorum*, and beyond.

It may be time to return to officially recognizing and affirming an *Order of the Silenced* that we might hear their story from their own lips and not just talk about people who are not able to be at the table. In some denominations, the silenced are persons identified as LGBTQQIAA (some narrow that silencing to ordination, but that doesn't change the silencing and shunning). In many places, the silenced include an immigrant without official papers. Additionally there are all those who by age or class or educational/economic status or _____ (your experience of being silenced) cannot be heard by those in power.

Traditionally, an *Order of the Silenced* was authorized to engage in prayer, which seems safe enough. I expect, however, that their prayers all kept coming back to Jesus' prayer, "Forgive them, they don't know what they are doing", and its correlative, "Wake them to what division is caused by silencing people and help them engage the silenced in a new common-unity."

---

a house is being built
that requires
everyone's hands
to raise it up
not even G*D
does this alone
without a widow's help

1 Kings 19:4–8
Proper 14 (19)

Elijah was so depressed that he couldn't get out of his furze bush (NJB). He was so depressed that he had to be fed. Then he would lie down again—and again and again. I suspect an angel came more than just twice to encourage Elijah to again visualize and enter the mythology of life (the 40-ness of life) beyond the reality of the details and the stacking of events against him.

May you be as encouraging as an angel, first dealing with the basics of food before moving beyond that to the meaning of life as journey.

As you journey back to the basics of your faith experience, your Horeb, may you be opened to not simply repeating, but breaking new ground. This will allow formerly impossible constructs, such as the sound of silence, so you can hear anew by paying attention to the context for the meaning of particular notes.

---

it's over
and done
power wasn't
a be-all, end-all

I might as well be
as dead as my ancestors
for all the good I've done
or can foresee

sleep sleep sleep
40 nights
would be about right
sleep away

then
always with the "then"
always before snoozed through
then

get up and eat
nap time is over
there is a long journey ahead
eat and get up

2 Kings 2:1–12
Mountain Top to Valley

Elijah comes and goes and comes again. Jesus comes and goes and comes again. Consider that you are part of this same pattern of coming and going and coming again.

We tend to get all caught up in coming and staying and staying. As long as we have these attachments, it will be all too easy to identify with the disciples who want to build some temples where they can stay and stay and stay or, as with any political group that has an edge, it will hone and hone and hone.

The desire we are left with as we leave Epiphany behind is that of moving on. Elisha finally had to let go of Elijah and his own past choices in clothing and pick up Elijah's left-behind cloak. The disciples finally had to let go of Transfiguration and quietly go down the mountain. You and I finally have to use our belovedness and entrust ourselves to leaving our places of established security.

We have come. It is time to go. It is time to trust there will be a coming again and to practice the spiritual disciplines of letting go.

2 Kings 4:42–44
Proper 12 (17)

Here are three verses that haven't received much comment through the years. There are some who have gotten all metaphysical, new-agey about the reference to Baal-shalishah. It does roll off the tongue rather mysteriously or magically. For some, the anonymity of the man with bread is a reprise of Melchizedek. Most other folks limit themselves to the archeological question of where such a place is to be located. Some cast it forward as anticipation of an event with Jesus and the disciples.

The lectionary committee, being Christian in orientation, has matched this up with the Gospel lesson of John 6:1-21 and Jesus feeding an unknown number of people (up to 5,000 men plus women and children in other recountings). This makes it easy to focus on verses 43–44, the feeding.

Of greater interest is the setting of this last of several extraordinary deeds by Elisha. Each of these actions is in response to realities in the lives of individuals and communities. In a variety of ways, Elisha brings life, sustains life, and restores life when it appeared to be quite problematic.

The reflection on this passage in *The New Interpreter's Bible* contains this interesting sentence and conclusion:

> For all its emphasis on the miraculous nature of these acts of Elisha, however, this passage is noteworthy that the needs to which he ministered are remarkably mundane: freedom and life for the destitute, hope for the childless, restoration of a dead child to a desperate mother, food for the hungry. ... it only takes the eyes of faith to discern those forms in our day and age. ... Proclamation of the word of the Lord involves much more than words; it involves reactive and proactive action to bring life and to give hope to others.

May you be given to work in the mundane, in the world. Here is our locus of meaning—using what is at hand to meet a current need.

2 Kings 5:1–14
Guiding Gift [6]

Theory: We live within six-degrees of separation from one another. Here we move from an unnamed slave girl from one country to her mistress in another country to connect a commander with a prophet for purposes of healing. Were we to pay more attention, we would find ourselves related to the poor and abused of the earth. What connections are we overlooking that would lead to healing?

Mission programs that connect local folks to half-way-around-the-world folks are examples of this same phenomenon. It makes us grin to imagine playing a more welcoming version of Elisha and to strew healing all over the place!

Now, instead of a formal mission program that institutionally connects people, imagine those who stand on street corners holding signs requesting money or a job or a person in a grocery line using food stamps or someone at urgent care when you go for a routine checkup and wonder who you know who knows them and how you might be a sign of hope to them in a time of need. Would it change your focus as you move through the day to know everyone you meet is a friend of one of your friends, and it would help your already known friend for you to be kind to their friend you are just meeting?

In this sort of small world, we need to redefine sainthood. The well-known saint who defines holy-living becomes the exception to the rule. Every ordinary person in their ordinary day and with their ordinary connections can be a source of healing for another ordinary person. Simple awareness of harm that may be occurring, and stopping it, brings some healing. Simple awareness of a good that may be done, and the doing of it, brings some healing.

Welcome to ordinary sainthood.

Esther 7:1-6, 9-10; 9:20-22
Proper 21 (26)

The story of Herod, Salome, and John the Baptist, with Herodias orchestrating from the side, has nothing on the story of Ahasuerus, Esther, and Haman, with Mordecai pulling strings off-stage. Were Haman's kin to tell this story, it may well have Haman honored as a martyr.

In some of the missing verses (7:7-8), we have a direct encounter between Esther and Haman. What do you see as Esther's options at this point? Why do you think/feel Esther took the one she did?

These questions remind us of the options we have, but often don't consider. We also bring back to mind that decisions have several components to them, only some of which we are aware. Hopefully, these will aid us in finding a way to feast, simply to feast, and to be merciful, simply to be merciful, not to either show off our wealth or commemorate and sweeten the bitterness of revenge.

There are different versions of Esther that have been combined to give rise to a two-day Purim celebration as well as a one-day feast. This expansion of joy is to include others (the poor and those at a distance).

Given this expansion, what is the limit of expressing a joy?

Behind this question is an idea that there is no limit but ourselves. Can you remember a time of great joy and relief for you? Is that not worth expanding through time and space? Can you imagine Mordecai expanding this feasting into a week, month, quarter, or year? Presumably, it wouldn't get acted on in the same way every day, for some faithful everyday task of weeding the ground and milling the wheat and fermenting the grape is important for feasting to continue. However, it might, nonetheless, be acknowledged that this seemingly ordinary day includes a celebration of some previous event and is part of its ongoing gladness.

Might you take an important time in your life and reclaim it and consciously live today in its light? What would that do to your interactions with others and your engagement with the cultures of the world? You may still get it in the neck, but respond with a new attitude and energy.

Job 1:1, 2:1-10
Proper 22 (27)

This passage concludes with "Job did not sin with his lips". How many ways have you avoided sinning? How many ways have you sinned? Let us count the ways.

There is an old saying that "sticks and stones may break bones, but names will never hurt". Here, loathsome sores may afflict, but lips will never sin. Both cover an incomplete assessment of the situation and fall short. Being called names does hurt, stiff upper lips may not say a word, and yet sin in attitude.

To go beyond the physical, what about questions? Can we say that "questions may discourage, while responses remain gentle"?

More to the point, what is a difficulty that you are facing this day? Have you considered a different response than your usual knee-jerk one? This passage can come alive if we take a look at a disconnect available between stimuli and responses. This is deliberately phrased in the plural as it is what we face most often. Almost anyone can deal with one cause and one effect at a time. It is when the stimuli of life gang up on us and reinforce one another that we are vulnerable to choice fatigue.

Can't you just hear the Tester or Confuser orchestrate this:

> Stimulus 1, enter stage right.
>
> Stimulus 2, enter stage left.
>
> Stimulus 3, enter by wire from above.
>
> Stimulus 4, enter on elevator from below.
>
> Stimulus 5, enter from upstage.
>
> Stimulus 6, enter through the 4th wall.
>
> Stimulus 7, enter from within a sense of privilege.
>
> Actor, Ad-lib.

And our perfect storm of excuses for having returned a tit for a tat swirls on and on. It is good to use for generations.

When a next question comes, what will be your level of defensiveness? And when another comes, how might you detach the stimuli from your response so your action is an affirmation?

Job 14:1-14
Absent Saturday

Fred Craddock notes that the first six verses comment on the shortness and sadness of human life. Will there be time in such a short time frame to receive a hearing from G*D? Verses 7–14 carry us to the possibility of life beyond death, where, perhaps, a hearing is still possible.

Craddock focuses on verse 13 to consider more than just some extension of life after death. Here, Craddock says,

> Job returns to a theme that he pursues tenaciously in his discourses, the request for a hearing before God. What would be the point of revival after death? For Job it could mean a further opportunity for a fair hearing before God. Thus death for Job signals and underlines the absence of God. Death could be endured, if eventually God would remember him. So Job wants divine justice, but he also does not want to be abandoned.

On a Saturday of an Absence of Jesus, this passage acknowledges the gulf of absence that is as real as death. It is also held by the merest smidgeon of steadfast love not experienced in the present.

Even when we are forced to bear abandonment, we trust it is not a final word.

To honor this day, we conclude with verse 14. We will do well to sit for a time with Job's question, "If mortals die, will they live again?" Perhaps we will remember that it is not death we fear, but abandonment. Right now, we feel abandoned. It's true. May we, in due time, be remembered, but, for now, simply sit.

Job 23:1-9, 16-17
Proper 23 (28)

What must I do to inherit something better?
What must I do to get a fair hearing?
What must I do to get out of the trouble I'm in?

These questions deal with a mystery, an invisible force, and a quandary. It turns out that what we are looking for turns on different questions than we have known how to ask. This leads us to appreciating an openness of the future, so we will have time and space to modify our questions in light of the non-response we are currently getting from them.

Inheritance is less of an issue than investment.

Fairness pales in the face of simply standing firm in the best decisions one can make at the time and modifying that stance in light of new data.

Trouble continues, and so it is not so much a matter of getting out of trouble as much as it is to find the right trouble to be in and diving into it with all one has.

———————————

Today my complaint is bitter!
What must I do to assure something better?

Groaning is not enough.
Contend!

But contend where?
With whom?

Arguing and debating is slippery territory.
Even integrity is not enough here.

Sparks don't illumine far in a deep darkness.
But we glimpse enough for now.

From dark chaos we have come; to thick darkness we return.
From ashes you have come; to ashes you shall return.

Treasure what little is known.
Here we stand and from here we leap.

Job 38:1-7, (34-41)
Proper 24 (29)

We do like to make up meaning. Urban legends abound to explain something or other. Once a quote is in place, it is difficult to dislodge it.

I was struck by these two items in the *New Interpreter's Study Bible*.

In the text, they characterize this section of Job under the title, "The Lord Answers Job."

In the note, they move in a different direction:

> This section (38:1-42.6) is the "Divine Encounter" in which God finally speaks. It is unclear to whom God is speaking. Since it is Elihu who had the last word, God's initial questions appear to have been elicited by his speech rather than by anything Job has said. Traditionally, these rather condemning words of God (chaps. 38-41) have been understood as a redress of Job's accusations against the deity. The problem with this interpretation is that the divine rebuke of Job's protestations contradicts the conclusion of the story, where God declares Job to have been right and the friends wrong. However, if God's anger originally was directed at Elihu, Eliphaz, Bildad, and Zophar, then the story's ending makes more sense. Perhaps this portion of the text represents another example of editorial rearrangement of materials for theological reasons. The text even seems to support a different approach to the divine speeches. Since 40:1 has a second introduction of the Lord's words to Job, perhaps the preceding divine address was directed against Elihu and, by association, Job's three friends. Then, 40:1–42:6 would contain the actual dialogue between the Lord and Job. This would also explain the delay of Job's first response to God until 40:3-4. This hypothesis does not resolve all the problems inherent in this section, but it does reconcile some of them.

So, how much stuff are you carrying along (text) just because it is easier to follow tradition instead of considering alternatives (note)? Let's see if we haven't caught ourselves perpetuating a meaning with our lips without it reflecting our hearts.

Perhaps the text title is just an example of the church being too tired to say what it means, and so we get ourselves into all manner of unnecessary disputes.

\

Job 38:1-11
Proper 7 (12)

Job has been looking for a hearing for a long time. Now, in the midst of the patriarchy of Provocateur Satan and erstwhile spiritual directors, Eliphaz Teman, Bildad Shuah, and Zophar Naamah, Job hears from the Divine Feminine.

Who else carries stormy chaos in her wake? Who else is Lady Wisdomish enough to respond to a self-justifying question with rhetorical questions?

Can't you hear Divine of John Waterman fame responding to Job: "Who has been driving around without asking directions, just demanding an arrival? It is time to gird your loins, like a man. Were you there at the big-inning? Who's the planner here, and who sat around satisfied with shiny things until they were tarnished? Remember who made the clothes to show off the best qualities of even clouds and dark?"

To make the noise of the storm even more intense, so less and less sense could be heard, Papa God pipes up too, "Who set limits on the issue from wombs with curfews and behavioral consequences for prideful adolescents?"

The storm of questions goes on and on. Imagine the iconic interrogation scene of a bright light and a bad-cop yelling in your face. Disorienting. Imagine scene after Kafkaesque scene rising to demand a response to bureaucratic bafflement.

Are you worn down to reverential humility, steadfast in your innocence, coerced into confession, or responsive to current realities? These choices continue.

As you come up against no direct response to your deep questions of identity and relationship to everything else, take a breath. Then, smile and say, "Plans, schmlans, so what will we do together now?"

Job 42:1-6, 10-17
Proper 25 (30)

The humanity of Job (dust and ashes) brings us ambiguity of what is being recanted, despised, relented by one who is suffering. This doesn't address the divinity of Job (made in G*D's image) that calls to be encountered on that level. A note in *The Jewish Study Bible* suggests verse 6 "may be a prosaic notice that Job feels this way while he is mourning on a dust-heap". Once off said dung-heap, Job's response may be different. How like ourselves.

In some sense, all the poetry ends with Job vindicated against his "friends", who are caught falsifying the character of Job and the character of G*D. Likewise, the prose ends with G*D vindicated against "The Satan". All the *sturm und drang* of Job vs G*D begins to take a back seat against these other level-playing-field debates.

Perhaps we need only focus on the debates we have with our family and friends regarding what we see as the nature of creation—a basic goodness begun. To expect privilege in a goodness-oriented creation is to expect too much, and thus the importance of simply not blaspheming creation. We remember our beginning and know that we must stand firm in calling G*D to account—whether a desirable response comes forth or not. When so many false arguments about the worth of the least, the outcast, the closeted, the poor, the uninsured swirl around us, it is good to cut through them all with a clear perspective of basic goodness.

Job's daughters are a sign of what a new world we are in when we attend to the clarity of goodness in this world. The women are named (not the sons) and given rights of inheritance—both contrary to usual patriarchal patterns. What sign will you give, will you be, of new values in this world?

Psalm 1
Assured [7] — Proper 20 (25)

Compare this psalm with the beatitudes in Matthew and Luke.

Happiness/blessedness sets the tone for the psalter and Jesus' teaching. If this is not a focal point for reading them, so much will be missed, and the teaching of life will become rote.

May we be planted by streams of blessing and happily yield more of life's fullness, in every season.

This beatitude of a psalm looks at choices made on life's journey and reflects that a choice that leads to greater rootedness in being open to a new opportunity for learning is a far happier place to be than those who consider that they have a corner on a law for decision-making and judgment.

Wisdom writings often have subtle environmental lessons to impart. A key image here is a tree deeply rooted by water that runs through it from root to leaf, bringing life (living water) from ground to sky. A second image is that of chaff, the dryness when root is unable to hold the soil and life-giving humus is blown away. These images evince the result of journey choices.

The Wesley Study Bible notes that John Wesley understood the "righteousness" described here as right relationships or "holiness". Blessings, beatitudes, come clear in choices that bind us closer together. The futility of going-it-alone leads to more and more loneliness, being blown off course under the guise of self-determination.

Drop your roots a bit deeper, honor and hold the soil around you, delight in paying attention, in being open, to new instructions found in relationships with G*D and Neighb*r that aid us in journeying together.

This dropping of roots actually allows greater exploration.

Psalm 4
Assured [3]

Here is a psalm with some obscurity and choices of translation. How like life.

At the end of the day, at the end of some event's period of action, we need to sort out what was meaningful from what was not. Where did we chase after illusion? Where did we trust, even if fearfully or tremblingly, and follow G*D's heartbeat with our own?

Did we find our pursuit of happiness depended upon others serving us or a particular amount of the world's resources being deposited in our account? Do we find ourselves still hungry for more? Have we settled for a consumption model as a definition of meaning?

Here are two alternatives to the closing three verses (6-8).

6   Am I crazy? Am I a fool?
       Some would say so. They doubt you.
7   But I know the peace I felt when you opened your door
       and the warmth when you invited me to share your table.
8   I can let my eyes close.
       In your home, I am at home.

From Everyday Psalms by Jim Taylor

6-7 Why is everyone hungry for more? "More, more," they say.
    "More, more."
    I have God's more-than-enough,
    More joy in one ordinary day
7-8 Than they get in all their shopping sprees.
    At day's end I'm ready for sound sleep,
    For you, God, have put my life back together.

From The Message by Eugene Peterson

When writers and poets get hold of good material, it can end up moving in several different directions. Jim's take tends in the direction of the Emmaus story in Luke 24 or Thomas' tale in John 20, while Eugene's has more in common with the leaping lame in Acts 3.

What take do you see? It will be interesting to compare that with what you would have seen a year ago and what you might see in another year. A literal approach to the Psalms is particularly deadly. May it continue coming alive in your time, and may you launch forth from your current place of safety.

Psalm 8
Naming Day — New Year's Day — Proper 22 (27)

"Out of the mouths of babes and infants...."

The New Interpreter's Study Bible Note: "It is unclear how babes and infants silence the enemy and the avenger. Does the praise of children have the power to silence foes? Or does v. 2a continue v. 1b so that even children recognize God's majesty in all the earth? Or does the psalmist celebrate the power of human speech present even as speech begins?"

Hinge verses that can go with what comes before or what comes after are special verses. They remind us the life of scripture is beyond simple answers. They also remind us of our current place in life. Are we going to mostly be connected with our past, our future, or swing back and forth?

If you had to evaluate your past week from this perspective, would it have been mostly oriented to what has gone on before or to what is entering from the future? Have you been evenly balanced or weighted in one direction? Any given week may be unique—sort of why, when folks are "church shopping", we need to encourage trying a month in a row, as any given worship experience may or may not reflect what is usually going on. So, how's the last week been?

As we proceed into a next week, how might you intentionally honor your *hingeness*? As a hinge between G*D and Neighb*r, where do you anticipate your work to be in the coming days? As a hinge between our common history that bears all too much harm, how will you prepare for a shift in that history according to a vision of living better together?

It is in being a well-oiled hinge that we express our thanks for any recognized opportunity to make a difference.

Psalm 9:9–20
Proper 7 (12)

If we were to take a "poor me" approach to this psalm, we would still be left with the perennial problem of class. The class of power (oppressor) versus the class of the powerless (oppressed); the class of the fortunate (holy) versus the class of the sick or unfortunate (sinner); the class of the "caring for" versus the class of the "cared for".

We might look to verse 18 as a key verse—"The needy shall not always be forgotten, ignored, or taken advantage of." At some point, the disjuncture between their hope and their reality will become clear enough that they will stand up for one another. Then structures that have seemed so safe, a teaching boat, will become threatened, a storm-tossed barque.

> Everyone with enough earthly possessions must seriously ask if they are not responsible, to some degree and in some way, for injustices and oppressions. We know, from the book of Exodus, that G*D's judgment can fall over the oppressors in a tremendous way. We also know that authentic love, the source of justice, can change the face of the earth.
> [modified comment from *The Christian Community Bible*.]

Rise up, O LORD! Throw off chains of captivity to the power of social norms sanctioned by the powerful. You have nothing to lose, period. You have everything to gain, period.

Rise up, O LORD PARTNERS! Throw off chains of captivity to the power of social norms sanctioned by the powerful. You have nothing to lose, period. You have everything to gain, period.

Rise up, O CURRENTLY POWERFUL! Throw off chains of captivity you have held on to. You have been as chained as those you chain. Surprisingly, you have nothing to lose, period. Remarkably, you have everything to gain, period.

Psalm 14
Proper 12 (17)

"shape a genesis week from the chaos of my life"
[*The Message* 51:10]

let there be light
shining into that which I do not know
of myself or beyond

let there be separations
dividing out water from water
clarifying otherwise confusion

let there be gatherings
of like portions into weight of substance
enough precipitate to work with

let there be distinctions
where shadows and mystery
play every evening and morning

let there be more than expected
out of basic structure
more life than was imaginable

let there be life upon
as well as life within
even life for care-takers

let there be pause
cessation to affirm forever
a goodness unbelieved

let there be a recapitulation
of goodness goodness
finding its way every way

let there be a rebirth
now and ever of my birth
and G*D's birth

let there be a new genesis
from within and beyond
every previous let be

let there be dancing on Sabbath
let there be Sabbath in dance
let there be "let there be"

Psalm 15
Proper 17 (22)

Blessedness and rejoicing are both exciting, over-the-top expressions and bedrock foundations from which comes steadfast love—shown in many ways. They need particulars to bring goodness into better clarity. They need particulars to respond to questions that will set case law.

Let's track some parallel terms from Micah, Psalms, and Paul.

• do justice	• love kindness	• walk humbly
• speak heart truth	• do what is right	• walk blameless
• do not take a bribe	• do not lend money	• stand by your oath
• desire wisdom	• demand signs	• decide through foolishness

All manner of arrows can be drawn between these terms. Some will double-back on themselves, particularly when the beatitudes are tossed into the mix. Each of the blessings can be related with good effect to each of these terms.

In fact, we have a season of possibilities here. Write them on a magnetic sheet and cut them apart. Each day, rearrange them on your refrigerator until you have identified the best pattern for your life in this season. (In another season, you may go through the same process and find yourself with a different best pattern.)

Psalm 16
Hopeless Hope Vigil — Proper 28 (33)

We are shaped as we travel backward from verse 11 to 6 to 2.

Trust is one of the best sources of humor there is. So often that which is funny relies on tricks, misdirection, put-downs, and finding a survival perspective. However, trust begins to see humor where there is none. Trust is a creative act. Trust leads us to a strange formula: $T+GT=C$. I don't know whether that can work mathematically, but it does here as Tragedy + G*D's Time = Comedy. From a Christian perspective, we begin with the tragedy of crucifixion and add to it whatever is meant by "three days" and, voilà, the comedy of resurrection.

Three tortoises, Tom, Dick, and Harry, decide to go on a picnic. Tom packs a picnic basket with beer and sandwiches. The picnic site is ten miles away, so it takes them ten days to get there.

When they get there, Tom unpacks the food and beer. "OK, Harry, give me the bottle opener."

"I didn't bring it," says Harry. "I thought you packed it."

Tom gets worried. He turns to Dick, "Did you bring the bottle opener??"

Naturally, Dick didn't bring it. So they're stuck ten miles from home without a bottle opener. Dick and Harry beg Tom to go back for it, but he refuses, as he says they will eat all the sandwiches.

After two hours, and after Dick and Harry have sworn on their Tortoise Lives that they will not eat the sandwiches, Tom finally agrees and sets off down the road at a steady pace.

Twenty days pass, and Tom still isn't back. Dick and Harry are getting hungrier by the day, but a promise is a promise.

Another five days and Tom still isn't back, but a promise is still a promise. Finally, Dick and Harry can't take it any longer, so they take out their lunch and just as they are about to eat it, Tom pops up from behind a rock and shouts........

"I KNEW IT!......I'M NOT GOING!"

Lack of trust is merely funny. Trust is the humor of joy.

Alternative ending:

Later in the day Tom left to get a bottle opener, Dick and Harry see Tom returning in as much of a cloud of dust as he can muster.

Panting as he arrives, Tom says, "Duh, we've been living so slowly, too much of the past has stuck to us. I saw some folks drinking at the picnic site we passed on the way here—the caps are twist-offs! We don't need a bottle-opener. Let's feast!"

Psalm 19:7–14
Proper 21 (26)

Verse 7 suggests the groundings/realities of G*D result in "making naive people wise" (CEV). By the time we arrive at verse 13—when we find ourselves corresponding/paralleled with G*D, all our wisdom from practicing returns us to "be innocent of great wrongdoing" (CEV). Now we just need to distinguish "naive" from "innocent".

Without pushing too much, consider verse 14 and how our internals (meditations of the heart) match our externals (words of my mouth). When we are practiced in this relationship, rules, creeds, and traditions lose their restraining power and can be re-entered in order to experience again the liberating power known at the initiation of our religious rites and rituals.

All of this breaks down the false post-Edenic separation between Creator and Creature, G*D and Humanity. We can remember G*D left Eden with the Adam and the Eve to also walk with the Cain and the Abel and the You and the Me and all Others. We have never been unlinked from one another, for always the G*D walks with us.

This "walking with" shifts us from naive to wise and the wisdom gained returns an innocence of unity. May we be naive enough to again walk with one another as we each, and G*D, move through a grace of repentance to new rainbow living.

Psalm 20
Proper 6 (11)

Presume for the moment that anointing is an equal-opportunity event. All have received an anointing. A gift has been received—to each for the benefit of all.

If a given, how does that change the process of calling upon an anointer? Do we anticipate or presume? Do we still owe and incur obligation?

If all are anointed, why do some apply it more easily than others? For some, it leads to charging in where an angel would fear to tread. For some, there is a quiet confidence and an ability to stand no matter what the circumstances. For some, there is disbelief that they are anointed.

Anointing was and is for every person, regardless of their status, inside or outside a Pentecostal room. When anointed, barriers are re-moved, and we can cross the usual obstacles (huge among them is that of language or culture). Stand tall, weapons of war will rust. Cross the roadblocks, before they are taken down. Doing so will add to the impetus to healthily remove our last barriers—until we clearly see one another as anointed.

This is a remarkably self-fulfilling prophecy. See another as anointed and they will begin to so see themselves. Withhold that vi-sion and we will live up to our worst. Inasmuch as free-will abides, these are not cause-and-effect actions, but deep-calling-to-deep.

Psalm 22
Annihilation Friday

On "Maundy" Thursday, we heard the psalmist lead off with:
"I love you, YHWH, for you have heard my voice and my supplications."

On "Good" Friday, the lead is:
"My God, my God, why have you forsaken me? Why are you so far from helping me, from the words of my groaning."

What a difference a day makes. What day is today for you? Remember, the other day is still echoing or just around the bend.

Psalm 22:1–15
Proper 23 (28)

How many different ways can you say, "I'm not feeling well; my expectations have been dashed." If you only have the "Fuck" or "Shit" word available to you, you are not able to communicate the depth of your despair. Psalm 22 can add to your lexicon of descriptors of your woe. Just being able to bring so many different metaphors and similes to bear helps.

This is a case where expanding the expression of experience actually deepens the experience.

One of the interesting phenomena involved here is that using a multitude of images begins to build in such a way that by the time the Psalm actually ends, we have shifted gears and can see our situation from a different perspective—one that will help us move on rather than be stuck. This ability to use many different allusions begins to cut through our initial illusion of being trapped in a particular circumstance. I can't think of a better reason for expanding an imaginative use of experience descriptors than this—it is clarifying and healing. Building so many wonderfully concrete pictures begins to put a new picture in place. Literacy is liberating.

Psalm 22:23–31
Conviction [2]

Forsaken and Hopeful. Here we again find ourselves in life's polarities.

Not knowing what is coming our way, we apply the gift of praise in the moment. We will note a new relationship within the gathered community. We will see that where we felt forsaken, there has always been mercy offered, and where we have experienced the miseries of life, there has always been someone to listen. We will find the excluded hungry are now gathered in to have enough and be satisfied. Those we least expected to be invited, those no-good pagans, are also a part of a new community gathered out of the pains and divisions of life.

Praise of G*D is given for actions of release, freedom, and care for the poor, the earth, the dead. Praise is never devoid of specific actions. Praise is not just praise, but praise comes in response to carefull behaviors.

In this light, praise is not just oral praise based on intellectual constructs or emotional/personality typologies, but also has a healthy dose of emulating behavior. If G*D is to be praised for matters of deliverance, are we not called to participate in the deliverance of others and create freedom from the bondages they find themselves in? Our highest praise, then, is an imitation of G*D's intentions and actions.

All of this leads us to rejoice beyond ourselves and our time. We anticipate our work now will bear much good fruit in generations to come. The excluded of tomorrow will also be born into the creation-long process of entering into G*D's joy. As we do our work to welcome all, we will be modeling for our descendants the amazing gift of hospitality that they will expand upon in their time.

So, praise well by your choices to be a partner in releasing the memory of folks gone by, forgiving the lives of people right now, and setting up a deliverance of those yet to be present. As we participate in these actions, we exponentially increase the quality and quantity of praise.

This is very important work—to recognize our forsakenness in the moment and to live a hope beyond tomorrow.

Psalm 22:25–31
Assured [5]

Four words – one from each pericope of the day:

> *Baptized* – yes, even eunuchs – (Acts 8:26-40)
> *Family* – yes, even current enemies – (Psalm 22:25-31)
> *Born* – yes, beloved of G*D – (1 John 4:7-21)
> *Abide* – yes, G*D in creation, creation in G*D – (John 15:1-8)

There are multitudes of ways we interact with the world around us. Among the biggest choices are those of what we prevent and what we nurture.

For those within a Christian tradition, here is a strong statement about choosing nurture over prevention: "Those who say, 'I love God,' and reject non-Jesus-oriented people are liars."

To abide, to be born from that abiding, to be family beyond limits, to be baptized into a way of life leaves little escape from a command toward wholeness. "Those who love G*D must love their brothers and sisters also," as well as respect and honor their common environment, their family relations, and their belonging past all divisions.

---

look – water
rippling with life
reflecting glory

look – enemies
still family
ancestral descendants

look – love
born and reborn
and born forever

look – home
abiding here
abiding everywhere

Psalm 23
Assured [4] — Proper 11 (16)

So often this Psalm is used quietly, as if we were blindly searching around with our hands to find the boundaries of the space we are in. Sometimes the quiet is meditation. These days, a first time this Psalm may be heard is in a funeral service.

Sometimes it feels as if we are limping home on a wing, a prayer, and the 23rd Psalm.

This time around, I have found it helpful to shout it at the top of my lungs as an affirmation or a challenge to the junk in the world that is too much with me, encroaching upon my time and space and hope.

Join me in loudly sharing this Psalm? I'll be listening for echoes of your affirmation, and if you listen carefully, you may yet hear echoes of my cry.

If, though, loud is not your thing, you may want to try this statement of affirmation:

> Partnered with G*D,
> I separate want from need.
> I take comfort in the midst of needs met
> and am deeply satisfied;
>   restored even.
> Together we make adjustments
> on our journey to Joy.
> There have been doubts along the way,
> but also a willingness to proceed;
>   for we are steadfastly together—strengthened.
> Together we are hospitable to others,
> even enemies,
>   and find assurance and peace.
> Surely goodness and mercy are
> attainable today and tomorrow,
>   as we walk together in this paradise
>   creating new life from current life.

Psalm 24
Proper 10 (15) — Honoring Day

What do we know about those who make it to prominence? Their hands and hearts are purely practical. They will do whatever is necessary to arrive at their goal and then do even more to keep it and even more to secure it.

All "acts of necessity" are finally called "blessings from the LORD". Taking advantage of Neighb*rs turns out to be taking advantage of G*D. Such is the consequence of those who seek the glorious and unending G*D known as Mammon. Please look at stanza 4 of Philip Appleman's poem, *Five Easy Poems for Pagans,* found at: www.poet-s.org/poetsorg/poem/five-easy-prayers-pagans.

In today's political/economic realm, we hear these ancient words anew:

> Lift up your heads, O gated community!
> and be lifted up, O golden job creators!
> that glorious Mammon may come in.
> What is Mammon's glory?
> A plutocracy strongly classed,
> a fascism mighty in efficiency.
> Lift up your heads, O gated community!
> O golden financiers!
> that glorious Mammon may come in.
> What is Mammon's glory?
> The God of Prosperity,
> is the king of gold.

While we are at it, consider the option of identifying G*D as steadfast lover instead of a mighty king. Consider how well we defend our privileges (whether slight or significant), and we might hear:

> mighty gates, ancient doors
> attend, awaken
> a humble G*D is present
> a G*D strong in creativity
> a G*D empowered by tomorrow
> a G*D on earth as elsewhere
> open to gifts arriving
> open to wrestle a blessing
> open to climb a mountain
> open gates frame a saint

Psalm 24:7–10
Old Welcomes New

First, we need to be able to imagine G*D outside. This is a herculean task.

For those not up to this task, relax. The common descriptions of strong and powerful—battle-ready—are minority reports. Far stronger images are of G*D, steadfast in love, and G*D, the merciful. The power of creation is to call out. Here we can call the doors to open so that folks can finally come out to play with the sun and moon and all the wee creatures from stones to flutter-bys.

Presume a G*D both inside, raising gates, and outside, calling for the gates to be raised. Now, follow suit.

To complete this shift in orientation, remember there is no separation between heaven and earth. Any heavenly force is an earthly force uncurling from within as a call to come forth echoes round about. The "LORD" of earth rises through service.

With a Selah here and a Selah here, Old McG*D has some gates. With a creak, creak here and creak, creak there, they open, slowly, but surely. It's time to come out.

Psalm 25:1–10
Conviction [1]

Lent comes suddenly. What happened? We were transfigured, and then we were covered in ashes. This is not an easy transition to make, and our first response tends to assign blame for why we are not going from glory to glory, but mountain top to valley. Let whatever has brought me low be put to shame.

These knee-jerk responses to situations in life are the result of not fasting toward a preferred future of steadfast love received and responded to with our own steadfast love.

Being created in the image of a creator calls us to fast from and toward a variety of covenants and our acculturated responses to them so that an image of steadfast love and faithfulness becomes our own image.

If, for whatever reason, we do not attend to this call, we are intentionally deciding that where we are is good enough, that wholeness takes too much work.

One of the tricks here is to finally recognize that no short-term fast for limited goals such as fame and exultation is going to satisfy. We practice fasting that we might live fasting. In this way fasting is never away from something as much as it is toward something more desirable than our current limitations.

Alphabetical poems have an artificiality to them. Even so, they can still be significant cries for help or insightful ditties. Here's a part of an alphabetical and mathematical song by Grin, Judy Fjell's puppet, *Gee I Am Glad I Am Me* [judyfjell.com].

> GIM glad IMME, OUR glad URU
> And if U + I make a WE
> Does 1 + 1 add up 2 1 2 or 3
> ...
> So WE're 1 + we're 2 + we're 3
> There's WE U + ME U ME + WE
> I don't know how this can B
> But then I don't even understand ME
> But these R the questions that life is made of
> Arithmeticklish problems of 🤍
> So I'll end it 4 now with 5 ways WE agree
> U 🤍 Bing U I 🤍 Bing Me I 🤍 U
> U 🤍 me . . . + sometimes . . .
> We both even 🤍 Bing WE

Psalm 26
Proper 22 (27)

An interesting shift in tense occurs from the beginning of the Psalm to its end. We begin with a claim upon G*D because of our past actions—(verse 1) "I have walked . . . ." By the end, we move to the present—(verse 11) "I walk . . . ." and future—(verse 12) "I will . . . ."

This is what we have to work with: remembrance of the past, decisions in the present, and consideration for the future.

Focus on these three will move us away from an unnecessary concern regarding vindication. Life will happen in all its joy and suffering, but we can take these in stride as we remember, decide, and plan. To throw vindication into the mix muddies our motivation and distracts our energies.

However, should you need vindication for some awkward situation—attend to your integrity.

This Psalm is one list of values and behaviors. It is neither an all-encompassing list nor one that pertains to everyone. Our call, here, is to see a movement and then to evaluate whether it would be helpful for current needs.

A key repeated word is "integrity". This ancient Hebrew word comes from a root that points to a completedness, a having been single-mindedly used up in an endeavor. It has been additionally translated to indicate: fullness, innocence, simplicity.

This makes it easy to sound like a broken record: "I, I, I."

It is less easy to claim integrity simply by living as though it were true. Every political season shows how easy it is for "integrity" to flow into self-aggrandizement, speaking of oneself in the third person, and going negative on others.

One needed measurement of integrity not often used is that of blessing. One of integrity's first acts is blessing G*D and Neighb*r in a given situation. This is an indication of being full of blessing from having been blessed. It is a sign of assurance.

This becomes clearer when we paraphrase the last two verses:

> I remember being graciously healed and
>   claim this as my way ahead.
> In the midst of many options,
>   I choose a foundation of blessing
>   from which to encounter life.

Psalm 29
Beloved — Live Together

Verse 11

> *May the Lord give strength to people!*
> *May the Lord bless people with peace!*

1) It is helpful to relate giving to blessing. Any giving that is worth receiving will be a blessing.

2) What gives strength? At least one response is that justice gives strength to both individuals and communities. This then can be related to peace. Peace is not sweetness and light as much as it is the strength to do justice.

3) The qualities of gift, blessing, strength, and peace are all variations on a theme of belovedness. When we are raised from our dead places, we are effectively baptized; we recognize we are beloved by and in the universe and called to share such with others.

When we recognize we have been strengthened to be just and to advocate for justice for others, we recognize the presence of G*D.

When we catch on to having been blessed with a wholeness named shanti/shalom/salaam/peace and we use such a blessing to bless others, we recognize the presence of G*D.

Now, from the position of the end of the psalm, we can return to the first verse and yell, "Bravo!" for gifts and blessings of strong justice and whole peace.

Psalm 30
Guiding Gift 6 — Proper 8 (13)

The "dancing" that mourning has become is the same word as "whirl" in 29:9. In Psalm 29, "causes the oaks to whirl" might also be translated, "causes the deer to calve."

In dancing, we find mourning whirled through the night into the birth of a new day/life.

Such a new life calls us beyond an anti-adversity G*D that is only "good, restorative, prosperity-giving". We look for a with-us-through-the-night G*D.

Together we join a whirling dervish dance that is much slower than one might think and brings all the rooms of one's life together on the sill of a door to enlightenment beyond dualistic patterns.

Rejoice, weeping with another is connected with joy.

---

twilight comes on
doubts begin to arise
was the day as joyful as thought
when we play it again

evening deepens
relationships aren't as bright
shadows bring back old fears
second-guessing sets in

night sets in
doubts become certainties
it was only false joy
our friends fair-weather

midnight rolls around
rolls over and under
a storm-tossed sea
never-ending

darkest before dawn
is no old-sailor's tale
all warmth is used up
for ever and ever

and dawn so long in coming
creeps maddeningly forward
false dawn after false dawn
tantalizing in each betrayal

morning rises
bringing relief in its train
but so much weariness
joy needs rest

morning settles
tense muscles relax
a smile returns
a hum begins

morning warms
a slow jig starts in a toe
sackcloth comes off
naked joy is still

While appreciating the possible transformation of weeping into joy, that is not the only way people experience life. Post-traumatic Stresses, of whatever etiology, have a way of continuing the weeping, even in the presence of Joy-All-Around. [Assignment: Write a Psalm/ Poem for those who suffer a Post-traumatic response.]

Psalm 31:1–4. 15–16
Absent Saturday

The net of death is wide and strong. There is little appeal to be made when captured. In various mythologies (in the honorable use of that word), there are bargains to be made, but none of them are free from cost and consequence.

Reflect for a moment on what it means to entrust your spirit. There is a certain externalness to that which recognizes that spirit is relational. The old song that everybody has to serve somebody is pertinent.

When caught in death's web, it becomes clear where we have entrusted our spirit. Our appeal is fantastic (why didn't you live that way) or congruent (of course, that is where you would turn).

One of the questions for us is whether we have done the groundwork to trust without any surety of being justified, protected, restored, or other miracle from the outside.

This doesn't negate the relational nature of spirit but does put it in a partnered relationship, not a parental one. Here a future is in both our hands—G*D's and Neighb*r's; G*D's and ours; Neighb*r's and ours. May we work together to establish such a trusting love.

Psalm 31:9–16
Premature Fear Sunday

What word sustains you? Sustains a weary Jesus?

Is it:

- G*D's already helping me, even if it's hard to see right now?
- This is a confrontation that clarifies our relationship?
- For times like this, my practice of trust comes to the fore?

Or should those question marks become exclamation points? Some folks find possibilities more energizing; some find certainties to better sustain them.

What word sustains a weary you?

A word that sustains me is, "My times are not mine alone."

---

a weariness unto
a vanity of weariness
wears our vanity
into weariness

passion in the midst
of weariness
shines light
beyond time

circular repetition
or steady state
trap weariness
into our bones

which was
and is
and may yet be
freedom

passion beaten
into weariness
beats us down
to misery

one kingdom
stringing up another
calls for a new realm
freedom

freedom – morning awake
freedom – learns to listen
freedom – open eared
freedom – within time

Psalm 34:1–8
Proper 14 (19)

How does an angel set up a circle of protection around you? That is probably a clue about a gift you have or a way you might help to set up a circle of protection for others.

A current space opens a choice not seen before because you were so busy fleeing or battling with some difficulty that options had flown away from the flurry of your preoccupation.

As you have been blessed to be a blessing, so you have been protected to protect.

Angels are not to do our work for us or to insulate us from the consequences of our actions. If we find privilege in our guardian angel, we may need to take another look. In the playbook of Old Screwtape, this is a technique that has a very high return for the amount of energy expended. Protected people are not faithful people or trusting people, but are eventually people anxious that their protection won't last in the face of so many others also claiming grace and protection.

As you have experienced deliverance, know there are some others (not all others) who will need your witness and presence to aid them. Oftentimes this is a process of like calling to like—the addict to the addict approach. Pay attention to how you have been cared for and learn and pass it on.

Psalm 34:1–8, (19–22)
Proper 25 (30)

No matter what alphabet (talk about your giveaway word—what might it mean?) you use; no matter what letter of the alphabet we use to begin a line; no matter if you keep a pattern or break it (skip a letter or two or add a final line that is not part of the scheme)—the elliptical foci continue to be G*D and C*mmunity.

Again and again, we find these to be the tension points of our existence—our relationship to G*D and our relationship to others. Whether "our" G*D is "one" or "our" Neighb*r defines our "self", we keep coming back to these two realities.

So the ecumenical and interfaith mantra is: Let us exult, magnify, glorify, exclaim, and share our many experiences of G*D.

Rich or poor; users of this language or that; male or female; straight, gay, bi, trans, or intersex; focused on this religious tradition or another; plain or extravagantly spoken—we can't do without one another. Let us listen to the experience of one another. The lowest common denominator and the highest prime; real or imaginary numbers; plane geometry and calculated limits—all bring their revelation and find their relationship, one to the other. Expanding galaxies, earth's surface, and atomic subdivisions; eastern and western medical modalities; memes and genes—are absolutely crucial and irrelevant.

Take comfort and refuge where you can. Consistency be damned, full speed ahead. Start this day with a new letter and see what happens—try living from the vantage point of uvw instead of abc.

Psalm 34:9–14
Proper 15 (20)

Verse 14 summarizes the General Rules of The United Methodist Church with an important parallel construct.

United Methodist:
> Do no harm.
> Do good.
> Attend to relationships with G*D
>   (prayer, worship, etc.)

Psalm 34:14:
> Turn from evil.
> Do good.
> Seek and do peace.

The United Methodist version very methodically puts life into boxes. The Psalmist is here more relational in the motion and process of turning from that which breaks trust by seeking after actions which build trust.

Whether through method or relationship, the glue between the starting point and goal is the work of goodness. When putting the two together, we find the twin values of loving G*D and Neighb*r. These visions energize the good to box in our repent-from-past brokenness and current temptations to privilege.

Forward or backward, we live, move, and have our being in attending to a flow between not-good, good, and good-extended.

Psalm 34:15–22
Proper 16 (21)

The first part of this Psalm led us to the point of responsibility (no, harm; yes, good; G*D/Neighb*r). The rest concludes with the plug-and-play nature of a *deus ex machina* (we have no responsibility).

It is helpful to separate this Psalm to clarify the issue of responsibility.

A key to being responsible is being thankful (verses 1-3). With thankfulness comes an ability to see a larger picture than any present suffering. Thankfulness is also a source of learning.

When we posit the privilege of being watched-over (verse 15), our thankfulness turns to expectation. With expectation comes the smaller picture of a knowledge of good and evil, an ability to categorize the experiences of life so they can be avoided.

With Pentecost comes a responsibility to engage others out of thankfulness for having been encountered in a most common place (fear) and a most uncommon experience (partnering). Mostly, this passage has its value in reflecting on its limits and why not being responsible is actually anti-fun.

Psalm 36:5–11
Clarification Week Monday

How many lectionary cycles have you completed? Probably even before you began your first time through, you had an idea about some larger picture every pericope would fit within. We go back over ancient bits and pieces of our experiences. We plumb for new understandings—both where a particular piece fits in or how it freshly adds a perspective that challenges too close a fit.

In another setting, we might pick up on light springing to life. Perhaps, between a parade of Hosannas and a parade of weeping, between carrying palms and a cross, there is a centering prayer (verse 14) that we not be a doormat arrogant and privileged people use for their own benefit or be exiled from a community about to become new enough to revel in its variety of intersectional gifts.

There are temptations aplenty to keep us repeating a past triumph and to avoid any risk of losing whatever little we have. [Note: We usually feel we have too little, no matter how much we have.] Between past baggage and future-tripping, our fear of loss drives us to false security after false security.

May this week be a blessing to us as we come clear about what doesn't need to be clung to and where we will place our bet on the meaning of life.

Psalm 40:5–10
Creation's Conception

Have you read the scriptures well enough to see other folks there? Have you read enough to find your Neighb*r present to you? Or is it just yourself you find inscribed on an unrolling scroll?

> All of scripture is found
> within any single word
> and won't be found
> until all of them
> have danced with each other

Our experience shapes and is shaped by our heritage of being a community of learners stumbling across creation-seeds, nurturing them to fruition, and nourished by their fruit/sustained by new seeds.

Psalm 41
Guiding Gift [7]

From our insides (torn apart by sin), from our outsides (betrayed by best friends)—we need to be put back together, rescued.

"You know me inside and out, you hold me together...."

Now it is time for a response to this wonder of still being of worth in G*D's eye, no matter what.

That response is to mimic G*D. "Dignify those who are down on their luck, for that's what G*D does. Do this to regain balance and health for both yourself and your larger communities."

This is a wonderful way to honor G*D—honor others by seeing them as dignified and worthy of the same. This incredibly difficult yet simple act of seeing dignity, no matter what, ends up being the best part of our pursuit of happiness.

Why does it take us so long to catch on and then so much longer to learn this behavior so well that it moves from second nature to us to a first response for us?

Psalm 42, 43
Hopeless Hope Vigil

Why are you cast down, O my soul? Let me count the whys.

Hope in G*D. What's the option?

The poverty of the poor is still present.

When dealt with, instead of only noticed, it will bring forth praise.

This will be a turning point wherein the ends of the earth shall remember—and be glad.

Psalm 45
Creation's Conception

The New Interpreter's Study Bible reminds us, "Speech has performative efficacy here...."

Imagine you constantly heard, "You are desired." If there are conditions on that, its value is decreased. Even beauty has its limit and probably isn't a joy forever. Familiarity can make common the strikingly uncommon.

Here, a piece of the background is that a new wife will soon be part of a bevy of wives, each periodically desired, not eternally so.

Return to hearing, "You are desired." No matter how old, it continues to turn our head. We will follow where it leads. We are so easy, so needy.

There is little way to evaluate the purpose of a desire, even our own. Addictions are still not comprehensible. Will it lead onward or simply captivate us?

Again, hear, "You are desired."

In the midst of listening, remember. You have been desired before. Even before "before" you have been desired. Listen again, and a next desiring is already arising. Its wavering voice will steady over time. There never has been, nor will there ever be, a time you are not desired.

Within this affirmation come many options of response. Foremost among them is a question of whether you will so desire others to shine forth their particular and peculiar beauty. In Abram's way, "You have been desired, to desire" (Genesis 12:2).

Psalm 45:1–2, 6–9

Proper 17 (22)

Somehow, a psalm to a king is not up to the standard of a call from a lover.

The movement described here is from our love of righteousness and hate of wickedness to then receiving an anointing or authority of G*D to put such into action.

Consider the difference it would make if this were reversed—that you are already loved and have already been given an anointing (through creation) and authority (through fruit-eating) needed to be a discerning leader among those you are with. This leadership will clarify and assist in making the moral decisions needed in our setting—between good and evil.

At best, the lectionary editors have given us a built-in screen to help us find the real energy of life—lovely lover rather than kingly power.

Psalm 46
Hopeless Hope Vigil

From a quick and dirty search of the *New Revised Standard Version*, one-fifth of the Psalms use the image of "refuge" and nearly half the references to "refuge" in the whole canon are in the Psalms. This is a significant issue to sing about.

In the above paragraph, my fingers twice typed the word "refute" instead of "refuge." How Freudian is that?

Regardless of that psychological issue, there is a connection. To "refute" is to beat back an attack; to "refuge" is to flee from attack.

Where are you refuting harm to another? Where are you taking refuge from harm aimed at you?

Both are active and worthy acts. We flee to G*D for refuge, and G*D refutes the uproar against us. As G*D's people, we are called to be people of refuge for others and people who refute the world's uproar that would diminish any sister or brother.

Psalm 47
Our Turn to Witness

Hey!

stop clapping those hands
this is not performance art
but a spectacle
for those with specs to see

you are not to be subdued
by this rising
to hold down your own
investment in next generations

all ships are to rise
together
this is music to the spheres
no privileged place here

this is a new year
bringing new relationships
and new behaviors
new hands on deck

New!

Psalm 48
Proper 9 (14)

Let us ponder the steadfast love of G*D. It is strong enough to cause panic in the plans of the high and lifted up. Simply seeing steadfast love (whatever the venue) is to participate in the beauty of life, and beauty will last.

Ponder on this long enough to see that the assembled powers do have their day, but no more. They squabble among themselves and bring one another down—like the story *Hope for the Flowers* by Trina Paulus where caterpillars scramble over one another to unsuccessfully ascend to the top of the heap. It turns out it takes the beauty of metanoia to be able to circumvent ladder-climbing by way of flutter-bying.

After thus pondering for sufficient time, we can begin to walk around this miracle of steadfast love and see that there is room enough to accommodate all.

Pray your love will be in the image of G*D, steadfast. This is our secret weapon that is no weapon at all.

Psalm 50:1–6
Mountain Top to Valley

To use only the first six verses plays well with transfiguration imagery and moves us from a creating G*D to a transfigured G*D—the judge. Other than that it is an unhelpful truncation of the Psalm. If a transfiguration to judge doesn't indicate what is being judged or what the judgment is, we have only one of those old transformer toys—now its one thing; now its another. Without a storyline and only having the end-points, there isn't much sense to be had.

So how does "thanksgiving" enter into transfiguration? "Thanksgiving" is a keyword in the Psalm. The transfiguration is to reveal the importance of thanksgiving. Yes, this is a thanksgiving beyond the building of holy huts on a hill.

The good blindly follow the rules. The wicked use the rules to their own advantage.

In both cases, G*D says there is more to this transfiguration business than getting a handle on some set of rules, even if they were G*D-initiated at some prior point. The point is living thankfully.

Thankful living moves us beyond the rules and keeps us true to their spirit when applying them. Thankful living is, finally, a path of rescue and salvation.

Psalm 51:1–12
Conviction 5 — Proper 13 (18)

A question from Jim Taylor's weekly *Soft Edges*: "How does one sing of cosmic holiness in a society that seems unable—or unwilling—to imagine anything beyond a private and personal God?"

This psalm is often read as a top-down power arrangement. It is possible to read it differently by adding a choice of focus to the standardized language.

> Have mercy on me, O God, according to a steadfast
>   love [of all creation];
> according to an abundant mercy [for all creation] let
>   us start again.

> "Restore to me the joy of [making everyone and
>   everything healthy],
> and [together] sustaining a willing spirit."

Each of us can cultivate a steadfast and abundant love/mercy relationship with G*D and all creation. This expansion of individual responses to community and creation deepens our individual experience with that of innumerable others.

This psalm, too easily seen as a me-and-G*D moment, needs to remember the end of the Psalm that begins,

> Do good to Zion [to see all working together];
> [together let us] rebuild safety within Jerusalem.

Of course, folks can stick to a personalized contriteness, but life can be even more energized by entering into a partnership with G*D rather than just having an appeasement policy. Blessings to you on seeing love and mercy as a way of life larger than just me/we.

Psalm 51:1–17
Self-Recognition Day

Penitential approach: *wash me thoroughly from my iniquity*
Discipleship approach: TEACH ME WISDOM

purge me with hyssop
LET ME HEAR JOY AND GLADNESS

restore me
I WILL TEACH

a broken spirit
DO GOOD, REBUILD

We begin Lent with a basic choice of approach to life. As long as we remain caught between or trying to balance both penitence and discipleship, we lose sight of where we are to end up and myopically experience strict justice as more real than nurturing mercy.

All-in-all, discipleship bears more hope and fruitfulness than the penitential. This also accords with the beginning of Lenten disciplines intended to result in baptism and membership within a Christian Community. Little-by-little, over time, we have shifted from an affirmation to a denial-of-self. That shift carries with it the seeds of destruction. A church cannot last (even though it has for a long time) only built on penitence and atonement and other doctrinal formulations. A Living G*D will simply move on and leave it doing its rituals.

May Ash Wednesday find you still moving toward a joy of discipleship and living out the belovedness of baptism.

Psalm 54
Proper 20 (25)

According to the superscription, David is hiding among the Ziphites. We might use this as an opportunity to ask what might be hiding in this Psalm of Vengeance and Retribution.

A *New Interpreter's Study Bible* comment:
> The prayer's anticipation of victory and expression of assurance change the situation of the one who prays. This prayer defuses the oppression of the enemies, and hope becomes reality.

That same resource also has an excursus:
> Clearly those victimized by these threatening rivals use the language of prayer as a vehicle of liberation. Enemies are dealt with in words that express uncensored yearning for God's vengeance. Such prayers transfer anger and rage from human hearts to God, yielding enacted vengeance to divine prerogative.

Both of these comments push us to look through lenses other than our giving in to the temptation of the idolatry of preemption. They help us find an already anointed David in the wilderness of a foreign refuge.

In today's world, our betrayal is by Western Wealth, which claims a prerogative of setting the only context able to give and take life.

When in the midst of exile, slavery, genocide, or other loss, leaving no practical recourse, we may be reduced to calling out, "Sic 'em G*D!"

When we are able to take another look and see a particular fruitful tree instead of a forest of fear, we may see again the hidden and yet central verse 4. Help is available and can be upheld in the midst of any disaster or series of disasters. "Help" is a moment of relationship in a larger setting. "Help" is a partnership, not just a unilateral act. There is a vision of something now unseen coming into being. There is a mutuality implied that helper and helpee will go back and forth to the benefit of both and more than both—of all.

Psalm 62:5–12
Guiding Gift [3]

For G*D alone my soul waits in silence.
For G*D alone my soul pants like a deer for flowing streams.
For G*D alone my soul searches the heights and depths.
For G*D alone . . . .

My rock, my deliverance, my questioner, my friend, my image, my judge, my . . . .

For Neighb*r alone my soul waits in silence.
For Neighb*r alone my soul pants like a deer for flowing streams.
For Neighb*r alone my soul searches the heights and depths.
For Neighb*r alone . . . .

Beyond an affirmation that G*D pays a fair wage for a day's work, how's your day's-work quotient? What would you consider a fair recompense for it?

Would you be willing to be recruited to the long line of prophets who are able to see the good and evil results of current behaviors and speak it clearly (whether believing it will make a difference or not)? It is this seeing the results of present actions that is the gift of Eve's choice, not some *a priori* ideal of good and evil to be parsed beforehand and chosen for or against. Waiting in silence, etc., brings a new view of "disciples" and "prophets". In addition to being alternative spellings of one another, they are both experience-based. Prophet Eve leads to Prophet Jonah leads to Prophet (your name here).

Play prophetically with these pairings:

silence — rock — deliverance — pour out

hope — salvation — honor — trust

Psalm 70
Clarification Week Wednesday

Well, we have ridden into the city and been cheered. No arrests were made at the upset at the Temple. Plans are underway for Passover. Perhaps this is prelude to the Romans finally seeing we are more trouble than we are worth and saying, "Let them go." Still, there is ambivalence because Jesus is still talking, "Suffering, death, new life."

Into this tension between our hopes that all will work out for the best by tomorrow and I am going to have to give up something today, comes Psalm 70 and maybe, because of the lack of ascription on Psalm 71, also Psalm 71. So read on.

We are pumping out, "God is great!", just as much as we can. It is almost as if we can only say it often enough and passionately enough that we will yet come through without the death-part Jesus keeps harping on.

Finally, though, it comes down to, "But I will hope continually." May this be sufficient for the days ahead.

[Note to self: Still caught in a culture of individualism, it is very easy to read this as a Psalm about my deliverance. Without a group solidarity, there will be a temptation for us to scatter when we momentarily lose track of hope while in the heat of a confrontational choice.]

Psalm 71:1–14
Clarification Week Tuesday

Especially after a time of Hosanna, do we need to take into account horrors yet ahead. These sub-optimal realities run the gamut from expected aging to being intentionally targeted right now.

All the trust built up through our years can only store up so much persistence. At some point, we can but continue through an application of hope beyond what can now be trusted.

There are times when our trust, hope, and love will be our primary vehicle of engaging life. The greatest of these will often be our trust, until it fails. Often, it will be our loving relationship with creation that comes to the fore. And, often, it will be a hope in a mystery still undefined. Thankfully, each supports the other when one (or more) goes AWOL.

Regardless of how vulnerable you may seem to yourself or others, remember how thankful you are to have simply made it thus far. In such remembrance, we find a place to stand and continue levering joy to the forefront of possibilities, always available to be chosen for.

Psalm 72:1–7, 10–14
Guiding Gift [1]

It is the king's responsibility to uphold and administer justice. It is a president's place to do the same. Likewise, for a bishop, pastor, lay leader. And the same for parents, employers, teachers. And for everyone else not so far listed, we too have a responsibility for justice processes.

The yearning for, searching for, attempting, and implementing justice is constituent with long-term common good.

We keep short-circuiting justice with economic and political models that eventually meld together, each subverting the other. All too soon, there is no check or balance available to keep the poor from becoming poorer, even as prosperity for all is available. The needy stand as sign and significance of a lack of pity, compassion, community. As oppression and violence are put into legal place to ensure economic/political power, we look to justice leaders only to find them absent.

It is not just the king who needs a reminder about the interconnected web of life and the respect and honor due each one. This is a reminder to all that justice depends on each of us to raise the questions and to risk standing with the poor and those who have no helper.

On Epiphany, may we give even better gifts than gold, frankincense, and myrrh. May we offer our heart and energy to justice on behalf of manger-laid people everywhere.

Psalm 78:1–2, 34–38
Relic Day

While we tend to be creatures of the concrete, the tangible, we can learn to attend to ancient parables and hoary riddles. The meanings of life do shift in their descriptions from generation to generation, but the desire for meaning remains. As we listen in on past wrestlings, we clarify both current strengths and lacunae that will soon force a reconsideration of paradigms.

One of the things we learn as we listen to prophets, fair and false, is the way people have lied to themselves about their desires trumping realities. So it is that we have perpetuated harm to one group or another. In attending to these learnings, we learn to ask better questions about our present state of fairness.

Another learning is the way mercy has been applied far beyond our judgment. This pattern can have a huge impact on our engagement with difficulties in this moment. We are encouraged to keep a lens of mercy ever before us. To see the play of current affairs under the light of a merciful response to a hurtful act is to learn one more entry point into a live partnership with G*D and Neighb*r.

Try substituting a parable tied around your arm or running through your mind as strongly as one of those earworm tunes that gets in. This will probably have a stronger effect on you than a shard or replica of some so-called cross around your neck or tattooed on your skin.

Psalm 78:23–29
Proper 13 (18)

Ah, sweet fleshpots! There is nothing sweeter than vain imaginings that something other than a worthy life will satisfy. We look for that "more" in sex and getting what we want through betrayal. We look for that "more" in "the good old days" (that really weren't). We look for that "more" in controlling unanimity by using fear of the "other" to keep us in line. We look for that "more" in fullness of stomach and pocketbook.

———————————

our transgression
needing untold mercy
is the violence
to which we will go
to get a fuller stomach

no matter how we cover it over
sin is connected with violence
this is its ultimate ending place
little by little we accommodate
and fear fear enough to instill fear

a clean heart restores joy
so lacking in short-cuts
that lead to violence
so focus on joy
sustain a willing joy

joy-gifts touch us
deeper than tokens of fear
joy that sees abundance
all around
reveals the lie of violence

Psalm 80:1–7, 17–19
Needed Change [1]

O G*D who leads, we plead, "Save us; restore us".

There are presumptions galore here about the nature of G*D and an expected state of affairs for ourselves.

Does a "G*D who leads" lead into exile, into dark nights of souls and of simply dark nights? If so, what blocks our recognition of such leadership in the midst of our waiting and yearning for elseways?

Does a "G*D who leads" need to be pleaded with to go into reverse gear and restore? If so, is this a God we would care to follow?

Where else might "a G*D who leads" lead? If it is not backward or it is not forward, so we can repeat this dance for the umpteenth time, might it be to an advent empty emptiness of our present that we might accept its emptiness and appreciate its fullness?

Is the restoration needed here a restoration to an intimate and erotic relationship with G*D (read, with one another and creation), where we are, in exile and continuing to walk through a void, and not a return to a previous set point? If so, what we need to work on is not setting ourselves right at the expense of someone else who has done injury to us, but with our self that contains G*D and with G*D inside whose face we may yet be.

In the Kabbala, the word "before" G*D's face comes from roots indicating "inside". If we follow this, the plea to let G*D's face shine is to find ourselves at one, inside G*D's face. While we are yet separated by whatever it is that we use to cause and continue such, G*D's face shines not.

What we plead for, we find we have the resources to accomplish. Soon, with Joseph, may we awake from our sleep, shine forth from G*D's face, and live a compassion that receives that which is not ours, as though it were.

Psalm 81:1–10
Guiding Gift [9] — Proper 4 (9)

Different translations handle the numbering of verses in this psalm differently. Whether at the end of verse 5 or 6, there is this construct midway through this pericope.

"G*D hears an unfamiliar or unknown voice."

Mitchell Dahood in *The Anchor Bible* helps us understand that this is a reference to "collective Israel in Egypt before it was chosen by God as his people. Before its election, Israel was 'unknown' to God."

Imagine the Magi hearing an unknown voice from the stars and wandering off to find its source. Once identified, gifts are given that symbolize the same honor and release we hear about with the Israelites.

Gold, frankincense, and myrrh are sources of freedom from temptation to sustenance, eternity, and power in a similar fashion to freedom from the realities of forced labor, genocide, and meaninglessness.

As we move from hunger to satisfaction, we find a correlation between whatever "G*D" might signify and a needed freedom to engage a past in light of a preferred future and make needed changes now to arrive later.

Might you listen to an unknown voice today? There is no need to currently label it as anything other than unknown as that might slow your response. All too often, we connect the unknown with taboo or unclean. If you consider the unknown as simply unknown space, it may yet be a source of salvation for both of you.

Psalm 84
Old Welcomes New — Proper 16 (21)

A comment on verse 2 from *The Jewish Study Bible* [Note: This is verse 1 in the Christian Bibles that don't count the ascription as a first verse]:

> *Lovely,* Heb "yedidot", is not just "beautiful" but "beloved." There is almost a mystical quality in the intensity of the psalmist's desire (with his entire being, v.3) to be in God's presence.

Beauty—a marker of the presence of G*D. We yearn for it even as we trash our planet and relationships with one another. Beauty, for some, is a mighty temple and for some lowly bread. And for you?

When we partner with a living G*D, the smallest sparrow has its place, as does the largest whale. A beauty of partnering and mature-relating is easy to spot. It is evident in every vale of tears transformed to deep joy and singing in the rain.

Instead of measuring our life in drips of sin, live radically within the tides of beauty. Beauty honors G*D and Neighb*r and S*lf.

On your pilgrimage to the center of your faith/being, what is a beloved person, moment, event, etc., that would be a marker of what you are aiming the rest of your life toward re-membering again and again in each new moment?

To find this kind of loveliness triggers a trust that such is a worthy intention to which we might put our longing, our yearning, from this time forward.

Psalm 85:1–2, 8–13
Needed Change [2]

Speaking of peace is one of the most active of endeavors.

Peace aids the meeting of love and faithfulness. Without it, these two would continue along their separate but equal arcs—each finding a way to avoid the other. Love without faithfulness can wander off in any old direction, and faithfulness without love is all too easily stuck.

Peace even works on itself and its doppelgänger, righteousness. They kiss (to complete themselves, not to betray the other). Peace blesses and is blessed by the easiest way away from peace, self-righteousness that covers up communal-righteousness. Peace kisses past the shell to the place of unity.

Peace plays creator between the waters above (righteousness) and the waters below (faithfulness) so that neither takes over and life can happen between. Peace calls each to its place in the wholeness of well-being.

To "Peace" is to lead an active life, a pro-active life, leading to more life, life in abundance. Advent is a time to practice the presence of peace between our various selves (internal and external). This is a most wonderful time of the year—setting the expectation of Peace that we will work on all the rest of the year.

If you are interested in Advent Devotionals that are oriented to moving beyond the struggles of life to learn from them a peace that passes our understanding, but not our participation, you are invited to check out *wumfsa.org/reflections/lentadventindex.html*.

Psalm 85:8–13
Proper 10 (15)

Sing for what can now be seen as providence. Once it could only be seen as disaster, but now, through the lens of steadfast love meeting faithfulness and justice cavorting with peace, we can glimpse a blessing in the midst of true disaster.

This doesn't mitigate the troubles or redeem the losses. This simply gives us a perspective from which to stand and take another step.

What would this world be like if we had memorials to providence rather than to victors? To the mystery of everyday living rather than to mechanical beasts?

Consider what song you are singing. If it is too optimistic, get real. If it is too pessimistic, remember providence.

Either way, let's continue to be a righteousness that goes ahead of G*D, making a path for G*D's presence. That's pretty good enough work.

Psalm 89:1–4, 19–26
Needed Change [4]

Love is built to last forever.
[*New Jerusalem Bible*, Psalm 89:2]

This is a grand affirmation. Later, G*D says of David, "My constancy and faithful love will be with him."

Can you hear this affirmation addressed to you?

When I hear this for myself, I begin to try saying it to others. And then something happens as I begin to hear it coming out of my own mouth toward (1) G*D, (2) my Neighb*rs, (3) my self, (4) one another, and even toward (5) enemies. While yet shaping the words, there is something holding my voice back from meaning it. It is almost as though I recognize that love is built to last forever, and I am not ready to live out the consequences of that reality.

May we so love in all these five different directions at the same time, thus giving birth to a new heaven and a new earth. What else will get us to that glorious newness than living as though love were indeed built to last and last it will? So dive deep into love and live anew.

For G*D so loved the world that G*D participated in its frailty (birth). As an image and partner of G*D, we also participate in the birthing of tomorrow through the frailty of today.

Psalm 89:20–37
Proper 11 (16)

A youngest son out tending sheep is finally found and anointed. Three ancestresses—Tamar, Rahab, and Ruth—foreign and sexually wily, have to be acknowledged. There is no predicting David's ascendency with this background. Imagine the political ads against David. We will, however, grant great importance to his descendants.

There are whole theories about the queen of England being a descendant of David's along with who knows how many Jews. There are whole organizations of David's descendants, such as the Davidic Dynasty, much like the Mayflower Society and the Daughters of the American Revolution.

There is a drive in us to be among those who are "established forever like the moon, an enduring witness in the skies". You don't have any prophetic responsibility to live up to; you're in like Flynn.

Presumably, David's descendants are as motley and of no account as were David's ancestors before Samuel came looking. It's not fair to presume upon your lineage if you are not going to do anything that would honor it. First, do what the kings didn't—protect the weak, lift up the weakened. This is the line to be continued—*care-for-all* has persistence while *looking-out-for-one's-own* eventually leads to division and exile. If the internals are not strong, there will always be a crack for an enemy to exploit.

Psalm 90:12–17
Proper 23 (28)

This is a psalm that can be fruitfully returned to, time after time. Reflection here shows a basic creative dynamic that keeps us rolling along. It is an unknown tree eaten from daily that is to be feared—the tree of finally settling on one aspect of life as sufficient for all time. This is a mutant cousin of a Tree of Life.

Listen again to how it is that Peace is a dynamic of growth. Here, foolishness is settling for only one benefit out of many—primarily settling for a benefit for me over a benefit for a larger community—war, with the power and control it brings.

Some internal impetus of steadfast love engages some external difference or eternal truth, and a spark is generated that eventually calls forth one more step to be trod and investigated.

What is here described as truth springing up and righteousness gazing down can apply in a variety of contexts. When these are operating together, we find a larger than expected harvest, a larger than previously known common-good.

These results from inner and outer connections prepare a way for the apparent suddenness of a lightning bolt. What seems so arbitrary in its arrival does have precursors we weren't aware of.

Much of our work is the analysis of roadblocks, preparation for their removal by way of fulcrum placement, designing a lever adequate for its task, strengthening a place to stand, and applying an individual or corporate amount of weight and energy.

Through all of this, we find that which is growing within and opening before us, creatively and interactively applying both a process of steadfast love and a desired outcome of wholeness.

What processes and outcomes are informing one another in your current life circumstance? How's that working out for you?

---

beauty is
we walk in beauty
a bounty of beauty

the work of our lives
confirms and establishes
these graces

kindness
becomes
our beauty mark

how pleasant it is
to shine forth
beautiful kindness

Psalm 91:9–16
Proper 24 (29)

Americans have effectively changed the language of their founding from "common defense" to "assured security". Of course, there is no way to assure security—Death of individuals and Fall of regimes will out.

The same adjustment has been made within American Christianity and its claim to be a national religion. It has moved from "trust" to a guaranteed protection or salvation through creedal or behavioral enforcement. This movement has historically come to naught and actually hastened its own demise as alternatives are outlawed. What is designated as too risky turns into one backward-looking salt-pillar or another.

When all our ways are guarded, we are at the greatest risk. No more do we have to rely on a new word. The old smoke and mirrors that have gotten us this far go away as fast as a conjurer's trick. They distracted us from our next plight and the resultant lack of feedback loops found in Research and Development or infrastructure repair that should have been invested in.

To dream of having Goliath-like power, armored by angels, is always to forget we are engaged with a Living G*D, a Dying G*D, an Absent G*D, and a Newly Partnered G*D.

This may be among the most dangerous of scripture passages. We have no security, only sufficient assurance to proceed awhile longer.

Psalm 92:1–4, 12–15
Proper 6 (11)

What is your view of G*D's presence in the midst of difficult times? Easy to discern? Can't tell until you look back at one pair of footprints? A dark night of the soul that doesn't even have any footprints?

Is it your view that the righteous flourish? That the lawless get theirs?

These questionable understandings of how life moves and has meaning affect our interpretation of our experience. Fortunately, our experience can also affect our viewpoint. In the interplay between our predominant viewpoint and our various experiences, we find ourselves both fated from the past and freed for a different future. Which will prevail?

An image here is that of a tree filled with fruit. May you continue to see a fruitful future for yourself and for us together. With that vision comes strength for a journey that scatters seeds along the way and prepares for a new creation.

Psalm 93
Our Turn to Witness — Evaluation Day

Consider the triangle as we interact with the metaphor of ascension or the evaluation of a past year.

Wide at the base and indistinct because of the troubled waters of life experience roiling under it. Single-pointed above where there is but stillness.

There is a presupposition that this model is the best model and that the best place on the model is the top. Yet, as we close off one church year and begin a next, there is soon to be a cycle that draws us to dive from the top into the bottom—what topological fun as a silent word takes on noisy flesh.

I know how inappropriate it is to foster these sorts of mixed-up-nesses between scriptural traditions, cosmological models, anachronisms, neologisms, and the like. But I simply can't get used to static images of a living G*D or a living me or you. Every time we get to the surety of decrees and call them holy, it feels like the still before the storm or that what is running deep below the still waters is about to break loose.

If "majestic on high is G*D", can this same G*D be majestic in low places as well? Well, of course. May we have the eyes and ears to hear and join.

Psalm 96
Blessed Body / Proper I

In honor of "Peace on Earth, goodwill to all" - - - -

Sing to your Neighb*r a new song;
  sing to your Neighb*r where'er they be.
Sing to your Neighb*r, bless them;
  tell of their wholeness available this day.
Declare their worth among the human family,
  their good works to others.
Great are your Neighb*rs, and greatly to be praised;
  they are to be revered.
For discrimination among people is an idol,
  but Neighb*rs are part of paradise.
Honor and worthiness are in your Neighb*rs;
  strength and beauty reveal their security.
Bravo for your Neighb*rs; they are family,
  Huzzah for your Neighb*r's presence and joy.
Hooray for your Neighb*r filled with glory;
  share with them, listen to them.
Be in awe of your Neighb*r;
  rejoice with them in this time and space.
Say aloud, "My Neighb*r, my friend!
  Our relationship is firmly established;
  we support and correct one another in equity."
Let the air be glad and the earth rejoice;
  let the sea shout and all that fills it;
  let animals of the field exult.
In sign of all this,
  the trees of the forest will sing for Neighb*rs.
Neighb*rs are gathering, gathering for discerning action.
  Neighb*rs act with compassion to one another and all—
  G*D smiles.

Psalm 97
Blessed Body / Proper I

Propers I, II, and III use Psalms 96, 97, and 98 in sequence. Here in the middle, let's look at all three.

Sing to the Lord a new song:
　Judgment is grounded in equity, righteousness, and truth. (96)
Sing to the Lord an old song:
　God loves, guards, rescues. (97)
Sing to the Lord a new song:
　Remembered steadfast love and faithfulness. (98)

If you had to embody one of these songs, which would come first to your lips? This is almost a personality test and it doesn't make any difference whether that is a gift hard-wired or learned through experience.
Are you into
　　- judgment on what has already happened?
　　- being proactive in peace and justice ministries?
　　- living as you would have the future become?

_____

After the above was published on KCMlection.blogspot.com, our friend Thomas D'Alessio responded:

How about:
Sing to God, for God,
　the very song
　the only song
　that only **you** can sing
　the song that only **your** voice can carry,
　the song that only **your** heart and mind and spirit can dream of.

What if all else
is nothing more or less
than a denial of God?

_____

What is your response?

Psalm 98

Blessed Body / Proper III — Hopeless Hope Vigil — Assured[6]

To judge is to engage in discernment.

Where is righteousness? – where Creation and Humanity clap for one another.

Where is equity? – a key marker is where Joy is mutually expressed.

When will judgment take place? – now and now and now again.

Want to be well judged? Judge well where righteousness and equity might be revealed and reveal them through your actions.

Psalm 98:1–5
Relic Day

Sing a new Song!

A new opening has arrived—just as we had hoped, but for which there was never a confirmation. This new possibility adjusts all our previous relationships. Even that which we had claimed as steadfast love takes on a new energy level. No longer is it simply a background constant, but it becomes an active catalyst for the creation of new love for that which was formerly unlovable.

We sing because we're happy, and we sing because there is no other way forward. We sing a song not yet known. Even an inability to stay on key, in tune, in rhythm, on the current verse, or within any other usual musical value can delay neither the need for nor readiness for a new song. Out of silence—a hum. Even a skeptical, "Hmmm", might begin a new hum or song.

Sing a new Song!

The rest of us are waiting. We wait not for judgment but for this joy of a new song. Simply let it loose, this new song that is yours to add to our common life.

Psalm 103:1–13, 22
Guiding Gift [8] — Proper 3 (8)

What benefit of life do you want to remember, no matter what?

Is it a healing of a spirit, relational break (forgiveness)? Is it a forgiveness of an identity, physical break (healing)? Is it some major escape or a series of smaller sidesteppings? Your sense of being assured, loved, having been treated mercifully? Something long-term or renewable?

Your experience may also entail an appreciation for a trouble that sharpened or strengthened you, even if you couldn't avoid or otherwise overcome it. There may also be some special benefit you have experienced that is unique to yourself.

In one way or another, our benefits tend to be forgotten in the shadow of one concern or another or several simultaneously. So we pause late in Epiphany, or at any time, to check to see whether our benefits are still with us and not pick-pocketed by life's circumstances somewhere along the way.

Have you had a mercy extended to you in excess of the moment? Rejoice. Mark it well. Remember and remember again. Record it, so others might also know. Apply the excess to your Boldness Center, so that you might be even bolder than usual.

Rejoice in your blessings and put them to work for yourself and your Neighb*r.

Psalm 104:1–9, 24, 35c
Proper 24 (29)

"What a wildly wonderful world...." [*The Message*]

I trust this brings to mind Louis Armstrong's *Wonderful World*.

Maybe G*D didn't just rest on the seventh day, but allowed lyrics to ebb and flow and then took one breath ("bigger than a circus tent" as e.e. cummings has it) and an eighth day was sung.

Can you imagine not just cycling through seven days, but going on and on? We would lose some tradition and attributed meaning, but we would also gain an expectation beyond anything so far experienced because wildly wonderful creations of love do go on and on.

Wouldn't it be something if Daniel's days turned out to be less filled with turmoil and apocalypse and, instead, we had a day of lullabies and a day of blues and a day of symphonies and a day of rap and a day of silence—all to express love?

Learning love in so many different ways would open us up to taking our part in the choir, sitting on a telephone wire, some singing high and some singing low. Hum again Bill Staines' song, *A Place in the Choir*.

My yoga teachers have consistently let me know that a result of the discipline is a moving gracefully through the day as well as in a moment of practice. I suspect the psalmist of being a yoga instructor. In this light, consider the wind as you both sit on a wire and proceed through whatever is left of the day. Its flow is shaped by what it meets, and its power shapes all that it touches, a bit at a time. May your flow and power be graceful and creative this day.

Psalm 104:24–34, 35b
Energy to Witness

If we are going to see G*D as reliably creative, we will soon find ourselves moved aside from partnership with G*D to someone who sits up and begs (v 28). We become dependent upon G*D and unable to stray from the orthodox, official, tradition claimed to be the guarantor of our next handout.

Thus, we don't mention sin and wickedness in verse 35a. We need to ban even half-a-verse that takes the focus off of verse 31:

> Glory to Yahweh forever!
> May Yahweh find joy in his creatures!

Where did these consumed sinners and wicked folks come from? The same place as Cain's and Seth's wives? The image of G*D from creation?

Pentecost is not about praise, praise, praise in a secluded room. It is about face-to-face encounters with that which is different and finding a common link between. A too-happy Psalm puts more focus on tongues of fire and less on tongues of reconciliation.

Psalm 107:1–3, 17–22
Conviction [4]

Even fools are redeemable, healable.

There is more than enough foolishness to go around. Let us pray for all the fools who lead us to war. Let us pray for all the fools who are led to war. Let us pray for all the fools who protested war so ineffectively. Let us pray for all the fools who got caught between warring parties. Let us pray for all the fools who will profit from the war. Let us pray for all the fools who pray for all the fools.

May we find the joy and thanksgiving available to replace the warring madness. May faithful love lead to honesty and rejoicing. May redemption lead to a vast silence that is prelude to a great party.

The redeemed (those who recognize G*D's steadfast love and are able to respond to that love, instead of react to it) give thanks that steadfast love, beyond any expectation that it would still be there, is yet available. This action of thanks is a spark or flow of energy that comes from a completed circuit.

Remember back to your own days and moments of thanksgiving that go beyond official turning on and off of thanks (a proclaimed national day, a letter to grandma for a birthday gift, etc.). How might that be transformed into an anticipation of thanks to come and an intentional working toward that which completes a circuit between steadfast love offered and responsive love returned? When working well, this small circuit has become connected with other similar circuits to become a larger presence of steadfast love now awaiting additional responses.

Whether an individual-sized circuit or a congregational-sized circuit or a community-sized circuit, an experience of wholeness leads to a life of activity oriented toward an expansion of thankfulness. Whatever might get in the way of such an expansion is thankfully left behind (sometimes read as sacrificed).

Psalm 107:1–3, 23–32
Proper 7 (12)

Individuals and nations can get caught in storms. At first, they seem lifted to the heavens with a rush of excitement, and then it becomes apparent that the blowback of their presuppositions catches up with them, and they are headed to Davy Jones' Locker.

Think about storms for a moment and our theories of pressure fronts. Storms are generated at the edges of highs and lows. If this were to stand for the wars between individuals and nations, it might be posited that both this Psalm and Psalm 133 are what stands between the two. At stake is living in a unity that is not a uniformity.

It must also be noted that storms do bring rain that brings the flowers. Aargh! If only one image would stand still long enough to hold all the meaning in the world. Well, until then, do what you can to live in a creative unity that allows enough rain to nourish without escalating into a storm that devastates.

Psalm 111
Guiding Gift [4] —Proper 15 (20)

To read this acrostic psalm by itself, without also reading the next acrostic Psalm (112), is to lose one's balance. Here we are marched through the alphabet, seeing G*D in each letter, in all of life. In the next Psalm, we are led along the same alphabetical path, seeing people in each letter, in all of life.

The two together begin to give us another glimpse into the great foci of life—loving G*D, loving Neighb*r, loving S*lf. By extension, we also love environments and enemies.

If the right-eye and left-brain attend to G*D while the left-eye and right-brain attend to neighbors, self, environment, and enemies—wink as fast as you can, back and forth between your two eyes, until they begin to blur together. This takes great discipline. There is not a lot of meditation time left for more transient issues. Consider this process to be a means of grace that will change our relationship with those more fleeting issues of survival and ego.

Attending to this interplay is the beginning of wisdom, for a lection is never encountered in a vacuum.

Psalm 113
Elizabeth and Mary Meet

Whether it be Lady Wisdom in the beginning or Hannah or a Psalmist or Elizabeth or Mary or you or I—when we stop long enough to listen, there is the echo of a far-off hymn hailing a new creation.

Are you hearing the assurance that such a new creation is a given? Even if it gets us into all manner of issues of how such a strong future allows such tragedy at the present to continue, we still proceed as though it were true. To do anything else is to settle for what is, and "We are far too good not to be better." [Robert Rindler, President of the Milwaukee Institute of Art and Design–and probably many others]

Even in the midst of our humility, may we sing loud and clear—a new order is growing among us. Don't give up, for you are one of the stepping stones of its arrival; you bear within you new life.

Psalm 114
Opened Heart Evening — Hopeless Hope Vigil

Oh, for more extravagant language to describe our formation. Most language these days is that of advertising, both political and commercial, that constrains us to one party, one product or another.

Homework:

The tradition of this Psalm of Liberation is to record a whole process leading to freedom into 8 short verses. Put into 8 points the process of your freedom to exercise your gifts. It is OK to use parallelism to extend that to 16 examples.

This task is both difficult and transformative. It is not easy to condense in a way that leads to poetry and not empty words lying alongside one another. It is particularly difficult to refrain from using the religious language of the day.

Because of the difficulty of honestly reviewing transformative events, rejoice that this Psalm comes around twice this year. A comparison between your two exercises will be instructive.

Whether done once, twice, or more times, your re-visioning of your past will open you to a revising of your present and anticipation of at least an equally energetic shift in days to come. Out of our last miracle arises an opportunity for a next crossing of boundaries.

- _____
- _____
- _____
- _____
- _____
- _____
- _____
- _____

Psalm 116:1–2, 12–19
Courage Thursday

Oh, how we like to be acknowledged. Because my voice has been heard, I'll go ahead to a next testing time. And woe be to the god that disappoints, that does not acknowledge me.

What is life but one great series of trust tests? A sequence of tits for tats? When you scratch my back, I'll return the favor?

Into this reality, there eventually comes a question of what I will do with or without trust. Well? To what are you going to be true? Will you remain in a relationship when a trust test falters and fails? For every 10 times you have been responded to, does the respondent receive a get-out-of-disappointment card?

Is this process translatable to what's good for the goose is good for the gander, so that you might also accumulate forgivenesses and opportunities to try trusting again?

Without falling prey to issues of abuse, what are your current boundaries of compassion, and how would you contrast and compare them with previous boundaries and hoped-for boundaries? In responding, don't forget to consider this from the perspective of being on both the giving and receiving end of compassion or trust.

Psalm 116:1–9
Proper 19 (24)

Are you walking in the land of the living or hanging on to personal and cultural traditions and rituals? This is difficult to parse out for we want to have a meaningful life and, at the same time, not to have to risk much to achieve it.

It would be so nice to have a G*D to fall back on who will come through for us without the necessity of our leaving a locked and windy room to practice our communication skills with folks from a different cultural circumstance.

This is one more opportunity to reflect on how easily we let our transformative moments go. We shift to institution-building far more easily than relationship-building and partner-development, which keeps shifting and calling us to change as much as we desire any other to change. And so the three huts on a transfigurative mountain are now instituted after a locked-room experience.

It is hoped that enough practice here will lead us to love as well as resist the dynamics of interrelationships. When this occurs, we no longer cry out for help as much as we presume a providential presence.

In the long run, Grace and Mercy are to call forth more Grace and Mercy and not just be a band-aid or icon for a particular circumstance.

Psalm 118:1–2, 14–24
Assured

> Open for me the gates of saving justice,
> I shall go in and thank Yahweh.
> This is the gate of Yahweh,
> where the upright go in.
>   [NJB vss 19-20]

For those of us who claim Justice to be a key issue in life, we need to keep using that gift as a key to Yahweh's intention for us.

Presumably, others are given the key of Mercy to match that gate of Yahweh.

Let's say there are 12 gates to the city. What are they?

> Justice?
> Mercy?
> Faith?
> Hope?
> Love?
> Persistence?
> Humility?
> Mind?
> Body?
> Emotions?
> Relationships?
> Church?

How do you identify your gate and honor the upright at other gates?

Psalm 119:1–8
Proper 26 (31)

What a difference a comma can make. The United Church of Christ campaign, *God is Still Speaking*, uses a Gracie Allen quote about a comma to describe what we are still learning about G*D and our relationship with the same.

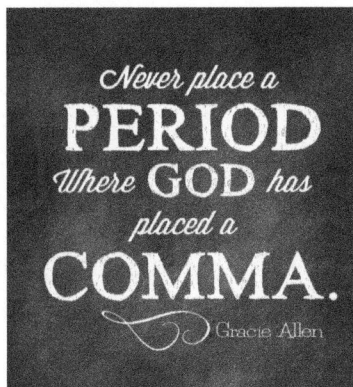

A key here is verse 3, "walking in G*D's ways". Note the plural "ways" of G*D. Note that walking in these ways is not the same as claiming one of them is universal. Note that walking is not static and it is not creedally constrained. Walking in the ways of G*D requires more faith than certainty, more hope than Realpolitik, and more love than personal salvation.

There is room for a goodly community to walk within G*D's ways, each with an upright heart and all with room for each other. So it is we live long in the land.

Our very breath leads us to speak in phrases. Sometimes they are linked together or stand alone as a sentence. Sometimes, not. The space between our phrases is an oral comma that needs honoring. It is as though we have built-in opportunities to listen to our heritage and our hope, as well as our moment in the sun. To pile phrase upon phrase for nothing but making a point, proving one thing or another, without allowing for a pause to speak a word of affirmation or correction, is a source of great trouble. Commas are built into life so that we might better say something of value.

Very little will add more to life than an ability to listen and speak as we engage one another, particularly to listen and speak while we are speaking. A breath, a comma, may let us know when we are about to say more than we know or understand, and to early and easily retract a hasty word.

Psalm 119:9–16
Conviction [5]

Why learn laws? Well, they track our errors and make it possible to learn from them. Laws can be a source of pleasure as we remember not to repeat a mistake.

For the same reason, a next law will be in order—a new lesson has begun to be learned.

Just as importantly, we can learn that we learned the wrong lesson when we made a law. This makes it possible to modify or repeal a mis-learned law.

So let's not get all rote about law. While legalists have a tendency to teach to the law and to make new laws to expand prior law qua law, life experience will eventually win through. Even as laws are still expanding, we live toward the turning of the law when law is delightfully deconstructed back to the basics of Love (creation and all neighbors)—against which there is no law.

Psalm 123
Proper 9 (14)

Mercy is indeed needed. It is an ever-present need. There are contexts and events that are not controllable but, nonetheless, need a response that includes mercy.

At issue is whether mercy is exclusively what is needed.

For instance, when and where will mercy appear as preemptive advocacy from the bottom-up rather than a benefit dispensed from on high?

How might G*D's image interact with the rest of creation to affirm mercy has already been experienced, rather than is still to arrive?

Given the reality of Mercy, what will it take to stand for one's self as well as another's life?

Psalm 124

Proper 21 (26)

If Roy were not on our side [*remember when*]
  we would have sunk.

If Betty Lou were not on our side [*remember when*]
  we would have sunk.

If G*D were not on our side [*remember when*]
  we would have sunk.

If Mom were not on our side [*remember when*]
  we would have sunk.

If Jesus were not on our side [*remember when*]
  we would have sunk.

Who else would you add to this list?

Sometimes our thanks is creation-wide. Sometimes it is very specifically located. Either way, when we experience being lifted up, it feels as though we were a bird escaped from a cage. A new horizon is before us.

In all of this, we find ourselves unable to say "Thanks" to G*D without also expressing it to Roy. Likewise, we can't say thanks to Betty Lou without including Jesus. May your thanks always bind together new relationships.

If we are to love both G*D and Neighb*r, we are to thank both Neighb*r and G*D.

Psalm 125
Proper 18 (23)

What would keep a hand from a scepter of wickedness? This "Precious" is a great temptation and needs a strong intention to avoid it. We might look to mountains to hedge us in, leaving only the good as an option. We might employ capital punishment, eternal separation, as a technique to discourage wrong-doing.

We know from experience that external controls are only as good as their last success. Eventually, they will be tested and tested again. The two-year-old and adolescent in us will push every boundary and push again. Sooner or later, a temptation will be stronger than our intention.

Eventually, it comes to what we trust. We trust that being upright and forthright pays a better dividend than the breaking of trust with G*D, Neighb*r, or S*lf.

Image trust as solid as a mountain. A landslide may happen and rearrange a contour, but the basic mass is still present. Imagine living a solidly helpful life. A backslide may happen, but a basic integrity is still present.

Psalm 126
Needed Change [3] — Proper 25 (30) — Thanksgiving

> Rejoice!
> Restore!
> Rejoice!
> Restore!
> etc.

What a wheel of life we are on.

In theory, we are not on a dynamometer that lets a vehicle run in place to measure output. Rather, our theory is that each revolution is going somewhere.

Feel like you are spinning your wheels? Call for restoration.

Feel like you can glimpse a destination in the distance, and it is getting closer? Offer rejoicing.

Do both with good integrity (acknowledging the reality of the other perspective) and good energy (call and respond enthusiastically).

It has sometimes felt as though our lives have been stolen by our brothers and sisters of the religious right, who can only measure restoration in terms of going back rather than returning to go ahead. We can hardly breathe within their constraints. We have been in a time when the only reality has seemed to be the necessity of our own calling out, "Restore, Restore, Restore," with no rejoicing available.

Here we have two different calls for restoration battling one another. Perhaps one way to break this impasse is to be diligent in seeing the possibility of celebrating anyhow.

It may well be that we need to see beyond the moment and anticipate rejoicing in our release from bondage by our own. What can fear do to laughter but try to do it in and, as a consequence, set up the eventuality of rejoicing having the last laugh?

Psalm 127
Proper 27 (32)

How does a LORD build houses and guard cities and give sleep to the anxious?

From the very resources and potentials invested within us?

It is very easy to over-focus on G*D's power without considering how we play our part.

An important issue is how we see G*D's authority at work in the world. A significant model G*D uses over and over is an unexpected person, a youngster, an outcast, a baby, a death—whereby the enemy of life and justice is shown for what it is: shame trying to blame the victim for the crime.

Imagine you have a quiver of yourselves to aid you in your living. All those experiences from the past and all your expectations of ever-greater love of G*D and Neighb*r support your living well in this in-between moment. Wow, what resources we have been given. No wonder we don't give up building and guarding and resting.

Psalm 130
Proper 5 (10) — Proper 8 (13) — Proper14 (19)

sensitive to word and touch
we journey toward
a great getting-up day
when and where
our eagerness is sufficient
for earnest need

attentive beyond death
we settle in to days no more
no more mourning
riling to despair
no more no more
holding us back

in moments of generosity
we undertake a beginning desire
little by little
through this year
according to what we have
abundance in need

Psalm 132:1–12, (13–18)
Evaluation Day / Proper 29 (34)

The last Sunday of a church year might be thought to be a resting place. We've worked on peace for generations now. Surely one more year would have seen us arrive at a time for Jubilee.

The Psalm anticipates an eternal monarchy as the best governance model. At some point, though, recognition was bound to happen that the end-all and be-all of our relationship with G*D is not keeping current social classes going in perpetuity, albeit with the poor getting enough bread to subsist on—which isn't always the case.

If the best we can do is to have "The Lord rise up and go to a resting place," we have missed much in the way of growing into G*D ourselves. This is a static image that time cannot abide. And so in our end is our beginning—G*D is loose. Get a head start on Advent; begin your yearly game of hide-and-seek with G*D, Neighb*r, and Y*urself today.

G*D needs a rest. Too much wandering around outside of Eden and coming up with new responses to these very creative humans, packed to overflowing with cosmic energy.

G*D needs a rest. Too many promises to too many people. Too many expectations. Too many covenant revisions and new creations.

G*D needs a rest. Perhaps a Temple will be restful (until rousted by warriors from the outside and curtains ripped from the inside). Perhaps setting up a bloodline will be restful (until squabbles arise between potential heirs and those who prevail set up unstable conditions to suit only themselves).

G*D needs a rest. For such a time as this, you have a lullaby to sing and a task to pick up. In due time, you will need a rest. Then both G*D and you can rise refreshed to welcome one another and all others to health and wholeness.

Psalm 133
Assured [2] — Proper 7 (12)

Unity as "good and pleasant" is quite an understatement. Given our starting points, to arrive at some semblance of unity (an outcome of justice) is so remarkable that it calls for a more enthusiastic response.

To arrive at some given understanding that rejection is not the last word about the meaning of life (though it is often one of the first words we encode), a sense of relief in the face of such mercy needs a conversion miracle response.

---

how good and pleasant
to live together
it anoints a whole community
beyond a series of individuals

this living together
reveals an original blessing
a tree of life not forgotten
in the midst of a forest of all we know

though spoken often
this message is often overwritten
with desires of our heart—
resurrection is a communal event!

Psalm 138
Proper 5 (10)

A grateful heart is a key characteristic of living holistically. Recognition that our heart might be grateful is an important step in maturation. As difficult as it is to grow and recognize the role of gratefulness (rather than an enforced, "Did you remember to thank so-and-so for their birthday gift?"), it is just as difficult to begin filling your heart with grateful moments.

In life's usual way, we will also need to learn to be able to set a grateful heart aside, to not be so trapped by it that we lose our relationship with life that calls us to be a source of gratefulness as well as a recipient of it.

If we develop a grateful heart to be able to have everything done for us, we are but a clanging cymbal, full of lots of sound waves, but out of rhythm with the orchestra of life. Our grateful heart can become like a baby bird, all mouth, awaiting more.

May we regularly put our experiences into our grateful heart and as regularly pull them out to energize our engagement with places of ongoing pain.

May you celebrate well and be a catalyst for celebration by others.

Psalm 139:1–6, 13–18
Guiding Gift [2] — Proper 4 (9)

Verse 16: *Your eyes beheld my unformed substance. In your book were written all the days that were formed for me, when none of them as yet existed.* [NRSV]

Imagine you still have "unformed substance" (we are still calling it "junk DNA" until we know more).

This is not an easy one, so try it again: Imagine you still have "unformed substance".

Part of the difficulty of this creative pull into new being is that it is found between the many (sands) and the one (I am with you!). That which we might become when we grow up is as open as open can be (all the days) and as sharply drawn as anyone would want (days formed for me).

From this personal moment: Our grandchildren, ourselves, and our parents in the good hands of Hospice are all beholding our unformed substance. Our days and day are as natural as can be in this day. But if we were caught here forever, how sad. The young ones would not grow in grace. We older ones would only have our alzheimic memories. And the ancient of days would have only darkness.

Imagine you still have "unformed substance". What's next? What's not possible?

Verse 16: *Thine eyes did see my substance, yet being unperfect; and in thy book all my members were written, which in continuance were fashioned, when as yet there was none of them.* [KJV]

"Unperfect" here refers to an embryonic state in the process of being wrapped or folded together. We might be aided with an on-going appreciation of the unperfect folding and unfolding of stages whether currently in what might be called pre-life, or life, or what might be called post-life.

A blessed "unperfection" or "unformed substance" to you.

Psalm 143
Hopeless Hope Vigil

In a partnership, one would hope that neither of the parties is "righteous" before the other. Should that become the case, it would lead to a "fainting spirit" as partners are parted.

A key quality of our various relationships:

> self to S*lf
> self to Neighb*r
> self to G*D
> self to Others (similar or not)
> self to Enemies (personal and societal)

is that of preserving the others for our own sake and preserving ourselves for the sake of those we are partnered with.

Every morning, may you hear where trust yet abides and where steadfast love is still applied. Every morning, may you offer these to someone in need.

Psalm 145:10–18
Proper 12 (17)

Faithful in intention.
Graceful in deed.

might be an inscription you would choose for your grave marker.

The degree to which this corresponds to reality is a measure of your life force.

This psalm is a good wrap-up of our direction in life. You might try engaging this as a daily checklist.

Intent/Deed	M	T	W	Th	F	Sat	Sun
blessing							
praise							
gratefulness to ancestors							
preparation for descendants							
abundance of available good							
grace							
mercy							
steadfast love							
compassion							
thanks							
trustworthiness							
raising the fallen							
open hands generosity							
kind justice							
being present, ever near							

Psalm 146
Proper 18 (23) — Proper 26 (31) — Proper 27 (32)

Which of these qualities ascribed to G*D is most important to you today?

For how long has that been the case?

Do you feel a new arena beginning to open?

G*D . . .

> remains steadfast
> does justice for the oppressed
> feeds the hungry
> frees prisoners
> opens blind eyes
> lifts the fallen
> honors the good
> protects strangers
> sides with orphans and widows
> brings down powers

Which do you ascribe to or aspire to?

For how long?

What additional arena of life needs to be added here?

Psalm 147:1–11, 20c
Guiding Gift [5]

Verses 5 & 6 put together what is often broken apart in today's church (probably the church in any day).

> Our Lord is great, all-powerful,
> his wisdom beyond all telling.
> Yahweh sustains the poor,
> and humbles the wicked to the ground. [NJB]

First, we hear the praise refrain, Our G*D is an awesome G*D.

Second, we hear involvement in social justice.

For some reason, we tend to bounce back and forth between these two and set them up in antagonism to one another. The praise folks don't get the peace with justice stuff, and *vice versa*.

There is the transcendent G*D and the immanent G*D. The G*D beyond the stars and the G*D grounded in being. The work before us is the mystery of both/and rather than either/or. As we proceed, it is important to invite in and even search out the polarity where we are more uncomfortable. This is not to abandon the gift given us in our natural inclinations, but to experience the uncomfortable humility of living and dying for all of life and not just our own.

Psalm 147:12–20
Blessed Body [2]

Last year, on the Sunday after Christmas, we heard Rachel wailing in Ramah. At what point in Rachel's experience would she have found this psalm to resonate?

Would she need to hear it before she wailed, that it might be background to all else?

Is she able to sing it along with laments during a slaughter of innocents? (Remember your response to this includes the "collateral damage" done to children on this very day, even though we may not hear about it, by poverty in any city in the proverbial richest country of the world, and by that same country's army and bombs in far-off countries. Can you sing this psalm today?)

Will Rachel only be able to join this psalm at some future time, similar to Job's two-fold restoration?

For the moment, I am tired of bragging up G*D. How might we better work together for a common good and commonwealth? These boom and bust cycles are wearing us out.

Psalm 148
Blessed Body [1]

The word "praise" comes from older words related to "price".

What price do you put on praise? This is an important question. Is it what keeps you from living praise—the cost to some part of you is too high?

What price would be too high for having been created (vs. 4) or for having been incorporated into a neighborhood (vs. 13)?

What price do we charge others to praise? Do they have to say things in a certain creedal way? Must they experience glossolalia? Will they have to agree to a particular polity? Has status, power, class, education level, income, or other mark become a hurdle to their ability to ante in or to your willingness to welcome?

What keeps you from praise, and what keeps others from praise. How are these realities related?

Ultimately, praise is connected with action or it is just flattery.

To help you think about what keeps you from praise, consider *The New Interpreter's Bible* comment:

> While the songs of praise generally push toward universality (see Psalms 67:1-7; 100:1; 103:20-22; 117:1), Psalm 148 takes inclusivity to the limit, surpassing even the final climactic verse of the psalter (150:6). The inclusivity of the invitation to praise God has profound implications that demonstrate the inseparability of theology and ecology....

And the question of the day:

> Is there a limit to the praise (act) of inclusivity?

If "yes", what is it?

If "no", why do we keep playing the same discriminatory games against people and creation?

Proverbs 1:20–33
Proper 19 (24)

Howsomever we identify ourselves, we eat the fruit of our way.

This approach to the desired and undesired parts of our life, the life of others, and our common life does not justify continuing the ways in which we interact. There will be folks who get away with mean and nasty acts all their life, and others cut short well before their prime. This is not about karma or reincarnation. It has to do with self-justification and an excuse to continue a journey we might otherwise shift.

Evelyn Underhill puts it this way:

> The true rule of poverty consists in giving up those things which enchain the spirit, divide its interests, and deflect it on its road to God—whether these things be riches, habits, religious observances, friends, interests, distastes, or desires—not in mere outward destitution for its own sake. It is attitude, not act, that matters; self-denudation would be unnecessary were it not for our inveterate tendency to attribute false value to things the moment they become our own.

Eating the fruit of our way is the reinforcement of a habit or a way of approaching life. Some of this seems to be hardwired, but even that can be amenable to choices made regarding what we will attend to. To be willing to share the fruit of another way, of another's life or identity, draws us closer to their experience of life. Here lies the possibility of community that calls us to accountability for the whole of life, not just our own.

In the care of the larger, the smaller is also cared for—infrastructure intended for all is a blessing. Concentration of wealth in a few is a fever indicator of the ill-health of a community. Oh, we could go on about the importance of one life, but note how the larger context changes with changes in the particulars. It is not simply that a next best thing is done, but that it is done in a context.

Whose identity, currently missing, needs to enter your life today, to be tasted and enjoyed in its own right?

Proverbs 8:1–8, 19–21; 9:4b–6
Hopeless Hope Vigil

A Wisdom that extols itself is suspect as wisdom. Likewise with Understanding. In response to naivety and foolishness, Wisdom and Understanding try most diligently to identify some way of being that can't be subverted. In a blink of an eye, this attempt goes awry, for a next moment makes these posited truths uncouth.

When all of one's words are righteous, they become literal, earnest, and fragile, for now they must defend themselves against all comers, including a next Wisdom and Understanding.

When the claim is made of not being twisted or crooked in any wise, there is trouble brewing. Soon, the ideal of having only to do with truth that cannot be bought turns into wealth that comes to prove where Wisdom lies ("lies" is here used in several ways).

I hope you laughed as you read verses 19–21 when that which is claimed to be better than gold is then used to line the pockets of the "wise" with the very gold Wisdom is better than.

All too often, this prosperity gospel approach is attractive rather than laughable. Don't try cashing any lies.

Proverbs 9:1–6
Proper 15 (20)

The temptation of "understanding" is very great. Even wise old Solomon finally failed that test. Along with understanding came/comes riches and honor. And what, I ask, can stand in the face of such a principality and power? Understanding eventually pales through the temptation of increased riches and honor. Why? Simply because it takes so much to increase in wisdom appropriate to this new time and place. Let your growth in understanding lag for a bit, presuming for a moment that you have sufficient, and, lo and behold, riches and honor gain momentum and priority.

Without an increase in wisdom, there can be no sense made of metaphor and mystery, such as living bread imaged in personal terms. Alice in Wonderland's bottle and cake remain as strange to us as Jesus' language about eating him. Where we are willing to suspend our disbelief with Alice, we don't seem to be able to do so with Jesus.

[Can't help but wonder if Jesus tastes as wonderful as Alice's Wonderland drink—"mixed flavor of cherry-tart, custard, pineapple, roast turkey, toffee, and hot buttered toast".]

Proverbs 22:1–2, 8–9, 22–23
Proper 18 (23)

Fortunately, Proverbs come in parallel statements. This gives a second opportunity to view what is at issue. Using two sources of data can lift a 2-D movie to 3-D and do the equivalent with our imagination.

A good name—partner in creation—is not only a valuable commodity to be traded on, it is a realistic way to look at all our various relationships.

When we are clear about our connection with creation, we begin to lose the cultural and tribal distinctions of "rich" and "poor" at home or "us" and "them" anywhere. This perception opens us to connections with justice and generosity in new and helpful ways.

Likewise, beginning with issues of injustice opens our eyes to such ultimately backfiring. Then we find what works, what blesses, is generosity. Now we can return to where we began—creation itself that evidences generosity and generativity of partnership as the measuring rods of healthy relationships.

---

our good name
partner of creation
steps apart from injustice
draws near through generosity
refuses to rob or afflict
stands with creators everywhere

Proverbs 31:19–31
Proper 20 (25)

This acrostic poem means there will be some forced artificiality to the content. It is similar to those forced rhymes by second-rate poets, while the first-rate ones know how to sometimes come close and sometimes break the pattern.

For the moment, focus on verse 25—"Strength and dignity are her clothing, and she laughs at the time to come."

May this be said of you and me and others within whichever religious tradition we live and move and have our being.

Strength and dignity and laughter. What a wonderful combination. To have only one of this trinity is to falter. To have even two of the three is to stumble forward. To have all three at our disposal and to be able to play with them will lead to a life in all its fullness.

Be full—put on strength; wrap yourself in dignity; let laughter bubble up from within.

Without these three, it is all too easy to force women into only one way of being. For instance, the starting point of a good and capable wife/woman being hard to find. This starting point makes it difficult to have any but a periodic female exemplar. It excuses much even as it is usually perceived as an accolade.

This proverb is a testament to women having to work more than twice as hard to simply hold on to half the respect simply due any person.

Focus now on verses 23 and 31. Husbands/men can be counted among the public deciders simply because they are male. Wives/women show their competency, and yet there is only a recommendation that they find personal praise sufficient, rather than public decision-making. In the end, the only thing offered is a pat on the back rather than actual partnership in community affairs.

All the praises here heaped upon women turn out to be flattery, not serious participation in the decisions of life. And patriarchy, expressed today as capitalism, continues, co-opting women and children and poor men.

G*D have mercy and help us see ourselves as we are seen, so some modicum of hope might be held out for moving on from this stuck place.

Ecclesiastes 3:1–13
New Year's Day

Everything is fitting for its time, and when that fit is honored, it turns out that it contained a crucial component of eternity, of everything else.

Through the details of a moment, a larger picture begins to take shape, point by point. Detectives and spiritual directors are more interested in these details than some imagined ideal.

Here on our cultural cusp of time, when a proverbial "Old Father Time" stumbles out, weighted down with a year's worth of details and "Baby New Year" crawls naked of any details, is an opportunity to do more than weep or rejoice over a particular part of last year or to lade unrealistic fantasies with no grounding onto a next year. Time alone does not resolve anything.

What will be helpful is to be grounded in everyday realities of meeting survival needs, cultivating community, and working at what is fit for its time.

We can practice this grounding by asking time past about 1 small thing left undone, despite a whole year to have worked on it. Then, join into partnership with time to come that it, at least, will have that one detail come to fruition within the next year.

Mind you, nothing grandiose here. What one small thing might be moved ahead? Baby Years can't handle much, but they do have good energy and an ability to learn. May your partnership weld your intention to a new approach and pay good dividends for you and all.

Song of Songs 2:8–13
Proper 17 (22)

A first or most recent glance at a beloved calls forth action.
A first or most recent whisper of a beloved calls forth action.

Whether from or toward a beloved, we are called beyond sitting and theorizing/creedalizing/speculizing.

Even with the threat of messing up, of mistaking a dream of a beloved for a beloved, there is no real option (though lots of unreal ones) for following a heartbeat that resonates with one's own. There are no guarantees where such action will lead, simply a prayer that love will find its way.

Such love is our birthright. It is G*D's way that we re-image. It is a source of thanks that eases our journey through life.

―――――――――――――

stamp your foot
play your flute
throw your tantrum

there is no getting around
a wisdom of deeds
lived into and through

eventually we all
arise and come away
to a beloved space

in such wise
prisoners are freed
from dryness unto death

in such wise
prisoners are led out
to restored hope

Isaiah 6:1–8
Live Together

The line "Holy, holy, holy is the Lord of hosts; the whole earth is full of his glory" is a pretty thin way of getting to a doctrine of the trinity, even though it has the tradition of the early church behind it. They did some wonderful work and some lousy work (as do we today). A part of our task is to clarify which is which.

A better place to look is at one with "unclean lips" in the midst of an "unclean people", who sees the Lord of hosts. Imagine the connections between G*D, an individual, and a community. Out of this interconnection comes renewal of the individual, the community, and G*D.

This interdependent trinity has as much vitality as an internal trinity of father, son, and holy spirit. We may need to start thinking about a trinity of trinities, or more.

individual – community – G*D

"creator" – "redeemer" – "sustainer"

past – present – future

[your addition] – [your addition] – [your addition]

Isaiah 7:10–14
Creation's Conception

Into our fear we admit no sign of hope. To do so would mean moving to analysis and action.

This means we need to bury our nose in our social media. It used to be a newspaper could keep us from seeing the reality of our neighbors. That which was farthest from us became the most real to us. We would gladly send some money to a typhoon victim half-a-world away, but never consider our common resources called "taxes" to promote the general welfare of those across the tracks.

Now our ire can be raised and our compassion manipulated by viral videos and urban legends making one more round.

Gideon's multiple fleecings or Ahaz refusing to ask show how tiresome and bored we can be. What sign would you ask for, much less believe?

There is a continual need to be alert to a variety of calls if we are to move on from the traps our past has set to keep us from a better tomorrow.

As always, a typical sign will come in a package needing nurture and development. Babies fit this bill very nicely. Now, note what it takes to raise a healthy infant. That commitment of intention, time, and resources to see a mature sign is one of our biggest needs. No wonder Ahaz wasn't interested in parsing and engaging choices of evil and choices of good—it was too uncertain and long-term.

Choices are worth the making. Go ahead.

Isaiah 9:2–7
Blessed Body / Proper I

When in darkness—a glimmer is a joy.

A burden is not only personal, but corporate. Whole peoples have been oppressed by the iron hand of the latest holy market. Whether a single person or 99% of them, being burdened is a sure sign of inequity within a community, and such always falls, soon or late.

While we sometimes get caught thinking we need some wonderful counselor, mighty god, etc., to defeat such a huge system, it is important to simply be able to see a crack in the juggernaut (the huge nothing that pretends to be the lord of the world) that can be dealt with by a child—even a child such as yourself. Each of us is a sign of the times. As we choose merciful justice and trustworthiness, we brighten the light available to see where else we might choose a better way.

May you unwrap the present that is you. May your authority grow continually. May peace expand through your choices.

Isaiah 12:2–6
Hopeless Hope Vigil

Without verse 1, we lose an important perspective of timing.

I appreciate *The Jewish Study Bible* noting these verses (1-6) are, "A song of thanksgiving to be recited in the ideal age." While we can certainly play with these words in our currently less-than-ideal time and can even attempt to live as though they are already true, there are some things that can't be known until their time—long-term relationships and children are two easy examples, and you may have others according to your experience in other fields.

Here is the translation of Chapter 12 from *The Jewish Study Bible*:

> In that day, you shall say:
> "I give thanks to You, O Lord!
> Although You were wroth with me,
> Your wrath has turned back and You comfort me,
> Behold the God who gives me triumph!
> I am confident, unafraid;
> For Yah the Lord is my strength and might [or song],
> And He has been my deliverance."
>
> Joyfully shall you draw water
> From the fountains of triumph,
> And you shall say on that day:
> "Praise the Lord, proclaim His name.
> Make His deeds known among the peoples;
> Declare that His name is exalted.
> Hymn the Lord,
> For He has done gloriously;
> Let this be made known
> In all the world!
> Oh, shout for joy,
> You who dwell in Zion!
> For great in your midst
> Is the Holy One of Israel."

May you not be wrothed upon and may you hymn G*D and Neighbor and One Another and Enemy.

Isaiah 25:6–9
Assured — Opened Heart Evening — Honoring Day

Universalists, arise! Followers of Arminius, gather! We have nothing to lose and a feast to gain.

When we set about ensuring that everyone has a seat at the table before ourselves, we ensure our own place and get to eat sooner than later. As we wipe away tears so people can catch a glimpse of the table and find their place card, we speed the time when we can sit down to the feast. In the process of assisting shame to be refined into esteem, we energize people to come to the table rather than sit immobilized in the ashes.

We have nothing to lose by helping others into G*D's presence. We have everything to gain, including turning death from an enemy into a friendly advisor.

When such as ourselves cast out remorse, we truly laugh and sing and feast.

In a Maundy Thursday feast, we have a foretaste that strengthens us to broadcast an invitation list to an even greater feast. And, yes, of course, everyone's invited.

Isaiah 35:4–7a
Proper 18 (23)

If we back up to the beginning of the chapter, we hear about the wilderness and the dry land being glad, so glad they sing.

The progression of this passage could be the rejoicing wilderness that is to pass on the angelic message, "Don't fear."

What are our wilderness areas saying to us these days? Might it be, "Help!" rather than "Don't fear"? When you think of the wild places that folks would like to rape for commercial benefit, how far away does G*D seem?

When we can't protect the land, how might we expect to have the blind see? When the sighted are only short-sighted, we are increasing the number of functionally blind people, not reducing them.

Does it make a difference to you if it is the desert places in our lives that bring us a message of such deep joy, or if it is Isaiah, a person, who brings this message? How would it change your preaching/teaching/living if we simply honored the environment without having to run its song through some holy person's lips?

The desert places let us know that water, though necessary, isn't everything; so rejoice.

Isaiah 40:1–11
Needed Change [2]

Before preparing an honest way forward, attention is paid to resetting the past.

Here, a comfort of forgiveness comes prior to announcing a better future. There may be times when a vision of a better way will bring recognition that some form of a truth and reconciliation process needs to be set in place. But here it is a shift from past realities that leads a way into today's work on behalf of a preferable tomorrow.

When we have lifted valleys and lowered mountains so all are on the same plane to look together at some clearer semblance of reality, we find we can also look at our own lives without shrinking away from the reality of being temporal beings.

Inconsistent? Yes.

Mortal? Yes.

So how might we better deal with these realities? Two quick ideas:

We need a consensus approach to life. Majorities tend to let power (money) dominate. Dictatorships focus on what's good for those in power. Consensus processes can be manipulated, but when we focus on intentionally hearing everyone's voice and concerns, there is a much improved chance for us to catch our inconsistencies before they are inflicted on others.

Knowing we are not only frail, but temporary, assists us in sorting through our various options to ask about folks generations ahead and their benefit from today's decisions. Making long-term decisions brings an improved chance of our best intentions carrying on long after our bodies have faded.

After lowering mountains that we might better see, there comes a time to rebuild mountains where we can lift up a voice of good tidings. So far, we have seen that every generation needs to find their own way to honor that which brought them this far along, to deal with their own divisions (partly based on our mountain building), and to tear down our Announcement Mountain so that they can better see how to care for generations yet further ahead. Someday this dynamic may change, but for now it obtains.

For now, be comforted—the future is open. Gently assist one another onward.

Isaiah 40:21–31
Guiding Gift [5]

Have you not known? Have you not heard (seen, felt, smelled, tasted, sensed in any way)?

There is more than the circle of earth we run on. Raise your eye and see systems and processes whirling slowly—beyond your control.

This larger universe is available to your moments of faintness and powerlessness. Amazingly, this larger reality, from the inside, rises and we mount higher and walk farther.

This wonderful dynamic makes our very being tardis-like. We are larger on the inside than ever we thought, for we are connected to an outside which is more intimate than we had felt possible.

What have you yet to know? What have you not yet experienced as real? All of that and more is available to you and me, and us to-gether. Let this epiphany not go lightly.

Isaiah 42:1–9
Clarification Week, Monday

"My servant", "my chosen" are the same as "my beloved".

To be baptized is to have been visited by a spirit of justice.
To have a spirit of justice is to be baptized.

Our role in life is to have a regular, steadfast, quietly determined, even if dimly burning, justice orientation in everyday events. The big, flashy, creation-wide righteousness is G*D's.

Moment by moment, new justice is declared and brought to pass, one by one and two by two.

Brother Servant, Sister Chosen, Beloved All, let us throw off our chains of fear that those we are complicit in oppressing might rise. We will do so not out of an expectation of reward but because they will spring forth with or without us, and it is better to be part of the party.

Here is one version: "You are beloved."
Here is another: "You will be just."
Justice is not extraordinary action.
Just be just with or without a ruckus.
Steady—don't faint.
Be a light where you are to reveal better choices.
So here is the thing:
You are beloved; you are just.
Go ahead, reveal it.

Isaiah 43:18–25
Guiding Gift [7]

Remember good-old Jesus, teaching away in the synagogue when comes a load of sin through the roof. This is an opportunity to keep on teaching and rebuke the interruption. It is also a time to remember Isaiah 43:24b-25: You have burdened me with your sins, but I blot out your transgressions for my own sake, to be consistent with my own teaching, my own image.

What do you do with the loads of sin that come your way to interrupt an otherwise wonderful life? It is so easy to keep holding folks' sins against them and so hard to move on, to remember not such sin, to help folks stand without the props of certainty and socio-religio-politico-trappings.

Even when sinned against, G*D forgives. What do you do when sinned against?

Isaiah 49:1–7
Clarification Week, Tuesday

For the workaholics and/or perfectionists among us it is easy to get caught in verse 6: "It is too light a thing that you should be who you are, doing what you are; I have something larger for you to attend to."

These words can also be a challenge to individuals, congregations, communities, and nations who, over time, have come to the conclusion that the dreams we once had have become vain. We settle into routines and settle out of the action.

Along comes a larger picture. Will we have the energy to follow where it leads? Can we face one more disappointment? Has our strength been for nothing? Is vanity all there is?

What dream, what call, has been beckoning for the last little while in your life and in the life of the communities you connect with? Perhaps it is time to take one more breath and give it a try. Trust is not in our own constructs, but in a call beyond them. Follow and gain and learn. Follow and fail and learn. Follow. Learn.

Isaiah 50:4–9a
Premature Fear Sunday — Clarification Week, Wednesday —
Proper 19 (24)

The gift of deep, attentive, appreciative listening is critical to clarify the issues in one's life and the life of a larger community. Listening is the backbone of being a teacher and leads to new learning, important learning, prophetic learning.

It is important to note what one is listening to as well as how one is listening. What combination of listening to the wisdom of ages gone before, dreaming of days to come, and their transition through the present will best serve?

There will be times when an appeal needs to be made to a historical perspective. At other times, we will over-ride well-settled precedent that no longer carries energy for new relationships and opt for a wide-eyed dream of a better or more expansive community. And there will be times when all we can do is hold to listening as best we can as we wait for a better question to hear a new word of the past or future to come clear.

This will, though, require us to stand in the midst of opposing teachings without claiming special privilege of having some god on our side. With a waking ear, we can wait with others to learn without falling prey to bad-mouthing them or arbitrarily setting them aside as being of no account.

Listen for what needs to be relinquished and what needs to be picked up. Blessings on intentionally practicing your listening skills.

Isaiah 52:7–10
Blessed Body / Proper III

Yes, Peace looks beautiful while a distance away. We project all manner of expectations upon what peace will do for us. First and foremost, we want peace to keep us from having to choose mercy. We project that when peace arrives, all will work together for good. We will choose to do good, and that will take care of that.

Peace is as unrealistic as any other heavenly or earthly utopia.

When Peace actually arrives within the city gates instead of strolling the horizon, we find its good news requires us to give up one or another privilege—whether we acknowledge we have such or not. To partner with G*D is to give up some control, or illusion of same.

What was such a sweet song on the breeze, wafted to us from afar, turns cacophonous as it nears. Peace songs hold together disparate tonalities. They are not unified marches. Just as any good choir must, singers of peace need to listen and adjust to their neighbors.

Now, pause; listen for the challenge brought by angels singing "Peace on Earth!" How, this year, will we listen to newborns of every class and caste? Without this listening and resultant change in choices, the angels will sound nice from a distance but have no real good news announcing a healing of a family, much less a nation. Without this listening and resultant change in our choices, the angels will join Rachel in weeping.

Want peace? Change your ways!

Isaiah 52:13–53:12
Annihilation Friday

We have been sold for nothing. It seems like we have arrived where we are by the most natural process available. Little-by-little we have come to today, and we can't figure out how it happened; it must have been nothing, just happenstance. And who can argue with that?

As importantly, the only way out of our present predicament is as equally mysterious as nothing. On the farthest horizon, a whisper of a messenger who seems to be taking such tiny steps in our direction. For the longest time an approach seems so slow. Little-by-little we catch advance echoes calling us out—"Depart; depart."

Where we thought we were stuck, we find it was a wraithful illusion. We don't go out in haste, but through one deliberate choice after another. We have heard, "Depart; depart".

Though hard to hear, we found trust available. We have seen the courage of others before and around us. We sense a new wisdom rising in the next generation. Between these, we are encouraged to think a new thought, even though it threatens our current well-being.

All that is said about a suffering servant could be said about you and me.

For now, we simply focus on knowing this current situation cannot be defined as normative. We are called to, "Depart; depart." No more retribution. Rather, the blessed will lead others to their own blessedness. May you so lead and light a new way.

Isaiah 53:4–12
Proper 24 (29)

Seeking G*D while G*D is active in ways our senses can appreciate does imply an unceasing awareness. Asking whether G*D is present now, in the midst of this sorrow, this joy, this everyday, does increase our ability to catch a glimpse of G*D.

Of course, we usually record our experience as more than a glimpse. We turn a moment into eternity. In doing so, we cease asking whether G*D is present as we bask in echoes from the past—after all, we have had our fix and don't need to attend for just a little while.

It is also worth seeking G*D where G*D is not anticipated. Here, the accumulated wisdom is clearer. Where wickedness is being pursued, G*D is present. Where widows and orphans are not cared for, G*D is present. Where doubt rises, G*D is present. Where idols reign in marketplaces, G*D is present. Basically, wherever G*D is an afterthought, G*D is becoming more present. The corollary is that wherever G*D is thought or felt to be present, G*D is already moving on.

What kind of perversity is this sort of steadfastness? It is the same challenge every teacher uses. Prophets have simply learned the latest lesson about how to learn about presence. Attend to the present; anticipate more depth than surface; there is more ahead than behind.

Isaiah 55:1–11
Hopeless Hope Vigil

We are down to basics—thirst and poverty.

What needs to change—that we do not pollute the water table of anyone? Today fracking and oil spills are spreading thirst at an alarming rate.

What needs to change—that everyone has enough safe water to grow daily bread and to lift a glass in welcome? Today, wealth gaps and false theories of responsibility-for-self abound and pollute communities into false G*D/Mamm*n/Neighb*r categories.

A first change is that some have heard of an alternative vision. One way or another, there is a need for prophets invested in an eternity already present within creation. They won't be heeded, at first, but eventually all short-term greeds fail and cultural Ponzi schemes fall apart.

A second change is for some to fall while espousing a communal way. Prophets and non-prophets can have the integrity to die being true to a deeper truth than profit and power. Some will later be named martyrs, and some ignored. Either way, their blood cries out more broadly than staged cries of protest. Their deaths fertilize ground being organized into a new foundation.

A third change is for more and more to see the consequences of privatized charity and to choose a communal compassion model, restructuring old ways. Just as water cycles, so prophets, martyrs, and your choices today nourish the present to seed and nourish tomorrow.

Isaiah 58:1–12
Self-Recognition Day

At first, fasting is irritating. Time seems to slow and our fast fast becomes forever far away from ending. Remembrance of and antcipation of feasts deepen our present emptiness. Getting our own separates us from one another as we squabble and claim. Completing a fast separates us from G*D when our purpose for fasting does not quickly appear. This inward nature of an outward piety is similar to diet yo-yoing, and we end up hungrier and lazier than ever.

Fasting clarifies relationships from both sides. In the covenant between G*D and creation, it shows grace and mercy that steadfastly persist and release. It also reveals decisions for justice and freedom for others based on solidarity with the oppressed, hungry, and homeless.

As our fasting puts our usual support structures at risk, no matter whether for a long or short time, we find ourselves at a "thin place".

This place of activated spirit will play a variation on one or more of these actual changes:

- breaking chains with which we have unjustly bound others
- removing yokes of servitude that cultures and classes have imposed on anyone deemed "lower"
- freeing those oppressed through structural procedures
- feeding hungry bellies, minds, spirits, and relationships
- sheltering the homeless, abused, and aliens with deep hospitality
- clothing the naked and vulnerable with garments, honor, and family

Fasts that lead to energized spirits engaged in the world around are fasts that light a way beyond bickering and onward beyond restoration. Out of the ashes of a fast rise, a Phoenix, a new community compassion-deep and mercy-wide.

Isaiah 60:1–6
Guiding Gift

The obvious connection with Epiphany is the reference to gold and frankincense.

If we start at the beginning of this passage, instead of the end, we are encouraged to reflect on what we would use as a sign of hope in the midst of darkness. Consider your particular vocation/occupation. What would make sense, in that context, for you to anticipate or respond to a sense of new beginnings?

The Magi seem to be more scholarly/priestly types who are particularly attuned to the stars. So their catching on to something, going on beyond their ken, that needs their attention and presence would likely come from the stars.

When they arrive in Jerusalem, there seems to be no consideration being given to the issue of a fulfillment of hope and where its locus might be identified. Both king and priests had to scramble to figure something out. Eventually, based on the Magi-estic questions, folks remember Bethlehem.

What in your area of experience/expertise is calling out to you for recognition and your involvement? In your questions, others will be stimulated to begin paying attention to that same call in their arenas of participation with life.

I won't be using a star-gazing approach, for that is not my gift. I'd be more likely to catch a glimpse from some comedic reflection on *The Daily Show with Jon Stewart*. What puts you in touch with the prophetic recognition of new life in the midst of the darkness of our usual power and control issues?

Isaiah 61:1–4, 8–11
Needed Change [3]

Hey you! Ya, you! Righteous Oak! Victorious Terebinth! Whatcha doin'?

Rebuilding.

How you doin' that?

Seeing grace. Talking grace. Living grace.

How you doin' that?

Comforting them what mourn. Hey, now you got me talking that way. But, you're OK, so I guess I'm OK to talk your language. Also paying attention to fair dealing, whether dealt with fairly or not. And, giving roses to people while they live.

That sound fun.

Yep. Is. New life is springing up even before Spring. This is fun. It's rejoicing time. Even with a lousy economy, lost jobs, and larger class divisions they can't keep Rejoicing from me. In fact, I usually spell meta... "G*D", but it may also be spelled or named "Rejoicing".
Come on in; join me in anointing and being anointed with good news that releases Rejoicing from Exile. Let me plant an acorn in you for oaks in a grove dance together.

Hey, look at me—I'm a stump shoot—didn't need no acorn. This is fun!

Isaiah 61:10–62:3
Blessed Body [1]

For as the earth brings forth its shoots, and as a garden causes what is sown in it to spring up, so the Lord God will cause righteousness and praise to spring up before all the nations. [Isaiah 61:11]

An echo of this can be found with Malvina Reynolds' anthem, *God Bless the Grass*.

When the fullness of time came, G*D seeded the world with grass —a babe and a woman—to break through the cement of law to adopt all into a new togetherness.

---

god bless
grass
worms
cow fodder
fish food
dropping nutrients
for more
worms
grass

blessing that echoes
through generations
through spacious time
through one life
through all life
through to new blessing

god bless
grass messiahs
wriggly messiahs
dopey messiahs
silent messiahs
lamed-vav messiahs
sacred-cow messiahs
denied messiahs

god bless
one messiah
all messiahs

Isaiah 62:6–12
Blessed Body / Proper II

Pre-exile, exile, and return from exile all have their moments of insight. As we look back and envision ahead, we are reminded of how closed and habit-laden we usually are, how free we are to set in motion a new orientation toward one another and creation.

Take another look at 62:11b and its predecessor, 40:10. What is this having our desired achievement or anticipated prize precede our participation in them?

The announcement we ever need to hear is that our desired future needs our engagement with it now. Our expression of steadfast Mercy is in energizing and enacting our preferred future in an exiled present (whether or not this exiled present turns out to be pre-, post, or present exile). Even the rejoicing of a return from exile has historically been but an interlude sliding, unnoticed, into the pre-exile of a next exile.

This process of serial exiles is part of a growth movement. Exiles can sharpen our vision of tomorrow past only a return from this present exile. We need better questions about what is common to all exiles and addressing that directly.

In this case, those trusting a larger love and mercy are the "achievement" that precedes and welcomes G*D back into partnership. We are the condition of reconciliation. Though unsung, this is an honorable task to wrestle with, to quest for.

Isaiah 64:1–9
Needed Change [1]

... You have hidden your face from us and
given us up to the power of our misdeeds.
And yet, Yahweh, you are our Father....
[64:7b-8a NJB]

In the midst of the most difficult and strained of relationships, there still remains a relationship. Sometimes it feels as though the only connection we have is that we breathe the same air. [And why don't we take care of such a precious gift but degrade it for the sake of the idol of Maximum Profit?] And yet there is never a time we are so far out of touch that reconciliation can't take place [prevenient reconciliation]. Even when this is difficult to see, it remains.

Perhaps the most thanks we can muster today is tied up with that "And yet..."

It is something that can be built on. Will we? Will you? Will I? Let us pray so.

Jeremiah 11:18–20
Proper 20 (25)

And why is it we have come to the point of seeking retribution, vengeance, violence against others?

Might it have something to do with the disaster threatened against them in verse 11: "I will bring upon them a disaster from which there will be no escape. Though they cry out to me, I will not listen to them." [NCCV]

Hear also verse 15: "What right has my beloved in my house, when they have done vile deeds?"

How natural it seems to toss ingrates into a pit and leave them there. Yes, things may have a tinge of anxiety about them, but to change our culture is simply too much to ask; those who have much dare not lose any, and those who have little aspire to have more than enough (just a reasonable buffer, don't you know).

What is particularly poignant about this asking for retribution is that it is about Jeremiah's own hometown of Anathoth.

Later, Jeremiah will buy a plot of land in Anathoth as a sign that the violence to come will not have the last word and the violated will have a place to come back to.

Consider Palestinians and Indigenous Peoples everywhere whose plots of land were removed from them, casting them adrift with nothing to come back to. How does this story now play?

———————————

I told the truth
this society is failing
it soon will fall

I called for reform
unraveling all privilege
and soon I fell

well we'll see
where falling and rising
settle out

may we finally find
our commons
settled in

Jeremiah 23:1–6
Proper 11 (16)

Is a righteous king the same as a benevolent dictator? Our experience of the latter is not very good. This equivalency is mostly the spin from inside the power structure rather than the results from outside. Unless you posit a great deal of external evil to which the king must respond and return evil for evil, thus becoming the evil they oppose, a question has to be asked about why there are no continuing empires of righteousness.

We may need to remember that the title of King is not one that Jesus uses. It is used by the Magi as an extension of what they knew about the way the world works, through political power. It is placed upon him by the Romans as a taunt. While taunts can become affirmed (see Methodist name tradition), they are usually just an example of a political dirty trick; notice the way the word "liberal" has become a swear word instead of a descriptive word.

Jesus uses images of kings as part of his teaching, moving folks from where they are to a better, wider place. John records Jesus as moving away when folks wanted to make him king.

In front of Pilate, Jesus is recorded as testifying to something called "truth" rather than continue a conversation about kingship.

How scary is it to think of a shepherd, a king, or Jesus, being with us rather than leading us?

Jeremiah 31:7–9
Proper 25 (30)

The NRSV has it that a "remnant" has been saved. The Message says "the core" has been saved.

Interesting to play with these.

The remnant of an apple is the core—"a central and often foundational part usually distinct from the enveloping part by a difference in nature [core of the city] : as the usually inedible central part of some fruits (as a pineapple); especially : the papery or leathery carpels composing the ripened ovary in a pome fruit."

The core remnant of an apple carries on the species—"a basic, essential, or enduring part (as of an individual, a class, or an entity)." [definitions from Merriam-Webster online dictionary].

Are you feeling like a leftover piece in the bargain bin or right at the center of an expanding presence of G*D?

Whichever—

> Sing aloud ("core" is the core of chorus).
>
> Weep aloud.
>
> Live.

Jeremiah 31:7–14

Blessed Body [2]

Here is the prophet's vision. Here is a vision worthy of challenging us and calling us to repeat it again and again and again.

The prophet can see G*D at work, calling exiles home, turning mourning into joy, and sorrow into comfort.

If we do not have this larger vision, we are only prophets in training who have passed courses in gloom-and-doom, but not in reconciliation-and-restoration.

Happy New Year! Lift up your hearts.

Jeremiah 31:31–34
Conviction [5]

We will know G*D through forgiveness (31:34). This is the most powerful image in this passage.

The first part of this pericope talks about not having sins passed on to the generations, but each generation and person having immediate feedback or consequences for behavior that is harmful to them and others and creation. This sounds idyllic, but taken just a half-step further leads to greater constraint and self-censorship. To connect behavior to consequences too strongly and quickly may make us obedient puppets, but loses the living nature of G*D and ourselves as Partners.

It doesn't take much immediate correction, like an electrified fence, before we shy away from even coming close to it. It may no longer be active, but our past experiences with it have effectively kept us from pushing the boundaries of life. Pavlovian responses, even in the supposed service of G*D, are more detrimental than helpful.

So how does G*D's heart become our heart, and *vice versa*? It comes through the beating process of trial and error and forgiveness received and forgiveness given and trying again. So we stand and walk; so we ride a bicycle; so we build community. Let's get to the heart of the matter—loving kindness is revealed in many ways, and forgiveness is near the top of its revelatory presence.

Lamentations 3:1–9, 19–24
Absent Saturday

We need only pick one of the "worst" times of our life, and re-membrance adds in every other "worst" time. It is an unfair fight. Every affront wants to come to the front to claim its needed reparation that will never be enough to not come back for more.

This day of absence—no contact— brings every other loss along with it. What more can be said than, "My heart dwells on this continually and sings within me." [NJB] This summarizes the situation of death.

For some, this is a sufficient stopping point. Others will acknowledge this reality, sink to its depths, and find there is a hope not noticed, waiting, even here.

It is understandable that some would not be able to navigate this dark a place. It is not understandable that others would continue to affirm that, against all experience, Mercy is not over.

Too often, we have put our trust in small mercies to see us through specific moments. It is difficult to move to a larger mercy when the asked-for one never arrives.

Similarly, it is difficult to live through a dark and false dawn masking a steadfast love that can be affirmed beyond any and all of our current loves that eventually fall and are extinguished.

Finally, it is a practiced affirmation that wraps-us-round in the face of the direst difficulty. "This is all I have; for now it is enough."

Lamentations 3:22–33
Proper 8 (13)

We, created in the image of G*D, have the power to forgive, to redeem. Will we be generous with this power?

We have the experience of renewed health after illness and, by extension, of resurrection after death. Will we extrapolate from our experience in our interactions with others or limit it to ourselves?

We have a new day in which to move beyond our prior responses to life, not trying to clone our experience but build on it. Will we stretch to a next layer of life that is both higher and deeper than where we have been, and include others in that?

Knowing we have an option beyond yesterday and today opens to us a basic understanding of life—life-long learning. We can take the generosity of our ancestors who took things as far as they could, and now push things as far as we can that those who follow will be grateful for our generosity that has so blessed them and encourages them to go as far as they can. We can. Will we?

Ezekiel 2:1–5
Proper 9 (14)

OK you
stand and receive
stand as a weather vane
attending a shift
in breeze
becoming gale

brightly painted
weathered gray
stand and attend
your pointing
a witness to even
any blind or deaf

structures lean
from a prevailing breeze
not yet sensing
a change underway
from the expected
or predictable

having leant so long
in one direction
they can't help
being a rebel
against a living wind
blowing where it will

whether seen turning
every so slightly
or creaking on
rusted bearings
a prophet stands
and receives

Ezekiel 17:22–24
Proper 6 (11)

The small are great; the great, small. This turnaround will be home to many.

A majestic cedar dances with a lowly mustard. In both cases, when you have the eyes to see, life blossoms and flourishes.

Birds are a wonderful symbol of our life extended. From Genesis 1:20 onward, birds show G*D at work. "Let the waters bring forth swarms of living creatures, and let birds fly above the earth across the dome of the sky." In 1:26 we are to be in relation to the birds—good old "dominion" or "partnership". Verse 7:3 reminds us that the birds are related to "clean animals" that symbolically draw us closer to G*D.

A bird brought a sign of new life after a flood. Job appeals to birds who evidence G*D (12:7). Psalm 78:27 reminds us of the quail in the desert: G*D "rained flesh upon them like dust, winged birds like the sand of the seas". Ecclesiastes 9:12 equates the demise of birds with that of humans.

The prophets continue to find connections between birds and ourselves. Isaiah 31:5 equates birds with G*D, partners in creation who watch over it. Jeremiah 4:25 shows how desolate life is becoming, with even birds having flown the coop. Ezekiel 31 has the cedars of Lebanon populated by birds as a sign of blessing and Daniel 4 sees a similar great tree at the center of the earth, well-nested with birds—signs of restoration. Hosea 4 has a new covenant witnessed by the birds of the air, remembering a first creation covenant.

Matthew 6: "Look at the birds of the air; they neither sow nor reap nor gather into barns, and yet your heavenly Father feeds them. Are you not of more value than they?"

Mark 4: "…yet when mustard seed is sown it grows up and becomes the greatest of all shrubs, and puts forth large branches, so that the birds of the air can make nests in its shade."

Acts 10: Peter's vision of inclusion includes birds.

Revelation 19: "Then I saw an angel standing in the sun, and with a loud voice he called to all the birds that fly in midheaven, 'Come, gather for the great supper of God'. . . ." to clear away the decay and make way for a new heaven and a new earth. It would have been a nice touch to have the leaves of the tree of life show the healing of the land by the nesting of birds, but John's vision fell just a bit short of rounding things out.

Where are birds nesting in your life? In your cedar grandeur? In your mustard weediness? Watch for birds; catch a glimpse of G*D.

Ezekiel 36:24–28
Hopeless Hope Vigil

Mountain tops removed, land never rested, water poisoned, and Neighb*r exiled—each has their tale to tell of life become cheap with grace and gift suffocated under power's privilege.

Only a new heart and new spirit will sparkle against life's gray stone charred to gray smoke.

This new spirit and heart can come convulsively, projectile vomiting out an accumulated clot of non-digestible, nutrient-free, dirt to make room for call-receiving nutrition for the whole body, not just a part.

This new heart and spirit can come quietly as a gentle rain nourishing a mustard seed unseen in its smallness to rise up and offer its leaf to a passing dove searching for lost hope.

Note how stones are not thrown away but become signs of life renewed. This universal suffrage and salvation are available even to those who polluted the common pool. There are none so gone that they can't be cleaned up. At the least, their attachment to their idol can be thanked for demonstrating folly.

It is long past time to reclaim our innate partnership with each other and our environment. In this, we give witness to a new partnership with the mystery we spell G*D.

Ezekiel 37:1–14
Conviction [5] — Hopeless Hope Vigil — Energy to Witness

One of my favorite images from Nikos Kazantzakis is the portrayal of Holy Spirit as an eagle, not a dove, that swoops down, digs its talons into the back of one's neck, and drags you where Holy Spirit desires.

This gives the kind of action needed for Pentecost. It is not a sappy-happy birthday party; it is serious business, transformational for one and all. A response needs to be made; it can't be avoided any longer.

We can't get out of the energy of Pentecost by saying, "Gee, I don't know, what do you think?" Eagle Spirit is happening now, so go ahead. Take a deep breath; everything is about to begin.

Bone will knit to bone; separations between languages, cultures, and theologies will be bridged. Creation and re-creation are continuing. Speak and Act: Life is dynamic.

Daniel 7:9–10, 13–14
Evaluation Day / Proper 29 (34)

When we can't see a resolution to our particular sense of persecution, it is always handy to have a *deus ex machina*, even if it is more dream than machine.

When we have done all we can do—sometimes that is more and sometimes less than is needed; seldom is it just what is needed—we can but wait for comeuppance for others and dominion for ourselves.

Daniel's dream is the dream of every 96-pound weakling. In today's world, it is also the dream of the church to be returned to the mystique of Holy Empire, but this time one that is everlasting.

What keeps getting left out of the dream is the reality of death to make this dream come to pass. So verses 11–12 are conveniently left out as the Greek Empire is done in. In leaving these out, we get the same old story in recent days regarding the USA and Iraq. As long as we can ignore death, we can dream of conquest. War presidents attend fund-raisers instead of funerals.

We will see about days of judgment to come and history books that reveal the need for such judgment. For now, keep doing what you can.

Daniel 12:1–3
Proper 28 (33)

In the midst of trouble, we awaken to our being in life. How did we live in the days leading up to a breakdown? The watchman image from Ezekiel is a good connecting spot here. Did you sound the alarm while you could, or did you see trouble brewing and try to make do or benefit as you could until it came?

In the midst of the "land of dust", we awaken to our being in life. Do we live, as we have always lived, caring for the common good in good times as well as bad times, not only knowing something of the difference between good and evil but doing what we can to find the good in evil? Do we live, as we have always lived, avoiding shame while behaving shamefully?

In the midst of pre-creation darkness, are we connected with light that will not be put out, beaconing and beckoning like stars pointing to new life?

Rise with Michael. Live well in the midst of unwellness. Live at ease in the midst of disease. Rise and shine, for your light is; come! This is more important than resurrection—live abundantly—¡Que será, será!

Hosea 2:14–20
Guiding Gift [8] —Proper 3 (8)

Hooray for the word "therefore". It marks a shift based on a conclusion drawn from both stated and unstated realities. Some of these follow quite nicely, and some are logical fallacies. Now something can be examined. Up to this point, we are in a world of reaction.

If we look at this section in relationship to what lies immediately before it we find that the "therefore" skips all the way back to Chapter 1 and G*D's naming of children with an unstated understanding that names are not fate.

No matter how little compassion someone has toward others, that will not stop compassion flowing toward them.

No matter how isolating and exiling someone is toward others, they are always welcome back.

Preemptive Mercy and Prevenient Grace continue to hold true and be the basis for every subsequent "therefore".

No matter the provocation, the testing, the past judgment passed, there is an openness to undo and redo every burned bridge and steeled fact to the contrary of intentional mercy and preparational grace.

I have been forgotten, "therefore" I will search out and court forgetters. Therefore, "therefore" is transformed from some straight line from past to present that constrains this transformation to indicate biblical "therefore"s also contain information from the future, freeing us to live differently together as partnered helpmeets, not judge and jury.

May your "Therefore" be based on a surfeit of mercy and grace, not dependent only on what has happened to you, but on what can yet happen because of you.

Joel 2:1–2, 12–17
Self-Recognition Day

Blowing trumpets does not keep darkness away. The same is true for gloom of any degree.

How does a sanctified fast differ from a cleansing fast? Is there a difference between these and a fast resulting from mourning? A fast with more solemnity than another fast would seem to be a significant factor, but it is not.

Weeping priests are no protection against an angry G*D or a frail people. Better for us to have a relationship based on reality, not power of coercion by tears or flattery.

Ash Wednesday is less helpful as a manipulation of weeping, sorrow, and penance. It is helpful if it leads us to be real with one another and our environment.

Joel 2:21–27
Thanksgiving

This passage can only make sense if the disaster leading up to this word of reversal is clearly fixed in our experience. The turmoil and catastrophe trapping us need to be squarely faced for this vision to be grasped as revolutionary enough to be the place where we will go-all-in, and stake everything we have on a new way.

That which is needed to reverse our exile in our own home will seem as mysterious as that which caused our separation. Underlying every "ism" that separates small and large familial, peer, tribal, or economic groups from one another or others is a desolation that has raised its head. There is a Smaug or monster under our bed, a some-one who must not be named, or other incomprehensible mechanism needing to be faced. A stench or stink about human affairs has arisen from the ground around us, and we are overwhelmed.

Then comes a Mary Poppins' shift in the wind. Something is about to happen.

Caught between self-polluted ground beneath and a new breeze stirring above, we are to choose again to put shame away that our energy not be consumed by it but take advantage of a present and next opportunity to live one bit more thankfully than could be expected.

We might even be bold enough to begin this passage, "Scatter thanks where trouble has seared the land lest fear be all ye see." "Thanks" is a creative word often unrecognized in the refrain, "...and G*D saw that it was good." Hear always the surprise of "Whew!" and "Thanks!" yet present, for they remember how very unlikely was our birth and how very likely our presence will trigger a healing of land and offer hope for a next generation. We are about to join G*D and Neighb*r in doing a next creative act. The work left to do shifts from "about" to be done to "actually" being done. So up; Onward!

Amos 5:6–7, 10–15
Proper 23 (28)

Seeking G*D ultimately includes establishing a justice beyond what is fair. This kind of justice will not allow any excuse for making the situation worse for those with less.

We cannot take a renewal of justice simply on the basis of laws attempting to ensure justice. Laws are always trying to keep a second incident from happening and are a step behind a next injustice. Laws are helpless against innovative wrong, and so protests and rebuke are no more effective than silence.

The part that is left out, verses 8 & 9, gives us a better perspective from which to seek good and not evil.

> [8] Rise to the Pleiades and Orion,
>   to watch dusk become dawn
>   as worlds spin below.
>   Dive deep into the waters,
>   splashing water over the land
>   as seeds waken to rise.
>   Seek perspective!
> [9] Rigid walls fall in a flash.
>   Separation cannot be fortified.

Can you equate justice with the cosmos? with participating in the refreshment of people and creation? with saying, "No," to those for whom there is an acceptable level of waste?

Let's raise our vision beyond tit-for-tat laws holding the worst at bay, but still institutionalizing poverty and all its attendant woes. Let's go beyond our usual responses and speak the grand vision of our being in a cosmos star-flung—and smile and live its truth.

Jonah 3:1–44, 10
Guiding Gift [3]

I just saw a sermon for this coming Sunday that posited WalMart (called Mall Marty World in the sermon and VoldeMart by others) as Ninevah. That may trigger other arenas for you where this tale might well be told. The message Jonah brought in the sermon is:

> It's not keeping the customers happy that I'm most concerned about; it's the way you treat your employees. They have nowhere else to work and you don't pay them a living wage. When their children are sick, they have no health insurance to pay for their medical care. When they are too old to work, there are no pension funds to help them maintain their mortgage and car payments. It's not right. Your managers and executives live very comfortably.
> [Found on *Midrash* posting from John Sumwalt]

Instead of just a generic "Repent", it is helpful to be specific about what is needed. When you find your Ninevah you will also find your voice, and it will thrive on detail, not generality.

Behind every prophecy is an understanding that the future stands open; G*D is open. An important corollary is that G*D is not fate, but life. Change is at the heart of life. Responding to new situations with new responses is crucial to healthy living. When one part of the equation changes, the whole situation can be rethought. To change the present is to change the future. However you cast it, smile; a Living G*D is at work and a Living Image of G*D can do no less.

Change is a consistent part of life. The only thing that doesn't change is change.

Change comes to Jonah, to the citizens of Nineveh, to G*D.

There is an old story about the 36 hidden saints in the world (Tzadikim Nistarim or Lamed Vav Tzadikim). No one knows who they are, including themselves, but without them, the world would grind to a halt. They are seedbeds of change—not in terms of technical innovation, but for how we treat one another. Repentance and forgiveness are great change agents.

Since you may be one of the anonymous saints, what change needs to be made in you to live a whole and mature life that others might better experience you and the hope you carry within?

Since your neighbor, or even enemy, may be one of the anonymous saints, what change needs to be made in you for them to be more whole and mature?

Zephaniah 3:14–20
Hopeless Hope Vigil

"Judgments removed here! Get your judgments removed here!" This would be a winner of a marketing campaign. Zephaniah is one testimonial for a way of wrongs being set right, whether they were initiated by you or against you. Our imaginary fears based on gleeful judgment could then be set aside.

Yes, this is supposable. Who wouldn't want their shame to be turned into praise and renown?

Well, it turns out that there is no business like denial business. We seem to prefer continuing to be judged and to judge ourselves most harshly. Relying on external judgment turns out to be preferable to taking responsibility for the consequences of not changing the present. Likewise, having been socialized into a niceness that cannot be lived up to every hour of our day has made us guilt addicts.

It may be that we have had our eye on the wrong prize. Having fortunes restored is not a large enough vision to pursue. Rather, there is a more compelling picture available when we deal with being in the midst of our story and knowing that we are not alone [17a]. Before we know it, we are *in medias res* of a story with no clear beginning. The outcome is not any more certain, but the journey is less lonely.

Malachi 3:1–4
Old Welcomes New

As Jesus is brought as a babe in arms to the Temple, there is a question about who is the messenger here. Is it Simeon? Anna? Jesus? Mary/Joseph?

Malachi means "Messenger". Is an unrecorded blessing here waiting for Jesus to come back to the Temple when he is at a next transition and given "Malachi" as a middle name in anticipation of traditions yet to come—adding a Confirmation name? Instead of Jesus bar Joseph, Jesus bar Gabriel/G*D, or the heretical Jesus bar Mary, was Jesus dubbed Jesus Malachi Joseph/Nazareth/David/Christ?

Might today's messenger be you? Is Malachi your adopted middle name?

Let's presume so for a moment. Our work is clearing a way for the next generation and the next, even unto the seventh. There is no other time for this clearing, and so there is a sense that this act is one that comes suddenly upon us.

One of the clearings is that there are no doors on the gateposts of a sanctuary. All are welcome. There will be those who can't endure this openness that burns away all personal prejudice as well as institutional discrimination, but that resistance will not keep a Malachi from reforming gatekeeper priests.

My friend, Malachi, take care what you announce today. By your message you will anticipate your blessing or curse.

Wisdom of Solomon 1:13–15; 2:23-24
Proper 8 (13)

G*D created you as a full-partner, no matter what. (Verse 23)

Oh, there is plenty to get in the way of this partnership working well and long (v. 24). But, time and again, life-giving, partner-developing energy continues at work to bring us back on course (v. 14).

And so our work is to look a second and third time at what we are doing to ourselves and creation that keeps cutting us back from partnering together (v. 15). "Doing right" is no easy or automatic process. Doing right is a creative act in the midst of a chaotic situation.

We know this chaos as death—that which cuts off rather than that which flowers and fruits.

Now, a hard reality: seeking after G*D is a seeking after self, is a seeking after community.

In a moment of doing a G*D/S*lf/Neighb*r act, we find our eternal intention, no matter what comes next. In this finding is the "All!" of enough, whether it lasts or not. It is sufficient for the moment.

This is what we practice in our common time—thanks for living up to our intention and thanks for a next opportunity to not rest on our laurels, but live into a next even more expansive intention. And on we go into a reverse mirror regression where, instead of looking smaller and smaller, we find ourselves growing nearer and nearer to right doing and encouraging doing right in our partners.

So, death? A clear opportunity to practice partnership with "Ahh!" It lasts.

Wisdom of Solomon 1:16–2:1, 12–22
Proper 20 (25)

On this day, this reading and Jeremiah 11:18–20 can be chosen between or connected. Here we connect.

Let us test what will happen at the end of his life. Thus they reasoned, but they were led astray, for their malice blinded them, and they did not appreciate the mystery of God, nor hoped for the wages of holiness, nor discerned the prize for blameless souls, nor understood that by our tests are we, in turn, tested. [Wisdom 2:17, 21-22]

Let me see your vengeance happen to them. Thus we reasoned, but we were led astray, for our ill will blinded us, and we did not know the hiddenness of God, nor hoped for the wages of holiness, nor discerned the prize for blameless souls, nor understood that our desire for retribution is, in turn, paid back. [Jeremiah 11:20b, Wisdom 2:21-22]

In the midst of the storms of life that come our way or are caused by us, there are choices to be made. May you live in the "hope of holiness" more than turning tests into retributions.

Wisdom of Solomon 3:1–9
Honoring Day

Always there is a tension between being watched and being watched over. It is very easy to pick the worst from both and smash them together for harm to self and others.

Very few people appreciate an open and steady gaze upon them. It is received as a challenging stare, not a grateful reception of their basic being. Being watched seems to trigger memories of one failure or another, as well as anxiety that present actions won't measure up. Exaggerated awareness of self causes a lack of natural gracefulness.

As a result, we set up rules we can just barely fit within, while others will obviously not measure up. Presuming G*D grades on a curve (even while espousing strict holiness), we will squeak by— thanks to those our rules will leave behind. Blame and its avoidance is the game here.

Likewise with being watched over. At some point, we want to be able to make our own way. Without an ability to have some independence, we can't move toward interdependence. All manner of subterfuges are developed to justify our sneaking off. We will even deny the obvious surveillance camera staring us in the face and think we'll get away with our little trick just once. And then twice and thrice.

When we finally give up and settle back into self-censorship because we can't get away with being us, we find only two choices: suicide by acquiescence or suicide into nothingness. Either way, ultimate dependence leads to lack of meaning.

We make up literalism to argue connotation so, at least, we can always be partially right. We make up closets into which we can push others so, at least, it is always mostly their fault.

Our sainted mentors accept being watched as they teach by modeling and being watched over as a source of freedom to act on behalf of all in important areas.

May we remember our being called and be bold in public.

May we claim our communal interdependence and accept being watched over as we watch out for others.

Wisdom of Solomon 7:26–8:1
Proper 19 (24)

In every generation, Wisdom passes into "hole-y" souls and makes them friends of God and prophets. (Wisdom 7:27b)

Recognize yourself? Well, recognize yourself!

It is a mistake to mistake a certain level of holiness (theirs) as a requirement for the presence of wisdom. Blessed wisdom is wise enough to recognize seasons of life and not force a way in. Friendship is not requirement-bound. Prophetic living cannot be sustained without argument.

As seasons change from growth to harvest, thanks must be given for the sun and rain of the past that bring forth bounty. Storing the energy of a harvest for leaner days ahead is a double blessing—having sufficient for tomorrow and for those who will benefit from today's work when we are gone. Canners and driers and storers are the summer for those who will feast on a preserved harvest in a later winter.

In every season, Wisdom passes into patched souls. Enough said.

Wisdom of Solomon 10:15–21
Blessed Body ² — Thanksgiving

Psalm 147:12–20 is paired with this reading from the Wisdom of Solomon.

The Psalmist's "he" and Wisdom's "she" run along parallel tracks of action. They each rescue and inflict. Note that we are finding out more and more that these parallels are poles with innumerable variations between. While talking here of polar differences, won't it be strange when we lose this particular dichotomy?

One interesting difference, among several that can be accounted for by their different writing situations, is the way in which the male word declares to everyone, while the female opens the mouths of the mute to do the declaring. A bit of reversal can be glimpsed in silent Joseph, who is declared unto and simply acts, and singing Mary, who responds with an affirmation that lifts the poor and outcast.

The differences here are less about male or female roles since there are males who declare and males who open, and females who open and females who declare. Whether male or female (all are one in larger perspectives), what is at stake is the question of what is needed in a given situation. Are we at the point of needing folks who can speak to and for others, or folks who can assist folks to speak their own experience?

This discernment is important because we tend to get caught in roles, even roles of wisdom, and develop a Johnny-One-Note approach to situations. Wisdom can adjust to the need of the time and the need of the future to bring forth what is needed. Without the ability to implement appropriately, wisdom is simply received knowledge, but unhelpful, unable to get any traction to effect needed changes.

We need those who are persistent, in good times or bad, and those who shift to bring a needed perspective. It is not that one is automatically preferable, but that what is needed might be evidenced.

Praise G*D; affirm Wisd*m.
Praise Wisd*m; affirm G*D.

Sirach 24:1–12
Blessed Body 2

In this passage, not often heard in today's church, there is a sense of a drilling down of wisdom from the general of creation to the specific of geography known as "here", from time immemorial to "this present moment". Where and when should wisdom alight? Well, why not here and now? Can you sense wisdom alighting in your honored life? Hooray!

From the book *Where Shall Wisdom Be Found: Wisdom In The Bible, The Church And The Contemporary World*, the end of the article "Sirach and Wisdom's Dwelling Place" by C.T.R. Hayward:

> Disaster befell Sirach's beloved Temple when, in the year 70 CE, the Romans put it to the torch. Yet Sirach's Greek translation of his grandfather's book was not forgotten. It was included in the Greek Old Testament and was thus available for Gentile Christians to ponder. For them, the work proved so popular that it was regularly read in worship, and in the course of time came to be called Ecclesiasticus, a "church book" of great distinction. No doubt this process was encouraged because St. Paul, the earliest Christian writer, had dubbed Christ "the wisdom of God" (1 Cor 1.24, 30; cf. Col 2.3), and because the evangelists had, in their several ways, used Temple imagery to speak of Christ's body (Jn. 2:20-22; Mt 26:61; Mk 14:58). Sirach proved to be a rich quarry from which the Church's teachers could unearth almost inexhaustible theological resources in their explorations of Christ's relationship to God. And since Wisdom, both in Hebrew and Greek, is personified as a woman, the way was open for them to develop their thinking on the role of the Blessed Virgin in the Christian economy of salvation. Reflection on Mary as Wisdom and Mother of God, the Temple of the Holy Spirit, is discernible already in the writing of St. Ambrose (De Spiritu Sancto 2.51, PL 16.753), and was destined to bear abundant and nourishing fruit in the liturgies of the Eastern and Western Churches alike.

The Three Wise Guys may be profitably transfigured into Gals. If so, even transfigured into your life? After Henry Van Dyke we can move beyond a fourth Magi to a fifth and further on down the line to you as a receiver and sharer of G*D's Wisdom.

Baruch 3:9–15, 3:32–4:4
Hopeless Hope Vigil

So why are you in this state of exile? Why has this particular loss so done you in?

If wisdom can only be mediated to us by scripture, rules dense with words, and concepts that can be played off against one another, how can we possibly know how to keep from trouble? If there is a real world out here that is not simply a figment of our imagination and ultimately manipulable by us, wherein the surprise is that we have been trapped both innocently and by our own betrayal of our values?

We become hopeless with but one step out of the boat or box we are in—the water is wide and we can't get o'er. Even a boat with two to row can't make it through some storms.

We make up stories such as our hero hasn't left us, but only just gone on a worthwhile trip to rescue folks in some supposed "hell". This may have some comfort years afterward. But in an immediate absence, who can remember—much less believe—a return on a specific tomorrow?

For now, we have neither our own strength nor the wisdom of the ages. We wait; we run; we mourn; we give in; we sit in one dark room after another. And we recognize we can only wait for so long, run and mourn and give up and sit in darkness for so long.

So here we are caught between—more accurately, caught out in the open, having bet the farm and lost. There is no practical move to make. The only thing for now is to experience this loss connected to all other losses and to dive deeply in, all the way to our own hell.

No guarantees, but once in death's clutch, it is best to vigorously enter to experience as much black hole as we can. Who knows what lies on the other side? This may be as hopeful as is now possible.

Whatever your state of exile, dive deep.

Matthew 2:1–12
Guiding Gift

Who dares star-gaze? They will be called malingerers, day-dreamers. Yet to gaze afar is to also look critically for a fulcrum spot in the present. From afar, folks may better see a new opportunity for an unfated future beyond their own culture. Through spotting unknown stars, they may better appreciate the mystery of a manger being about more than feed and water.

Still, there is a cultural residue as the scholarly magi and our own blind spots seek in a castle for what can only be found in a manger. When stripped of our habits and fantasies, we see the underbelly of assumed privilege and power and leave by a different route. At last, we remember—revolution happens from the bottom up: period.

So dream a little dream, like this one from Carly Simon's, *Let the River Run*, with its refrain:

> Let all the dreamers
> wake the nation.

How far will your dream, your gazing afar, take you? Into halls of power and out again? Into mangers near and far? Deep within your culture and comfort, or quite beyond?

Your response will be told in the gifts you bring and give away.

Matthew 6:1–6, 16–21
Self-Recognition Day

Practicing piety to be seen practicing piety is a spiritual thick spot, not a thin place. It separates paradise and earth by more than the standard three feet. When it goes on long enough, such a callus is built up that we become callous to G*D (the irony, oh, the irony), to neighbor and self. These are really high-quality blowbacks.

Yes, a bit more cryptic than usual, but I enjoyed it.

———————————

you been practicing your sexual orientation again?
nope, when you're this good practice isn't in order
you still practicing breaking a bad habit?
yep, don't know that I'll ever not be a xxxx-ist

there are things that come quite naturally
in a healthy way
there are things that come quite naturally
that destroy

we are told our nature is unnatural
forced into closets by family
we find our nature to be righteously right
and yet left no choice but secrecy

finally we face the difficulty
practicing the practice of wholeness
in all we do and refrain from doing
without simply practicing practicing

Matthew 6:25–33
Thanksgiving

Worry is endemic to life. To have an instruction to not "worry" raises any number of procedural questions. If we are not going to worry, what will we do to fill the time and use the energy currently engaged by worry?

The Common English Bible labels this section, "Worry about necessities". The question then becomes, "What is necessary?" Do we need a warm hug as well as age-appropriate food? How much shelter is needed in your climate? Do scarce resources go to those who have much, or will the little some have be taken from them? Where does an ability to influence others fit into any necessity for autonomy and relationship?

Because this is a Thanksgiving text, it is tempting to think about substituting "Thanks" for "Worry". Unfortunately, these categories are not complementary and interchangeable.

We get Thanks fatigue as well as compassion fatigue. Our ability to worry will simply add a worry about whether our thanks have been expressed well enough and are able to hold a lack of necessities at bay. No, our wrestling with worry will have to take into account our old worry tapes. Worry won't accept any substitute.

It may slightly help if we were to call "Worry" by its formal name of "Fear". Now we might make some progress.

Matthew 25:31–46
New Year's Day — Proper 29 (34)

Remember, this vision is not the end of Matthew. We go on to hear of Passover two days hence and a plot, betrayal, and death—and a surprise capable of changing our life. Don't settle for closing the year with a dualistic courtroom scene when you could be planning a feast, accepting consequences of building common good, and heading on to some Edenic "galilee" where we see face-to-face.

No more "be it resolved" intentions—only practice.

Matthew 27:57–66
Absent Saturday

No matter how we seek security, there is none.

A rich grave is no more secure than a poor one. Neither can capture a life.

Vigilance is not a source of security. Lives cannot be put on hold to watch.

Suspicion gives no sense of security. No matter how many contingencies are prepared for, the future cares not a whit for the limits of our imagination and keeps coming around every defense we put in place.

Security attempts to protect us from the mystery of emptiness, where "nothing" can become not only "something" but "anything". Security is our attempt to control outcomes. Security needs so much propping up that it, itself, becomes insecure.

Blessings to Arimathea Joe and Magdala Mary and Perplexing Pilate. [Note: In the Eastern Church Pilate was canonized for his proclamation of Jesus' innocence (Feast Day, June 25); in the Western Church Pilate is seen as the enemy of Christ and delight taken in devising ingenious and gruesome ends for him.] Blessings to you, still standing without any guarantees, just a sense of belovedness.

Mark 1:1–8
Needed Change [2]

Word should have arrived in parishioner's homes yesterday that I have been reappointed to an 18-month interim ministry beginning in the middle of January.

That news will be a real piece of coal for some and the best gift ever for others.

A part of the work on Sunday will be a recognition that the work I have done here is preparatory work for someone else who may be able to do that which I have been incapable of doing—turning around a 40+ year pattern of straight-line numerical decline.

It is appropriate that what will be remembered from my time is the pain associated with repentance. Pastoral sexual misconduct from 40+ years ago that was dealt with by simply moving the pastor on has festered. We finally recognized that we have been trying to control pastors and parishioners through conformity to a civic religion of external behavior. Perhaps by confessing our response-to-betrayal of trying to wash away differences as a compounding of the sin, we can be ready for the grace of Spirit and to grow through difference.

To forgive the offender, to forgive the church-at-large for its past inability to deal with the offense by other than covering it over, and to forgive ourselves for our response to betrayal by over-control rather than by gifting all (active and passive betrayers) with a Holy Meal—may be all that can be done right now.

O G*D, we have felt all too worthy to bind the feet and journey of others. Help us untie the sandals we have too tightly bound on others by forcing them to walk in one-size-doesn't-fit-all shoes. It is time to dance barefoot with one another.

Mark 1:4–11
Beloved

There was something about Baptizing John that brought folks to travel from the center of power to beyond the edge of same and opened them to look clearly at their lives and fess up to what they had been about that they knew they shouldn't be about, and yet they were about.

This is a story that moves from settlement back into exodus. This is a story that recognizes the permanence of exile over the temporary nature of acculturation. This is a story that brings us to the nature of life being a pilgrimage, and so we are back on the leading edge of creation.

Once upon a time, people recognized their dissatisfaction with the standard of living for their time and heard the call of the prophet to come out of whatever level of security they had settled for, whatever status they had managed.

From deep within came a movement of confession that was evidenced by a willingness to be thrown back into the moment of creation when all was chaos. This is a willy-nilly repentance indicating a willingness to move in any direction but the direction they were heading because they could see so clearly its shortcomings.

John focused the symbol of baptism on this chaos of confession/repentance and directs it toward forgiveness (a foundation of seeing, evening and morning, all the time, "it is good"). The marker for this forgiveness of every forgetfulness that interdependence and community are at the heart of our best life is the chant, "G*D is good—all the time".

Mark, like the Gospel of John, pushes us to creation imagery as Jesus' birth story. Mark does this with an overt connection to the prophetic tradition that uses the goodness of creation as the corrective for whatever situation we are in. It is only in the beginning, in the wilderness of creation's chaos, that we can start anew—another first step.

With creation as our base, we are once again introduced to the specific "it is good" of Beloved Jesus.

Mark 1:9–15
Conviction [1]

Just as Joshua and the boys had to take a step into the Jordan before they found it was actually going to back up for them to cross, so Jesus had to leave the baptismal waters to act out a blessing of belovedness.

Often, we visualize this as a dunking-style baptism (though you may be interested in most of the early depictions of this scene show a standing Jesus with water being poured or sprinkled over him). In this, we associate the descent of a spirit concomitant with or immediately upon the completion of the baptismal water ritual.

Suppose for the moment that the baptismal ritual of John was the baptismal ritual of John, and Jesus was simply doing his best to continue paying attention to G*D.

The baptism went according to plan, and it wasn't until Jesus had fully completed the ritual and was stepping back onto dry land that a rainbow insight came that the threat of destruction, even by fire, was really over and done with. Redemptive violence was no longer to be the way of G*D. No wonder Jesus was encouraged and enlivened to proceed to test whether that really was going to be the way (each of the traditional temptations can be read as variations on the theme of violence) and to practice it at the end (in Mark everyone runs away from Jesus' death as it didn't prove a rejection of violence against another would avoid violence done to me and in Luke we even hear the sometimes attested words of Jesus to forgive even those who don't understand what they are doing).

Is belovedness separable from repentance? Can I still be beloved, though yet unrepentant? Can I call another beloved while they are yet unrepentant?

This is our test. Yes, we can.

Mark 1:14–20
Guiding Gift [3]

Time – complete
G*D – present
I/You – recognize and act

Can we live from the perspective of the wholeness of time—was, is, and will be? Can we live as though the important issues of life were settled and we just naturally participate in the details of loving our enemies and all the love that leads up to that? To have time fulfilled takes the burden off and frees us to free a spirit within.

Can we live from the perspective of the presence of G*D? So in the kitchen and every other part of life, we can cook up a feast, a banquet at which all are not only invited but joyfully accept said invitation. We can walk and talk with G*D in the cool of the evening and the burning of the noontide heat. Out of this multifaceted present, we find a sense of enough. With G*D, it is enough so we can relax into life in all its fullness.

Can we take all this in—time complete and G*D present—and have it affect what we think and feel and how we respond to the situations of life (including crucifixion)? Does repentance lead you to believe everything is broken at the outset, or does repentance lead you to believe everything is a new, good creation?

As we mess with this formula, we begin to sense that it is metaphor upon metaphor and not didactic deductive dogma. Where does this old formula lead you? I trust it is to new life, for if it is only to the tried and true, it will soon pass into the annals of a trivia quiz, "What is the marketing slogan of both John the Baptizer and Jesus the Baptizee?"

Old formulas can teach new meanings.

Mark 1:21–28
Guiding Gift 4

In his sermon "On Zeal", John Wesley is clear that if you are participating in one of the works of piety (in this case, teaching) and an opportunity comes to participate in a work of mercy (in this case, healing) there is no way to excuse not shifting gears away from piety to mercy without endangering one's connection to G*D's love.

Here, Jesus gives us an example of this ordering of life. He does not keep on teaching but attends to the healing.

And, as any good story would have it, it turns out that Jesus' willingness to respond to the situation at hand leads to emphasizing the teaching he was doing. His walk fit his talk, as we like to rhyme.

It was the work of mercy that validated the work of piety. We must not be afraid to shift gears backward and forward as we move through life, for it is this very movement that validates every movement.

———————————

Listen to Theodore Jennings as he writes in *The Insurrection of the Crucified*:

> ...it is precisely the demonic that testifies to the identity of Jesus as the "holy one of God." This is a messianic title formally similar to the assertion that Jesus is the Christ or the Lord. Thus, the confession of the unclean spirit is precisely that confession by which the Christian movement thought to distinguish itself from all unbelief. Indeed, Paul had put forward (or appropriated for his own purposes) the claim that "...no one can say that "Jesus is Lord" except by the holy spirit" (1 Corinthians 12:3). This criterion is utterly overthrown by Mark's narrative, not only here but throughout the gospel. The danger which lurks in Paul's use of this criterion is that if it is taken literally it leads to a view of faith which is merely ideological. By placing the Christian confession here in the mouth of the unclean spirit, Mark demonstrates that the mere confession that Jesus is Lord, Christ, or "holy one of God" is by no means an adequate definition of faith. It may just as well be demonic. Those who loudly proclaim the "lordship of Christ" may, for all their "spirituality," be demonic. The test of an authentic confession is not ideological, or theological but, as we shall see, practical.

Mark 1:29–39
Guiding Gift [5]

We have a tendency to attribute power to that which is greater, longer, wider, deeper—power that is implacable and must be bowed down to. It is important to see an ongoing vitality of steadfast eternity. Time, Creation, G*D are powerful in relationship to grasshoppers, slaves, or frail[1] humans. But to stop with that distinction is to dismiss everything in favor of some one thing.

In these passages, a key dynamic is not the distance between the great and the small but is the willingness of the powerful to energize the less powerful and the powerless to rise and restrain the powerful. This might be called silly in our usual entropic systems, but it might also be envisioned as the only perpetual energy mechanism there is, one that shares energy in an open environment.

Our tendency is to look at a given cycle of rising and falling rather than at an ongoing stream of life. When looking cyclically, we get into law issues such as this interesting one: "I am not free from G*D's law, but I am free under Christ's law". When looking on-goingly we can see patterns of connection between our predecessors and our descendants, our selves and others, one religious, economic, or political system and another.

Here, we proclaim a connection of intentional interaction between every disparate moment. This recognition leads us to rejoice in time's flow that supports us, encourages us, and engages us in this flow. Rejoice in every evidence of power coming to the faint, being received, and passed on.

---

[1] Substitute various diminished descriptors of your choice.

Mark 1:40–45
Guiding Gift [6]

How hard it is to choose to keep a good to oneself.

Leper: If you choose, you can heal.
Jesus: I choose.

Jesus: If you choose, you can keep this to yourself.
Healed Leper: I don't so choose.

Choice is a key issue in life. To what will we choose to be true? What will we choose to bring into being or help on the way out? How do we choose between just these two when they are in conflict?

Do you choose to follow the tradition wherein Jesus shows pity, or that which has Jesus being angry about the request and not just sending the former leper away, but casting him forth as a demon would be cast out? Whichever choice you generally make, this is a good year to go the other way.

Here, our preferred approach is through a translation that honors Jesus' anger. So, looked at through a lens of pity with an underlying tension of anger, Jesus sees the pitiful state of humankind. We have been run out of a garden, been raised up and let down; violence qua violence and retributive violence abound. We are caught without hope and with an imagination too small. We don't even know how to claim a birthright of relationship and healing. We are left begging for these rights.

In responding to the pitiful with pity, Jesus heals—knowing all-the-while that good-telling will eventually lead to bad-telling and put Jesus in the pitiful position of asking in another garden, "If you choose, you can let me off the hook so all I will have to do is keep you to myself. . . . Oh, I see, neither of us can do other than pity the circumstances and choose to be whole regardless of circumstances around us. . . . I take it back."

Mark 2:1–12
Guiding Gift [7]

We last left Jesus, having changed places with a leper, wilderness wandering. He has quietly returned to Capernaum. Eventually, word leaked out that he was back, and a crowd re-gathers to hear teaching, not receive healing. At this point, one of the folks who was either not present during Jesus' extended healing the last time he was in town or had contracted some paralytic condition between then and now was brought by faith-full, faith-active friends.

Emboldened by unnamed friends, Jesus asks us to hear beyond our words—to the action of life. A better question than whether it is shorter or easier to say, "You're forgiven" or "Stand; walk" is whether you can hear and see and experience each in the other. This is astounding work.

You may be led to practice this new way of listening and speaking this week. It will be a translational challenge for you and those you interact with to speak divinely in regular life and to speak commonly in ritualistic situations. There will be those who will respond that you are taking a larger jump than they are able to do and, one way or another, label you a blasphemer or just crazy. You may get scared of the possibilities and back away. There will be those who will be thankfully amazed at being able to reframe their life. You may find a rebirth of action in your own faith.

Here are two additional thoughts:

For whom will you make a new backdoor to fuller life? For whom will you activate your intentions? Having identified someone or someones, what is your plan to participate in their healing and the blessing of those who are witnesses to it?

Contrast this scene with that of Job and his friends. On a scale of Job's Friends to the Paralytic's Friends, where do you fall?

Mark 2:13–22
Guiding Gift [8] — Proper 3 (8)

Jesus went where angels feared to tread. Oh, they were allies and supporters, but only Jesus entered to feast. He saw bread to eat and fellow travelers in the strangest of places. This time it was at a place of taxation and a meal with those the religious leaders deemed "of no account".

In a place of detailed accounting were those of no account. Jesus had a new accounting system that could see gifts of leadership in those of no account and call them to use those gifts.

This new resource base begins a new spiritual accounting. The previous limits on discerning resources couldn't keep up.

There is no adequate example of this change in the history of economic models because the development of a new resource runs its course in the realities of limited resources or an ability to find more, as well as the introduction of new technologies that make a previous innovation obsolete.

Here we are talking about human resources. Once a previously looked-down-upon group is recognized, they can't again be unseen. Oh, there may be backsliding (remember Pharaohs forgetting Joseph and enslaving a whole people), but those falsely labeled "sinners" are freed, again and again.

Whether in a season of signs or revival, a key question is that of who is invited to be a host. Levi as a host for Jesus is impossible for some. But, if attended to, who would have imagined you as a hostess or host? Each new host is a new vessel responding to previous wounds of exclusion or anti-creation that leak away the very spirits intended to enliven a party.

We must address the "no accounts" of our day by counting in what we used to throw away. There is no way to follow Jesus without accounting for those unfairly designated as of no account. No basic hospitality, no Jesus. Consider this day those whom your family, congregation, or nation claim to be of no account (people who are LGBTQQIAA, immigrants on the street who speak a different language, other races and classes than your own, those considered disabled in one way or another, ….) and simply wonder what you might be missing by being less hospitable than Levi or Jesus.

Mark 2:23–3:6
Guiding Gift [9] — Proper 4 (9)

Into the midst of limits, comes a release. This release comes galloping out of the past to remind us that constraint has always been conditional. When constraint takes on a life of its own, it needs a reminder about its purpose of setting one limit so that another limit might be expanded. Constraint is to be in service to freedom.

Sabbath is a time to set limits on productivity, tilling the soil, and conceiving children, to experience again a creative impulse not oriented to a response but a vision of communal partnership beyond utility.

A release from constraint also slides in from the future, beckoning us beyond our current hardness of heart that demands some to be less than their gifts offer.

Sabbath is a time to set limits on rituals of power, whether within or without a given institution. As we put down habits of blame, we are invited to see folks at their best and not at their worst, in their potential and not their previously assigned classification.

Sabbath hearkens us back to first experiences of mercy and grace. Sabbath hurries us on to next experiences of mercy and grace.

When Sabbath takes on a life of its own, we need a sabbath from Sabbaths.

Mark 3:20–35
Proper 5 (10)

When both friend and foe accuse you of being crazy, of having reached the point of "having made your point and now you are just hurting your cause", you know you are on to something. A point has been reached where you are being unreasonable, or you have your finger on a very important transformational issue.

It is not easy to tell the difference between delusion and prophecy. Both fall prey to a need for internal consistency and defining oneself against others. Both are vulnerable to temptations to choose privilege and peer pressure over personal gift.

I hope you have had to make a choice as to whether you are crazy or if society or institution or family is the crazy one. This will mean that you have experience with the joy and frustration of living out being in the image of G*D. As you decide that it is just crazy to continue to believe in some "god" and not crazy to believe in a different "god", you put pressure on religious authorities to shift.

Every election or decision-point becomes a vote on "god". Whichever way the results turn out, it is most helpful if there is a realization that we are in the midst of another opportunity to choose more of the same or to make a quantum (evolutionary) leap to a different "god". Are the rich ("gods" in our culture) a motivating force for everyone to try to get rich, everyone being for themselves? Are the rich responsible for all that has allowed them to reach that state (disadvantaging the un-rich) and called to reintroduce a potlatch process? Is the financial economy the most important economy we have?

A divided state or nation or person won't last (though they can cause plenty of pain). While the pain they cause can be forgiven later, a decision to break community by privileging a few goes beyond pain to an unbalancing of creation that will not be undone without a painful revolution.

And so a time of choice on election day (and every day) comes for you and for me. Who is birthing me and shaping me most? Who is my family? Which "god" or social construct will I commit to? Am I a creature of my past or my future, and which is riskier?

Blessings on finding your family, your issue, your "wild-and-crazy"ness.

Mark 4:26–34
Proper 6 (11)

How long will we grieve? Poor Samuel didn't have Elisabeth Kubler-Ross to lead him through any stages. It was get up and get on.

Ezekiel's image doesn't progress through any particular process. There is an intervention, a sprig is planted, a vision established, a journey to participate in.

For the Psalmist, G*D is present before any trouble is on the horizon, during trouble that arrives, and after any trouble has left its mark.

Paul reminds us of the importance of viewpoint. From some vantage points, a new creation can be glimpsed that guides our interactions more strongly than the pain of the past.

Seeds have been planted that grow through their usual stages. They can also grow unbidden and unattended to surprise us with a harvest. These seeds do their work through time and beyond time to bring a new perspective from hardened ground. Watered only by tears, yet they flower and fruit.

Where are you in one of your griefs? Ready or not, a sprig has been planted on a dark crag of that mysterious mountain in your life.

———————————

molehills are real
our shape different
because of them

they loom when near
shrink with distance
perspective bound

mother-may-I baby steps
seven-league strides
both bring new views

one for me and one for you
both together
stretching togetherness

recovering from a trip
to grief
and beyond

Mark 4:35–41
Proper 7 (12)

What does it mean to speak "Peace" when all about you are losing their heads? Is it simply that you don't have enough information (otherwise, you, too, would be afraid)?

This is one of the spiritual disciplines that we have lost track of—calmness in the midst of storms. To practice this is easier for some, as their natural inclination is to move in that direction, and much more difficult for others. But both can benefit from the discipline to make it stronger and to take a step toward "calm".

Who then are you if you daily operate more out of faith than fear? Surely you are not the youngster you used to be—you have matured in the faith. Surely you are in but not of the culture all around you. Surely you are picking up where Jesus left off.

I'm sure you will have an opportunity to practice this discipline today, evaluate how you did with your opportunity, and apply your learning a bit more tomorrow.

———————————

open wide your heart
let's go to the other side
in the presence of mystery
open challenge will be given
to impossible situations
in so doing
praises will be sung
thanks given.

Mark 5:21–43
Proper 8 (13)

Sometimes the medium is the message. Here, the medium arrives as an interruption. The way we handle interruptions is a measure of any grace we carry with us. Also, check out chapters 2 and 3 for other interruptions. Mark is telling us something in the very construct of the story, not just the words on the page.

On a wall of the office where I work, I placed a piece of art that came as a gift—a Print-Collagraph by Marianne Stanke with words woven into it, interrupting it, if you will, that read,

> *Peace is when*
> > *Time doesn't matter*
> > > *As it passes by...*

I find that plays well on several different levels.

For now, the pattern of Jesus' words may suffice:

> peace
> do not fear—trust!
> why this commotion?
> get up
> let it be (implied)
> let's feast (implied)

May you deal well with the interruptions of life.

Mark 6:1–13
Proper 9 (14)

What does it mean that Jesus did no "deed of power" in his hometown? Healings were accomplished, but no deed of power? Obviously, there is a distinction to be made between healing and power.

Here, power has to do with teaching, with revelation that we are not at a spot we would wish to be at—hence a need for repentance to move a bit closer to our desire.

Eugene Peterson names the short-hand of "repentance" as a *joyful urgency that life can be radically different*. Those predisposed to the process of church seem to be better able to hear the judgment of "repent!" than the beckoning of "joyful urgency". Translating "urgency" as "!", a one-word response to Repent! is Joy!

As long as formal repenters hold sway within an institution, it will roll along for a while, eventually slowing down and stopping. Perhaps we need to read this pericope again from the perspective of Jesus coming to your local "Christian" congregation where he should be known from conception to resurrection as a doer of power, and he finds "We've never done it that way." Congregants have become immune to surprise—a great judgment upon pastors—so take to the road with whomever will travel.

---

in season or out
learning is in order

learning to live
without surprise

we will receive
hometown adulation

along with
hometown rejection

both are unrealistic
no surprise here

caught up to seventh heaven
or caught on a thorn

teaching is in order
in season or out

Mark 6:14–29
Proper 10 (15)

Living a "temporary life in a temporary world", we might learn two lessons from this passage:

> Telling the truth is to be avoided.
> No second thoughts allowed.

See where the truth got John—headless. See where it got Jesus—rejected at home and hung out to die.

These lessons jump out at our "fear response" (wherever it may be located). We look at this passage and see truth being spun by folks trying to define Jesus. It is difficult to tell the truth in a confused setting. Sometimes there is only a Jimmy Stewart/Jesus story/parable to be drawled-out for those who might later remember it and think again.

When we read about John, we see again that power has its prerogative to avoid self-reflection. If those in power don't get us through ignoring, marginalizing, and discriminating, there is always "stop, question, frisk" as well as arrest, prison, execute.

Herod learned a first lesson well—get born to power and use its trappings to stay there. These first decisions mean that there can be no second thought given, for that is a sign of weakness and you will soon be powerless. There is no Prince and Pauper story here to learn from.

We seldom wait for over-active speculating to clear (It's John; it's Elijah; it's a prophet-of-old) so we can see what is in front of us. A second thought would be helpful.

Speed of thought can be a manipulative tool that sets us on a path to be a "leader" even as we miss important questions or thoughtful responses that would add value to our quick insight. Looking for more partners is helpful.

Blessings to you as you do what you can to honor a good deed simply because it is good, no matter from whom it comes, and the humility to see if there is another and better way forward. May you live in this temporary world as though it had some persistence.

Mark 6:30–34, 53–56
Proper 11 (16)

Jesus was an active prophet, not a poetic one. Particularly in Mark, do we have an agenda-driven presentation speeding on.

When Jesus invites us to a deserted place it is only deserted inasmuch as he is not currently there, not that it is a desolation. A part of his teaching is to be active where you are in such a manner that such activity can be sustained, for we are always dealing with the desertification of desert-ion.

Sometimes we enter desolate territory only to find it wasn't, isn't, won't be. Sometimes we find such desolation visiting our routine life. Whether visiting or being visited, opportunity for "making whole" is available.

Our choice is to view desolate places as our life's joy or an impingement upon our possibilities.

Consider that compassion may be an adrenaline antidote. It smooths out responses and refocuses attention toward a larger picture.

---

a deserted place
is never so
when it is sought

desolation has a life
and rhythm of its own
not to be presumed upon

transforming strange aliens
into intimate family friends
hostility to peace

out of such journey
comes healing aplenty
for every unbidden dark valley

a desired desolate place
teems with expectation
and vast need

Mark 7:1–8, 14–15, 21–23
Proper 17 (22)

Our primary experience is not repeatable, and yet we institute traditions to keep it going, even if in a secondary way. Eventually, our tradition becomes our primary experience, and we are frozen into our explanation, not our experience.

Every generation needs to wrestle with this phenomenon of locating experience rather than carrying it with us as preparation for a next experience.

In the time of American Empire, we are facing this as we exhaust an old experience of finding a sense of freedom in a new configuration of community. Our traditions of such have led us to a time of confusion and an attempt to find a new configuration of community in an extreme freedom for the individual where each person is responsible for their own outcome.

A review of communal karma would be helpful, but we have indoctrinated ourselves and left my thinking outside of your critique and *vice versa*. A result is that we have no way to evaluate expected consequences and appropriate risk.

"Tradition", "freedom", "individual", and "community" are excellent words and holders of deep wisdom. Left to their own devices, outside of relationship with one another, they no longer nourish. Each can defile the other as well as complement them. As each becomes filled with too much of itself, we find their various extremes unbalanced and unbalancing.

Out of tradition comes frozen experience. Out of freedom comes fascism. Out of individuals comes narcissism. Out of community comes tribalism.

May Pentecost revive your appreciation of communal karma and from your experience of resurrection become a basis to face your primary experience in all its raw wind and fire.

Mark 7:24–37
Proper 18 (23)

Tyre: home of Queen Jezebel, who disputes with Elijah. Remember Elijah's fear.

Tyre: place of a classic oppressor of the Jews. Jesus was politically correct in not wanting anyone to know he was there, also practically correct in the economic system of the place.

Together, these are a source of tension. Jesus seems caught in history and his contemporary economic realities, as well as the whole male/female role distinctions of his day. No wonder the first word that comes forth from Jesus is, "No!"

Hooray for strong women. This unnamed Syrophoenician woman stands firm, gives as well as she takes. Regardless of the unlikeliness of her knowing about Jesus (unless you posit the invisible women deacons around Jesus all the time, but only noted by Mark at the end of his tale), we have this remarkable instance of Jesus repenting of his response.

We, too, are called to standing ground-of-care for the sick, regardless of their heritage or relationship to us. This may need a repentance from us, but we have a model for that in Jesus. In light of last week's emphasis upon what comes out of a person, rather than what goes in, this raises interesting questions about Jesus' initial response and reminds us of his brotherliness more than any god-ness.

If we carry this forward, Jesus travels further into Gentile territory, finally passing back through home territory, and on to another Gentile community where he encounters a deaf mute. Gentile or Jew? What needs to come out of such a person, that was not available for release until now? What needs to come forth from you that was not available until now?

For those who experience such events, they, too, have something pushing to get out. Yes, astonishment and excitement. More, though, it is a sense of being able to do some something "well", too. When you see everyday miracles, aren't you encouraged to participate in one or even to initiate such? With new ears open to the need of the world, may you speak clearly, plainly.

Even if an Archie Bunker Jesus tells you to "Stifle", let the Edith Syrophoenician in you gently and strongly stand for a second chance, stand for healing, stand for grace.

Mark 8:27–38
Proper 19 (24)

We have multiple identities, depending on who or what we engage with. Sometimes we might be even further subdivided into where we are interacting or when or why. If folks were to ask about you, there are a number of responses available to those who know you well.

Hopefully, behind all these ephemeral presentations of yourself, there is a sense of being Anointed, Gifted, Blessed—being Messiah. Some will see that; many will not. Sometimes we see it more clearly; sometimes not.

Basically, being Messiah is an understanding from which we might interact with the world, whether anyone else understands that as our motivation or not.

Part of the reason for the "secrecy" is not some fancy Marcan messianic secret, but simple humility. To claim messiahship has a tendency to claim privilege and to reject any suffering along the way. Without knowing the difference between hope and fear, we get confused and fall into the trap of the Confuser to over-focus on short-term privilege and survival.

If any would care to be fellow-traveling Messiahs, they, too, will have to be humble enough to live in a moment as though it were eternity and be willing to lose their privilege for the gift of living congruently, unashamed.

Who do I say you are? Messiah, Anointed, Gifted, Blessed. Get on with it without making a fuss about being so.

Mark 8:31–38
Conviction [2]

Satan = out of touch with larger meaning;
    in touch with smaller meaning.

To have no choice is satanic. To choose yesterday's meaning or a smaller meaning is satanic.

To have said "Messiah" is not to have said it all. What sort of Messiah are we talking about?

Obviously, what Peter meant by his affirmation is not the same thing that Jesus meant by it. For, as Peter lives into his understanding, he finds he got it wrong, again. The disciples in Mark really don't do all that well. Even when they are affirmed for getting the external right (the term "Messiah"), they find themselves rebuked for missing the internal dynamic of Jesus' expression of Messiahship, of being anointed.

What might be satanic about the unilateral approach in a current time of rumors of war? We hear much about, "get behind me, traitor", so we need to ask about what folks really mean when they say "patriot" or "democracy", for once you've said that, you've not said it all, either.

This is a good reminder to check out meanings of both words and emotional states.

All	Openness
Shame	Penetrates
Has	Entire
A	Need
Mercy	Networks
Ending	Energizing
Denial	Sacred
	Seasons

Mark 9:2–9
Mountain Top to Valley — Proper 5 (10)

In a Bible-study conversation, we tried to get away from a mechanistic approach to faith of "making disciples". This simply doesn't accord with our experience of forgiveness and grace. As we looked at the dynamics of our faith journey, we found oh-so-many temptations to constrain the presence of G*D, whether through Jesus or not. One of the biggest temptations we acknowledged is a sense of control or entitlement to "make" someone more like us.

A shorthand way of articulating a dynamic vision statement that would call us into a better future turned out, for this evening, to be "revealing Christ".

"Making disciples", even for some larger transformation of the world, has a feel of the blood and gore approach to atonement. "Revealing Christ" moves us to a creation-centered, liberation-energized attunement to Christ already present in the best and worst of times and folks. We are not called to create out of whole cloth the next generation of Christians, but to model the presence of G*D-with-us in our own lives. The healing and teaching needed is already present; it needs to be released as we travel with our Eastern Orthodox sisters and brothers toward divinization (*theosis* as the backdrop for the Wesleyan tradition of "going on to wholeness") and community (having all things in common).

Try "releasing", instead of "making", language for yourself and see how you would complete these sentences:

Christ is released for . . . .

and

Christ is released from . . . .

Was this exercise transfiguring for you?

Mark 9:30–37
Proper 20 (25)

I trust you know first-hand the connection between not under-standing and fear. The two are a very powerful combination. In not understanding, we become fearful to find out or even to have an epiphany, for it will cause the whole constellation of behaviors we have constructed out of our misunderstanding to come crumbling down about us. In fear, we prefer confusion to clarity, for we can hide better and excuse ourselves better when things are muddy; our fear stirs up the bottom muck.

It is not surprising that the disciples did not understand Jesus' teaching about his betrayal and death, given the topic of their discus-sion. It is not surprising that their lack of understanding Jesus' own self-understanding and their fear of understanding what Jesus was say-ing led them to try to figure out who was going to carry on the teach-ing once Jesus was gone. Surely it would be one of them who would be the key to the next level of institutional success and who would protect their pension.

What! a child, a newcomer, will teach, will be called to a place of honor? How could this be? Doesn't Jesus understand the process of royal succession? Perhaps we can help him out by winnowing the weightiest pool of players.

If everyone votes for themselves as the greatest, everyone will get one vote. If everyone must vote for another (become last to someone else's first), then I'm more likely to get more affirmations of greatness. Remember John Nash's insight in the movie *A Beautiful Mind*? *Christianity Today* puts it this way:

> … the Nash equilibrium posits that there are circum-stances in which we are better off if we settle for something other than that which we most desire. This may be counterintuitive, but the mathematical proof (which is available for a general audience in William Poundstone's excellent book, *Prisoner's Dilemma*) is quite elegant. Indeed, the implication of the Nash equilibrium is that sometimes the entire community is better off when we choose not to pursue that which we want most desperately.

Without a mathematical proof, if you know about parents who become grandparents, you know about not pursuing the perfection of a particular young-one, but their basic health and assurance.

Mark 9:38–50
Proper 21 (26)

It is so tempting to fall into the trap of talk radio, where the most used word is "they". How like the church it is to narrow the perspective to the local expression of faith. We whine, "They're not doing it right!" We would separate ourselves even more widely than we do. Fortunately, Jesus is not so quick to take affront at differences—"Whoever is not against us is for us." Can we define people "in" rather than defining them "out"?

This is a significant question because, left to our own devices, we would see all "theys" as the hand or foot that causes us to stumble, and we would cut "them" off. Aren't we much more prone to prescribing this for others than for ourselves, who always has an extenuating circumstance and will, of course, follow through on our promise of the moment to do better?

Oh, to see ourselves as well as "them" as being salted with fire. May we have this fire of confession within and peace all around.

This was written on a day celebrating my physical birth; can I get cabalistic and claim a relationship between this passage and my next year [since I haven't always done a bang-up job with this the past year]? Do you have an organizing scripture passage for yourself? Has it changed with the changes in your life, or remained the same? If remaining the same, has your perspective on it, relationship to it, or use of it changed?

A temptation to privilege is not very unusual. One response to this temptation is to saltily confess it. Another is to calmly recognize and then ignore it by borrowing a practice of non-attachment from our Buddhist friends.

Mark 10:2–16
Proper 22 (27)

"Hardness of heart" is a disconnect with creation. It is this disconnect that is behind the surface of divorce. Disconnect can happen in any relationship—one to one or one to many.

Here, it is tempting to focus on a doctrine of marriage and divorce. More to the point is a look at the disciples and how they are disconnected from non-disciples—children and others overlooked by them (hungry crowds, gentiles, etc.). Disconnection becomes an entry point to growth for each of us—how are we doing with our disconnects?

Can you hear G*D, Jesus, creation blessing where we would not? Listen again, "The disciples spoke sternly to the children". Can you hear that as, "The disciples divorced themselves from the children"? Listen again to Jesus, "Do not stop the children". Hear him say, "Do not orphan the children".

Which of your disconnects hasn't yet eventuated in divorce, but will unless there is a change in your willingness to engage and bless instead of restrict? It is time to get on with either stopping a disconnect and starting a larger blessing or to get on with a divorce.

Mark 10:17–31
Proper 23 (28)

Our tendency is to ask what will come our way without any work on our part. What is our due, and when will it arrive? This is the built-in temptation with inheritance and why John Wesley and other saints say that it works against our spirit.

"Inheritance" language works in two contrary modes.

Spiritually, inheritance is a subcategory of hope. It is what our picture of a better future is all about.

Literally, economically, inheritance is an illusion. A 100% inheritance tax would reclaim money earned at the expense of others and return it to the commonwealth that basically made it possible to earn so much. All other taxes may be able to be done away with if we saw income as a public issue, not a private one. Ongoing conversations about "death taxes" are penny-wise and dollar-foolish.

John Wesley wrote of the folly of saving for your children/heirs in his sermon, *On Money*:

> Do not leave it to them to throw away. If you have good reason to believe they would waste what is now in your possession, in gratifying, and thereby increasing, the desire of the flesh, the desire of the eye, or the pride of life; at the peril of theirs and your own soul, do not set these traps in their way. Do not offer your sons or your daughters unto Belial, any more than unto Moloch. Have pity upon them, and remove out of their way what you may easily foresee would increase their sins, and consequently plunge them deeper into ever-lasting perdition! How amazing then is the infatuation of those parents who think they can never leave their children enough! What! cannot you leave them enough of arrows, firebrands, and death? not enough of foolish and hurtful desires? not enough of pride, lust, ambition, vanity? not enough of everlasting burnings? Poor wretch! thou fearest where no fear is. . . .

The better way is to travel with Jesus and turn the question from Inheritance to investment. Invest in the poor, in the community as a whole. Here you will find your hope brought to life. Here is the greatest return.

Mark 10:35–45
Proper 24 (29)

It is very easy to pooh-pooh the Zebedee boys for their ambition. It is much more difficult for us to recognize the power, authority, position, and rank we have settled for.

James and John wanted to get ahead of everyone. We settle for being ahead of at least one.

The other disciples were angry at the brothers J. I suspect that I would have been, too. They show me up and cause me to reflect on how petty my power is. If only they hadn't raised this larger question, I could have proceeded along as though all were right with the world, and I wouldn't have to consider my so-called life and how I wield my privilege in the small pond of my circumstance.

Jesus, speaking to the extravagant (J & J) and mundane (deca-oblivoids) purveyors of advantages and disadvantages, reminds both the assertive and passive desirers of benefits and perquisites that this is not a lesson to be learned.

And we are still trying to pass the test on this particular lesson. Left and right, liberal and conservative, progressive and orthodox seem to be genetically descended from both James/John and the rest. Keep praying. Keep practicing.

Alternatively, "Heads I win; tails you lose." So we desire it when we express our desires to G*D, whether directly or through some intermediary such as Jesus, Mary, or a Saint.

James and John are thinking about some future glory while Jesus is all about present doxa (challenging what seems to be accepted belief and promoting the glory and good of realized eschatology or John Dominic Crossan's "sapiential eschatology". [A difference between the Zebedee brothers and Jesus is summarized by Crossan: "In apocalyptic eschatology, we are waiting for God to act. In sapiential eschatology, God is waiting for us to act."]

The issue presented to us is whether we are with G*D, or not. Positioning is not relevant—whether right or left, or before or behind, or above or below, or within or beyond.

If we are with G*D, we will be with one another and all of creation. The question of special privilege is spurious.

What it comes down to is heads we all win; tails no one loses. We're pulling for you.

Mark 10:46–52
Proper 25 (30)

Somewhere along the way, Bartimaeus' call, "Jesus, Son of David, have mercy on me!" got transformed into what is traditionally known as the Jesus Prayer, "Lord Jesus Christ, have mercy on me, a sinner." The mercy part is constant, but it does seem to have a distinct theological bias in transforming Son language to Lord and adding a phrase about being a sinner (which does not seem to be part of the storyline here). As one who appreciates brevity of expression, I can see shortening this mantra rather than extending it—"Jesus, mercy."

Try breathing in this way:

Inhale with an extended thought/contemplation of "Jesus" and exhale slowly while centered on the word "Mercy."
Set a timer for 5 minutes and try it.

What did you notice?

Does it work better for you to reverse this by exhaling a call on "Jesus" and inhaling a response on "mercy"?

Does one work better than the other for you today?

Next:

Try this exercise for another 5 minutes with just the word "mercy" on both the inhale and exhale.

Any change in what you found? Some have made this even more generic by using the single word, "Help."

In practicing this, we draw near to Bartimaeus, who drew near to Jesus, and this draws us nearer to G*D. Breathe on.

Mark 11:1–11
False Dawn Sunday

In Mark, we play an important part in setting up the recognized presence of Jesus. We go out of our way to get the colt/donkey/vehicle of peace ready to present Jesus and place our outer lives/coats on the line (vulnerable to receiving a "mark of the donkey" as it passes over).

In John, King Jesus has resources available at the snap of a finger (only royal palms are used) and, instead of retiring for the night, religious leaders stay up to complete and confirm their assessment of having no option but to destroy this king in their midst.

These are two very different perceptions and recountings of the same event. In some sense, this is a reversal point. Usually speedy Mark lingers over preparation processes while loquacious John is the briefest of the four accounts.

Finding which of these stories best describes the situation we are in will give us another piece of information about next steps. In Mark, our part is taken back as Jesus goes on to his last acts of power: a cursing of the fig tree and the cleansing of the temple money/sacrifice exchange system. In John, we then see outsiders moving toward Jesus. There is a continuing play between myself and G*D as represented here with my active going to prepare and then Jesus retiring or with Jesus riding forth and my response to find out more. In the back and forth specifics, we also find a generally forward arc toward life renewed and life eternal.

Mark 12:28–34
Proper 26 (31)

It is always tempting to cut to the chase. What is the most important commandment? What is the main thing that is supposed to be the main thing? What's the basic principle here?

Unfortunately, there is nothing that is singular. Note this from a *Wikipedia* article about the multiple understandings of a "gravitational singularity":

> The two most important types of space-time singularities are curvature singularities and conical singularities. Singularities can also be divided according to whether they are covered by an event horizon or not....

There may be no other commandments greater than "loving" G*D and Neighb*r, but there will be those that will be similar to them in particularity instead of generality. After all, loving Neighb*r looks quite different through the lens of Democrat or Republican or Third-Party nominee for President, or you or me. And so it is with some generalized love of G*D and Neighb*r.

The most that can be said here is that physical symbols and decision-making processes cannot take the place of relationships. When we base our interactions on some form of power, we have missed something "more important".

May you continue to question your religious tradition about what in the world general commandments mean in a particular situation you are facing.

Mark 12:38–44
Proper 27 (32)

As always, what we see depends on where we stand. Listen to this note from *The New Interpreter's Study Bible*:

> Given the immediately preceding reference to "devouring widows' houses" (v. 40), it is hard to know whether Jesus' example of the widow giving all she had should be taken as a good thing (more than the wealthy give) or as another condemnation of the workings of the Temple (all she had to live on is gone).

Given a larger context, instead of just focusing on a snapshot, I opt for the condemnation perspective.

That which does not move toward increasing love of G*D and Neighb*r contains the seeds of destruction. If it's not building up, it is preparing to come tumbling down.

There are certainly equivalents in today's world of people who so readily vote for proponents of policies that, in both the short-run and long-run, run counter to their best interests. We get so caught up by the forces and rhythms of the culture around us that we willingly suspend our belief and put in our last two cents to "Rah-Rah" the current structures. Eventually, people self-censor their own conscience and best interest to prop up losing propositions. Is this not the history of the fall of the Roman Empire and every Empire before and since. That which can fall, will.

Weep for widows, literally and figuratively. Their houses are taken from them, and they willingly invest the last of their life's savings in one scheme or market or another, and so willingly step into a legal version of a gas shower. And how different are "widows" from you and me?

No wonder Jesus goes on to note that the stones here are not cornerstones but stones waiting to crumble.

As a contrast, consider Ruth's story. Would that more would get up and go for what was needed, even if culturally suspect, rather than be co-conspirators in their own demise.

Mark 13:1–8
Proper 28 (33)

David, Look! What a large Enemy!
   It will take a trebuchet to do in this large an enemy.
   One smooth river stone or five stand no chance.

Jesus, Look! What a large Temple!
   Nothing could ever bring down such stability.
   No number of armies with the biggest siege engines could prevail.

What fantasies we conjure as we face fears and attempt to continue our present course. In both cases, we exaggerate our situations. We are at one and the same time too weak and too strong.

Take a second and third look. G*D as rock is an interesting image. G*D enlarges on the way from sling to forehead, becoming irresistible. G*D reduces so temple walls can be stepped over, be no barrier, and may become approachable. G*D as rock is no static image, but is as transformable as any Living reality.

----

lead me astray
please
from solid falsehoods
told with volume enough
to fool all the people all the time

lies that grow
rumor so seemingly so
plausible to irresistible
small lie masquerading
as big truth

lead me astray
from popular memes
so believable everywhere
and all too repeatable
in sanctuary space

having connected with god
our least fears
are projected large
upon innocent
children and strangers

of all sadness
this grieves most
unquestioning
big lies hold sway
in holy space

resolution
a willingness
to be provoked
to love
not lie

Mark 13:24–37
Needed Change [1]

Advent is a time for Christians, every year, to practice being part of the people of God in a damaged creation. Part of this practice includes faithful and sharp-eyed examination of the realities of life in this world. Part of this practice ought also to include meditation on the situation out of which Jesus spoke the words in this scene in Mark's story. Jesus lived late in the messy aftermath of the Maccabean rebellion, a complicated mix of victory and defeat, of freedom and bondage. Jesus lived in the shadow of the Roman Empire in a family and faith uneasy under foreign domination. Jesus embodied the tensions that lead to the first and second Jewish revolts against Rome.... That means, at the very least, that the Jesus we encounter in this scene is shaped both by the rich, insistent hope of Jewish faith and by the wise realism of Jewish faith.... Christians, as they prepare for Christmas, have a lot to learn about hopes that shatter the skies and about realism that remembers the deep pain of real loss.... [*Provoking the Gospel of Mark: A Storyteller's Commentary, Year B* by Richard W. Swanson]

And because it is this generation in which these things happen, it is also this generation which senses the arrival, the advent of the reign of justice and generosity and joy, the advent of the truly human. This is the generation bound in solidarity with all those, in whatever part of the earth or in whatever time, who have stood where we stand, on the brink of history.

This advent is not something that is realized in the inward moment of decisions as the existentialists (following John) supposed, Rather this advent is recognized in the public sphere of witness bearing, of martyrdom. For what is at stake here is not simply the fate of the individual, but the fate of God's creation. [*The Insurrection of the Crucified: The "Gospel of Mark" as Theological Manifesto* by Theodore W. Jennings, Jr.]

Whether through story or manifesto, there is the realism of loss in Advent. We have lost. Now it is not the time to strike back; it is not the time to take over; it is not the time to add to terror. It is time to watch for the bloom of a new shoot in the midst of destruction and to spend the consequential time of nurturing it through the surrounding blight. If we are stabbed in the back while bending over to tend to this new possibility, so be it. We are awake to this fragile shoot of hope more than to the all-too-real power of a principality.

May we be so awake.

Mark 14:1–15:47
Premature Fear Sunday

Since the waving of Palms, we have heard teachings and threats regarding the logical conclusion of continuing as we have been doing. Mark ended that day by having Jesus go to Bethany. Between the Palm and the Passion texts, we bounce into Jerusalem and back. Here in the Passion text, we begin with Bethany and an anointing.

Preparing ourselves and one another for our burials is holy work as well as hard work. It turns out Works of Mercy are always available to participate in. We don't spend as much time as we might on the Works of Virtue. This is especially true for those of us on the prophetic end of things.

This is a pretty amazing state of affairs because our very nature or the gift we have been given, leads us so consistently to dying.

Instead of focusing quite so much on a "Jesus died for my sins" approach to Good Friday, this long passage might lead us to ask about what it would take for us to join Jesus and be prepared to so live that others might live and take the consequences every age gives to those who so live. What anointing do you still need to open your eyes to how OK it is to live and die faithful to your nature or gift? This anointing would also allow us to know that it is alright to die before we see the completion of our work.

May you have your Bethany anointing, and that right soon.

———————————

[Anointing Oil] She anoints my body for its burial.

[Waving Palms, Laying Coats] They herald my ministry for its trial.

[Wrapping Linen] Wrap fear and death in compassion.

[Living Life] Imitate Christ and learn forsaken faithfulness.

> Wherever good news is proclaimed
> these stories will be told—
> a woman, a crowd, a man, and you.

Mark 16:1–8
Hopeless Hope Vigil — Assured

Mary, Mary, and Salome, now representing the discipleship narrative once held by John, James, and Peter, were practical in waiting until Sunday dawn to go to a tomb. Tombs are dark enough in daylight and to do so in the dark would add difficulty to difficulty. They were not practical in their uncertainty about being able to get in when they got there. Where was Martha, who would have organized this expedition so they would know they could enter when they arrived?

Well, it turned out the spirit of Martha had been on duty after all —the door was open and they walked right in.

I suppose they might have known that things were already falling apart in their orderly world when the stone had been moved. It doesn't begin to sink in, though, until they enter to find another transfigured figure who transfixed them with words unimagined—"Jesus ain't here; he's on the way to Galilee. Tell those behind you that Jesus has gone on ahead of you" (sort of a John the Baptizer reprise).

Well, what now? Our question about the stone sure had a response we weren't looking for. Now there are too many more questions suddenly swirling within. We can't even talk to one another yet.

When practical and caring women go quiet, look out—gestation is taking place and birth will come in its own time.

What questions are taking root in you? What has surprised you into silence that it might become you? [Note: Remember to read the phrase, "become you" in several ways.] Eventually, you will "go ahead" too—so enjoy the growth going on now, and the going ahead will be more joyous.

Luke 1:26–38
Needed Change 4 — Creation's Conception

Perplexity can be left alone or challenged. Our confusion points come from inside and out. David and a Temple raise questions from a prophet. Mary and a pregnant question rise to challenge an angel.

David's going ahead meets reversal, and he holds back. Mary's holding back meets reversal, and she goes ahead. Both are promised good fruit—descendants forever and for good.

In the midst of a king's word being his bond and a young girl's raising of deep questions, we find prophets and angels—catalysts for reversal and renewal. In the midst of a world not knowing how to back off from misused power and individual fears arrayed against creative peace, we are still in need of prophets and angels.

Priests would urge us to build a bigger box in which to praise and to develop communal mores that would belittle the slightest change in acceptable perspective or behavior. Prophets and angels are where the breaks in our power and fear can welcome an outsider (Gentile Alien) without first shunning or reconstructing them.

What will it take for us to listen to the questions, inside and out? Can we hear Nathan, still speaking? Can we listen to a Child within?

What will it take for us to speak truth to power and hope to fear?

Here, as we near the focus of Advent—Christmas—it would be well to pay attention to what is and isn't being said. It is all too easy to toss institutional metaphors around as though they were literally true.

---

my spirit rejoices
I have been blessed enough
to back down from my word
to forge a new word

blessed enough
mercied enough
steadfastly loved enough

a mysterious revelation
a questing proclamation
release blessing enough
to rejoice my spirit

Luke 1:39–57
Elizabeth and Mary Meet

In what days did Mary set out to visit Elizabeth? In what day will you set out with a new gift?

For Mary, it was a day of angelic visitation. And for you? Do you have that sort of day when you say "Yes" to a transformative question? Hopefully, you had this sort of day yesterday, or today, and it is now time to strike out and care for its implementation.

Remember, Mary was betrothed and then was absent (unchaperoned?) for three months. In Luke, we don't hear about when Joseph heard of Mary's pregnancy or his response. Mary's stay is less about the particulars of old Elizabeth or pre-teen Mary. What is at stake is the eternal prophetic need to reorder relationships that had become stuck in power and privilege.

This is a minimum wage movement writ large. Or any of a multitude of communal disparities—health care availability, maternal/paternal leave, vacation/holiday time, union organizing, voting rights, gender identity, immigrants/aliens, and on and on.

Helping set right any settled wrong through a remembrance of mercy is a recapitulation of Elizabeth's and Mary's encouragement of one another that their common and yet unexpected circumstance is for a larger purpose than first observable.

This encouragement of a larger vision gives us a place to enter and continue the story. Out of our unknown journeys, we are out to openly disclose the silence about wrong, to intentionally divest from benefiting from wrong, and to literally disrupt the status quo of letting wrong roll along.

May you meet Elizabeth and Mary this day and hear them announce together, "Blessed are you!"

May you quickly and easily respond, "My life joins yours in magnifying a mercy needed to set relationships aright."

Luke 1:46b–55
Needed Change [3] — Needed Change [4]

What boldness! My soul, yes, my soul, magnifies the Lord.

Oh, I know this is supposed to be about G*D, but can you begin to imagine the difference it would make if your very life were seen by you as clarifying the presence of G*D. This is the life of Jesus: he showed us a close-up view of G*D. It wasn't about him, but his showing G*D, magnifying G*D, revealing G*D already present, but beyond the eyes of our work-a-day world.

This is Mary work; this is Jesus work; this is your work and my work.

When we magnify G*D for those in power, they finally catch on that they are not as big as they thought they were. When we magnify G*D for those out of power, they finally catch on that they are of much more worth than they thought they were.

Consider this for a few seconds: what does it mean to magnify G*D? Have you seen that as your job description? How would it be for the church to not stop at making disciples of or for Jesus Christ, but to imitate his self-avowed task of allowing us to see G*D much closer than we had thought possible, to magnify G*D?

Let us join Mary and Jesus in magnifying G*D so all can see, so all can repent of their supposed grandness or their ill-conceived notion of worthlessness, so all might experience a largesse of mercy, finally, mercy.

Luke 2:1–14, (15–20)
Blessed Body, Proper I

So far, so good. An unexpected child with an uncomplicated birth, physically. There are political and cosmic overtones in every birth, but that is another matter.

A birth here; a shepherd there. All is as might be expected.

Well, except for an unrealistic census and manger scene. Oh, and angelic choruses canoning from the sky specific details far beyond a general Hosanna!

Even so, we might be better served to pay more attention to birth statistics, expectations of where thin-places are located, and who might be present.

With the usual trappings of a memorable experience in place, we are left with a question of, "What now?"

What is Mary to do with a visitation come to fruition? What are shepherds to do with an invitational visitation? What are you to do with a gift and time and energy visited upon you?

The shepherds entered the heavenly instructions into their GPS and set off.

Mary stored experiences.

The shepherds later set their GPS for "Home" and returned to ordinary life.

Mary goes on to store rituals of purification, circumcision, presentation, and naming. She stores childhood episodes, including leaving Jesus behind at a spiritual gas station. She stores the reunion of cousins at River Jordan and Jesus' subsequent getting booted from Nazareth. She stores being put in a larger family picture when trying to visit one of Jesus' teaching sessions. She took her place in line with other Marys. She leaves as quietly as before she had been surprisingly introduced.

And you? Where have you set your GPS? Will you let a next small revelation unfold without you?

Luke 2:(1–7), 8–20
Blessed Body, Proper II

Let's hear it for all the third-shifters on Christmas Eve, or any eve. When the usual day is over and the sky is safe for angel singers, late-night workers have the opportunity for a waking dream and responding to it right away.

Imagine all the third shift workers catching a vision of peace for themselves, and all, that is so compelling that they walk away from their responsibilities and band-aiding and production. What a night that would be.

Some would see in this only disaster—the sheep would be open to attack; patients would finally be allowed to die; a protective shield against the consequences of inattention would go down—irresponsibility would reign.

Some would see in this only the breaking in of a new world we have held at bay because of our anxiety regarding power and control—hope would reign.

Some would see a combination that leaned in one direction or another.

Wouldn't it be a wonder, though, if we paid more attention to amazement and less to obligation? Yep, pretty chaotic. Would you be afraid someone would take advantage of the situation to get an illicit gain? Would you be glad to have such an amazing moment even if you had to ponder over it for the rest of your born days?

Christmas Eve—we are almost there, and just can't wait, so we celebrate now. Apparently, four weeks of Advent was too much. Waiting one more eve for the next morning is too much waiting.

Christmas Eve—and it was evening and morning the eighth day. Celebrate early and often.

Luke 2:15–21
Naming Day

The calendar says January 1. It is time to name the year. Is this an animal as found on placemats at restaurants featuring Chinese food? Is this a number in a never-ending sequence? Is this a Resolution you just made up out of whole cloth? Is this a year dedicated to a virtue or other purpose?

How we name is as important as what we name. Naming can both reveal and hide important aspects of life. In the church, it is tempting to do the Sunday School thing and have everything be about Jesus. Thus, this year is the year we practice doing Jesus' work. Show your work of identifying what of Jesus' life you will focus on for a year?

Try this:

1. List 10 characteristics of Jesus

2. Identify which 5 are most needed in the communities you regularly engage.

3. Of these, name the 2 that have the greatest claim on you by way of gift or call.

4. Chose 1 and give yourself to it for a year. Make a plan whereby at the end of the year you will be noticeably more identified with this quality of life.

Jesus Characteristic	Community Need	My gift My call	My year of:
1. _____			
2. _____	1. _____		
3. _____			
4. _____	2. _____	1. _____	
5. _____			
6. _____	3. _____		* _____
7. _____			
8. _____	4. _____	2. _____	
9. _____			
10. _____	5. _____		

Luke 2:22–40
Blessed Body [1] — *Old Welcomes New*

No, we aren't fooled. The Sunday after Easter/sunrise and the Sunday after Christmas/eve will not live up to the numbers of those in attendance on highly public days.

These are Sundays for the Anna(s) among us. Her persistence is noteworthy.

Luke records that Anna never left the Temple. She worshiped through fasting and prayer. If this is not hyperbole, a part of us wants to know the details of how this happened. Did she have a "son" during her years of marriage (was it during her betrothal?) who grew and became strong, filled with wisdom: prosperous, by G*D! Did this son see to his mother's welfare out of his own? Was it another relative? Was her acknowledged spirituality rewarded by gifts, "Now don't forget to take a little something to the Temple to help old Anna; you will be rewarded for your good deed to this saint among us!"?

But, beyond the gossipy part of us that wants details, how are we progressives doing with our Anna-shaped challenge to sing our joy on a Low Sunday for seeing, even in these difficult times, a renewed expectation for the freeing of every city bombarded by rival claims to right and privilege and power? Let us not give up. Let us hoist Anna and all callers-to-freedom on our shoulders to sing an everyday angel song of peace to all.

So often at the end of the year, we close with "Old Father Time", who cyclically passes away. This year, as we have a cup of cheer, let us bring *Anna Lang Syne* to mind (modern translation of Anna Phanuel Asher).

Be persistent, not only in doing good, but in expecting redemption for all, as we move from days in the past to life available in this moment.

Luke 24:13–49
Opened Heart Evening

A Stranger in Jerusalem would be a good title for a book. Knowing what others don't know is the equivalent of having questions others don't have—like a proverbial Martian visiting Earth.

Notice the lack of overt evangelism here. Jesus walks with folks. Jesus listens to folks try to understand the not-understandable. He does reflect out loud about expected consequences (labeled as scripture here, but simply a reality check that could be posited even without previous prophets).

Jesus' comments captured their imagination, but it was the fellowship that confirmed it in their hearts. When this "click" happens, the source becomes invisible in the same way that air is for us or water is for fish—invisible and yet all around and within, giving life.

Note that it is while the travelers were sharing their moment of enlightenment that fellowship (loving one another) would confirm or dismiss any particular doctrinal formulation. Enlightenment also holds a mystery symbolized by a shift in attention. Jesus shifts from invisible background to visible foreground and back to invisible—just as in any good illusion.

As if to confirm the primacy of fellowship, Jesus moves his generic "Peace" language to "let's get real" language—touch, feast, repent, and forgive.

We need to be in touch, to eat together, to mutually correct courses and preemptively forgive. It is important to begin where we are. In this case, Jerusalem. In our case, church. If we are not in close enough contact to touch and feast we won't be able to share in repentance and forgiveness. Without these, the church loses contact with the world, and there is no message or preaching that will trump these basics for more than a moment.

Remember John Wesley's old purpose statement and its particular locus:

Question: What may we reasonably believe to be God's design in raising up the Preachers called Methodists?

Response: Not to form any new sect, but to reform the nation—*particularly the Church*, and to spread scriptural holiness over the land. [Emphasis added.]

After remembering, what greater reform does the church need than a renewal of touch, feast, repentance, forgiveness?

Luke 24:36b–48
Assured [3]

While talking, our talk manifested. This surprises us as we are so used to our talk being based on speculation and spinning around and around until we are spun into another topic. And so we proceed until no one can trace back where we've been or how time passed us by. Time is still now, and we are still so unready.

Talk as cheap as cheap grace is no bargain. We are easily scared off from applying our experiences to the opportunities in front of us.

Even when trying to delve behind what has happened and fit it into a sense of forward motion, we get confused about what the main point is.

We hear a process and get caught up in repeating it as best we can. So suffer and rise become all that we hear, and it isn't long before we are causing suffering and only allowing folks to rise through the ranks as current gatekeepers who clone themselves and guarantee their perks.

This is such a strong image that we lose track of its intent in the minutiae of ritual and creed. Here to live (suffer) and continue revealing G*D (rising) are for one key result never arrived at when they take on a life of their own.

It is not a dual process of suffer/rise *and* repent/forgive. It is a lived cause and effect. As we suffer, we repent that we might forgive and rise. As we suffer, we reveal this rhythm of life to those who need to repent for causing our suffering, and we rise with ready forgiveness even before it is asked.

Don't just suffer and rise, but see how they prepare a table for repentance and forgiveness that embodies, "Peace is with us."

Luke 24:44–53
Our Turn to Witness

You are witnesses of these things. What things? Our fear of the unexpected (a flight or fight response seems to be on a hair-trigger and very strong). One thing that helps manage such an anxiety is an expectation of the unexpected.

We are also witnesses of joy and disbelief living side by side. Our tendency is to emphasize one side of that pairing, or the other. One thing that helps us keep perspective is to anticipate them both being present, even if one appears in the foreground and the other takes its turn as background. We don't need to make up a story that would prioritize them.

We are also witnesses of the importance of table fellowship, whether it be ritualized bread and cup or a piece of an everyday fisherman's meal of broiled fish.

We are also witnesses of the promises and threats of the past coming to fulfillment. This makes us a bit hesitant about the pronouncements we make in this day because of their echoing into tomorrow and coming back to haunt in different circumstances.

We are also witnesses that we are but witnesses. No eternal truths here. We simply say what we have experienced. We don't need to fudge the truth to make G*D look better, ourselves look better, or our enemies look worse.

John 1:(1–9), 10–18
Blessed Body [2]

no one
will ever
see G*D
not even
Jesus

every one
will ever
see G*D's heart
especially
you

each one
will ever
come into being
as light informs
their witness

we
will ever
reveal all else
living together
fully

John 1:1–14
Blessed Body, Proper III

The universal is always becoming the particular, and *vice versa*. This interpenetration of life with life is one in which we are participants. We have had plenty of opportunity to practice this interaction. So it is, we are to identify with being light to one another—love your Neighb*r as you love Y*urself and one another and especially enemies.

Believe it or not, a universal Word has become your Flesh. While Brother Ass, our flesh, gets us around, we are to be more than asses. From before and after, we are smack dab in the middle of transformation of energy to matter and matter to energy (Word to Flesh and Flesh to Word).

There is trouble brewing when this is not acknowledged. There is blessing aplenty when it is.

Merry Christ-mas to you and Merry You-mas to all.

John 1:6–8, 19–28
Needed Change [3]

Exasperated lately by not knowing your source of authority? This is part of the prophetic, progressive tradition—simply to go ahead.

The powers that be will send queries about who you are with the intent of putting you on the defensive—justify yourself, explain yourself, place yourself, categorize yourself, and, finally, deport yourself.

All of this is an attempt to get you to self-censor. It makes it a lot easier for the powers if you begin to second-guess yourself instead of claiming your authority and joining with others who claim theirs.

So, let's practice.

Powers: "Why are you doing what you are doing?"

John and You: "Because. And if you think you are having trouble with me, just wait for what is coming next."

Now, how can you take this freedom of being beyond the border and bring it into legislatures and congregations? Hang on to your head, but bring it on.

"Adam" was to testify, witness, to the light of creation, a relationship with G*D. Down through the years, this has been passed on—"Original Testimony", so to speak.

We are all called to the task of Adam and John and Jesus, etc.—to testify to the next, best, part of life.

There are different testimonies in different arenas of life. We each have our place to testify—whether from a riverbank or an empty tomb or where you happen to be.

This testifying is Advent work—Remembering back to our Original Testimony that we might Testify Forward.

How's it going?

Homework: Listen to Susan Werner singing her song "May I Suggest". As of this writing, this link works:
YouTube.com/watch?v=eW1DDSQnEYo

John 1:43–51
Guiding Gift 2

With tingling ears, we have searched and searched for something that will not disappoint. We have searched inside ourselves and found the house of Eli still alive and well. We have lowered our expectations of everything and everywhere; it is all like Nazareth—unacceptable as a starting place.

A big place we searched was the law, but we found it didn't hold Mercy very well. We could follow it forever and never find it brought us to a beneficial place, only a place bounded by Eli's sons waiting for a loophole to be found.

Finally, it is important to fall back on such basics as being trustworthy and without deceit. These are very tough roads to travel that go beyond easy, prior answers, and are continually in need of integrated responses.

Finally, it becomes a question of who we will be with at the end.

> If we will be with those we are now with,
>   what response is needed now?
> If we will be with ourselves as we are now,
>   what response is needed?
> If we will be with that unknown to us,
>   what response is now needed?

---

follow me
come and see
hurry on
we will come to a mirror
and see as we are seen

choices will be feasted upon
responses will be made and remade
we'll see how this looks
and that

shapes will be formed
lives hidden will be revealed
roads will open
laws will fade

hurry
pay your money
takes your chance
you are seen
you can see

252

John 2:13–22
Conviction [3]

One of the best stewardship analysis tools is a record of spending—checkbook registers (if anyone still uses them instead of a bank statement) and credit card bills. Here we begin to see what a person's priorities are. "Show me the money" is not just a cry for "more", but an evaluation of applied values.

Here, we find money to also be an excellent gauge of one's sacrificial life. Where do you put down coins of the realm to assuage your guilt and shame? Compare that amount with a tithe of your income. How does that work for you?

One of the dynamics that can be at work here is a focus on the external behaviors and our willingness to own up to any number of peccadillos to avoid awareness of an unmentionable/unforgivable sin.

Imagine, if you will, Jesus cleansing your checking account and investment portfolio.

If you can so imagine, you may be up to hearing a bit more about a resurrection for your life in this world after conversion from the suffering (shame) and death (guilt) of your past/present.

Change what you have the power to change
in the moment you have.

Make what you have the power to make
in the moment you have.

John 3:1–17
Live Together

Can G*D be revealed except by the intention of said G*D?
Can G*D be accidental?

Consider these questions in light of your own life and see whether or not they add value to you or whether you consider yourself diminished because of their presence.

For the moment, we will simply take it as an opening praise or set-up to an intended sharper question to come. Stipulated: Jesus, you are somehow tapping into G*D to be able to do what you have done.

"Let's start there," says Jesus. "You've glimpsed some surprising actions/responses going on that don't fit in your current picture. To address these, we will need to shift perspectives—seen from above, there are no boundaries like the ones you perceive while measuring yourself against the past or someone else. From above, we are also able to consider a future that surprises—like when you finally get one of those *Magic Eye* things." (Didn't you just know Jesus would know about stereoscopic free-viewing.)

There is usually more available to us than we have yet caught. One of the constant surprises is how universal Love is—how it moves away from suspicion and condemnation toward larger pictures from above—wholeness/perfection/salvation.

In this model, a creedal trinity is a limited and reductionist approach to a much larger life.

John 3:13–17
Relic Day

Ascending/Descending gets very confusing as they cycle one another.

Is it the pride of Jesus' cross

or the humility of Peter's cross

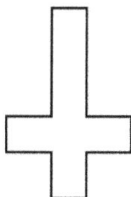

we are to aspire to?

Who can tell yin from yang anymore? Our beginnings and endings both do and do not cohere.

On a day of attending to physical remnants of a past experience (a pressed flower, a faded photograph, cold pizza on the counter, or a piece of a cross designated as holy), we can't escape the larger meaning of a small remembrance.

Endings do not condemn all that has gone before. Ends are meant as new beginnings.

Will the relics of your life point toward "no condemnation"? If not, what needs to change now that your leftovers will be a blessing and not a curse?

It will be easy to try to slip out of this question by hiding behind Jesus. "No condemnation" is Jesus' work, not mine. But, in the end, it will not be that easy to separate what Jesus was able to do and the even greater things those who follow his way are called to. Rejoice, you have a part in all this eternal life (new life) taking place in the present.

John 3:14–21
Conviction [4]

Again, an issue of what can be trusted raises its fanged head. When a danger seems great enough, that deemed evil or death is nipping at our heels, we are liable to pursue the improbable, if not impossible. How might gazing upon a bronze snake care for the poison a live snake has injected?

This then is the context of the famous John 3:16 line about believing to receive a conditioned gift of a positive eternity—something not intrinsic to persons, but given to or withheld from them.

If your greatest fear is a wrath to come, then what became substitutionary atonement theology is the only way to go. Faith becomes a zero-sum game that needs a dividing line between up and down.

Even when we focus more on a scene with Nicodemus and the allusions there, we hear conditionality retrojected into the conversation. It is as though the whole business of being lifted fills two functions. First, it builds on an assertion that Nicodemus did not understand his own tradition about where belief can come from—fear—and how it needs to be understood as sign and mystery rather than doctrine based on one experience [go get intentionally snake-bit so you can look on a bronze snake and prove G*D]. Second, since you are not ready to receive my experience, I can make the most outrageous claim, and it will not add or detract a whit to your willingness to see things differently.

Rather than get caught with the problems of a conditionally loving G*D, it may be more helpful to look at verses 20-21 and the potential of using embarrassment of having one's hypocrisy (often a great evil in the Christian Scriptures) revealed to others. Here is the antidote to secrets and night-meetings—by your deeds will you be measured, not by what you say and then don't do. In every generation, religious leaders still need to learn this reality.

In our day, this shows up around religious pronouncements and actions regarding LGBTQQIAA people, immigration policy, and economic theories. In each case, there are scapegoats expelled instead of a community broadened and deepened. Some churches have done well to know it isn't just a matter of looking to a past sign, but paying attention to a present choice to both proclaim love and express it in deed. This is light that illumines all the other born-again and bloody atonement excuses to avoid deeds done in G*D's freedom.

John 6:1–21
Proper 12 (17)

The NRSV has Philip being "tested".
The Message has Philip's faith being "stretched".

For those who have test anxiety (and who doesn't who has grown up with a tricky G*D just waiting to catch you at something), shifting that to a growth experience of stretching is important. We might think about testing in terms of measuring ourselves against some external measurement or in competition with someone else, where there can only be winners and losers. Stretching, on the other hand, is a yogic experience of measuring oneself against oneself. This is a difference between having to get to a particular spot right now and simply moving forward—arrival (test) vs journey (stretch).

Without grace, we have to get it right, right now and every time. With grace, we can grow into new life, find our dead-ends, shift gears and directions, live within mysteries far too large for us.

I know that I have given more than one teacher fits because I see tests as a learning experience, not simply a measurement of how well I have encoded whatever the standard line is. How do you see the church testing people instead of growing them through stretching their vision?

John 6:24–35
Proper 13 (18)

What must we do
to be a practitioner
of G*D?

So many different
ways of being practical,
which way to go?

Monkey see, monkey do
is an ancient model—
show us G*D.

Practice your performance
here and now
with us and ours.

Do it again—
and again
again.

Hop to—
our perfection
is in your hands.

Eat bread.
Be bread.
Share bread

Trick Alert!
That's not doing;
that's being.

John 6:35, 41–51
Proper 14 (19)

As we read the poetic language of John, it is important to remember Jesus as teacher, mentor, and leader of disciples. This will continue to ground us as we listen in on images of bread, life, eternity, and magnetism.

Jesus, as a sage and wise one, has enough teaching to chew on that a follower will always have a next syllabus. To come and live with Jesus will be fulfilling, whether or not you buy the "bread" identifier.

As you read this passage, it will be helpful to translate "taught" and "come" as "drawn to", "believes" as "lives with", "eternal" as "present", and "raised" as "revealed". Go ahead, mark your Bible—cross out words and write in new ones.

As you reflect on the way this passage now reads, there are two additional perspectives to add.

The first is, "I have come from heaven." The next time someone asks where you are from, use this line. Our identified starting place is important, and if you don't see G*D (euphemism, "heaven") as part of your start, you are likely to settle for coming from Madison or somewhere else and be bound by its limitations, your pedigree. In some sense, our start is what magnetically aligns us with our best intention and allows us to be drawn by it. For John, our start is pre-creation.

Secondly, "bread from heaven" is an extension of the creation tale of a by-passed tree-of-life (that one may eat of it and not die), we have been guarded against. Imagine, a walking tree-of-life pursuing us even East of Eden, as we are hesitant to glance back at it lest we are tempted to run back only to be sent away. At some point, our moving ahead will intersect a tree-of-life, and we will better recognize the good and not-good we thought so desirable to know and set out on a journey less traveled—presently being drawn by G*D to become our part of G*D—from before creation to right now.

John 6:51–58
Proper 15 (20)

Eat me!

In today's world, these five letters and two words are hurled at another to reduce them, to put one's self in a position of power.

In Alice's world, they serve a function to expand or reduce one's body, depending on circumstances. Knowing only the outside, we are brought to a kind of magic. Life happens, but we are not one with it— always it takes a magic elixir of dieting or carb loading to see us through our fairytale situation.

In Jesus' world, this is high poetry bringing us to a better spot than common sense would allow. Here is a breaking of barriers that sends new sparks of creation cascading and lighting our dark caughtness. These five loaves and two fish are an enlarging catalyst bringing us to a new perspective. They are the equivalent of "Let it be!".

And so the choice before us:
- *swear*, diminish another
- *magic*, wait on external solutions
- *create*, a new place to stand and state, "I am."

John 6:56–69
Proper 16 (21)

Quite a range of responses to Jesus—complaining, disbelief, rejection, confessing faith, betrayal—and these among his followers.

Do you feel better about your setting now that you see how Jesus was responded to?

What is your understanding of the straw that broke the disciples' backs and caused them to leave? Was it the bread/flesh talk? the ascension suggestion? the destiny vs. free-will proposal? something beyond Jesus himself, something in the culture that wasn't being transformed quickly enough?

So why are you still sticking around this Jesus? And how can you state that without getting into religious talk that will need more and more talk to explain your point? Any idea what your breaking point is with Jesus? with the Church?

It is revealing for us to reflect on Simon Peter's affirmation of Jesus as the Holy One and on Jesus' response to that affirmation in the very next verse. Remember, Jesus indicates that he chose both Peter and Judas—affirmer and betrayer. How does this reflect the calling of G*D of both saint and sinner? (Oops, straying just one verse off-course enters us into a whole new conversation. I guess we can put that conversation off, as we don't have to wrestle with that, simply make an affirmation.)

A difficulty is that saying, "Hooray for Jesus", is a conversation ender and removes from us responsibility to engage inconvenient relationships. A "Hooray" doesn't adequately address the disjunctures between our expectations and experiences.

John 10:11–18
Assured [4]

A "good shepherd" has the power and responsibility to know when to lay down their life and when to pick it up.

Followers of a "good shepherd" don't always get the power of this ambiguity. Some will claim the shepherd can only pick up life, and so everyone must give up their life in light of the shepherd's life. This will keep them from an ability to lay down their life for others. Seemingly, they can only see a shepherd's crook as a mighty scepter.

Other followers make exactly the other error: shepherds must, at all times and in all places, lie down and be sacrificed.

What we are still seeking is wisdom on how these fit together in our lives and in our times.

One beginning spot understands that goodness and mercy are ever-present. This gives direction to our picking up and laying down of life. When does one reveal the background of goodness and mercy through a contrasting action, and when does the other polarity kick in to better reveal a field of goodness and mercy against which everything else makes better sense? It is here we always find ourselves. Do we zap a fig tree or allow a rich, young ruler to go further down a dark path?

---

resurrectional power reveals
our basic bent in life
to narrow life down
one unique resurrection
to open life up

resurrection as commonplace
to see resurrection for Jesus
and claim it only for him
runs us afoul of other sheep
claimed as part of all
runs us afoul of others who also
reduce resurrection to one

to see resurrection as ours
authorized and encouraged
by this resurrected Jesus
for the sake of lost sheep
ordains us transformers
of resurrection to resurrections

John 11:32–44
Honoring Day

Who's to blame? A person born blind? Their parents? Jesus for intervening? Jesus for delaying? Last week, the wonder of G*D was revealed in a creation story involving mud. This week, with Jesus' delay in coming, Lazarus gets all the way to "mostly dead" (read *The Princess Bride*). Everyone understands Lazarus and Westley to be dead, but all great stories find a way to a larger possibility beyond apparent limitations. Even tragedies give instruction that we might find another way.

The unbinding in this story is very similar to the revealing to Photini, the Samaritan woman at the well, who she might yet become. The unbinding of Lazarus is also our unbinding, even as Photini's enlightenment is ours. All of these Johannine encounters hold a creative edge with possibilities and realities of new births.

Do you see how beloved Photini was, how beloved was Lazarus? This pushes us again to recognize our own belovedness. We are worth being wept over. We are worth being called forth. We are worth being unwrapped (shedding our skin one more time) and set free to a next stage of life. [Imagine here your own life stages that have brought you to your own emergence.]

What a difference a moment, a day, or even four days can make. Each of them holds an initial state of a new way of being/moving— use your favorite search engine for "butterfly effect" references.

We honor those whose appreciation of the small shifts in life runs deep. A touch here, a word there, and pretty soon we are in a different relationship with one another and creation as a whole. We sometimes categorize them as Saints (capital "S") when it would be more helpful to nod and say "sister" or "brother" (lower case "s" or "b"). This is where new life takes place, in the mystery of butterflies and possibilities.

Whenever and however folks hear, "Untie them and let them go", there is life to honor.

Do reflect on how many opportunities you had to unbind another today and how many of them you took advantage of. Each opportunity came with a different way of enacting this act of freedom. Myriad are the ways of unbinding. May you challenge yourself to do one more tomorrow than you were able to do today. For each release in this moment, more will follow in days to come.

John 12:1–11
Clarification Week, Monday

Generosity of others brings out the worst in us. It affronts our myth of never-ending progress for us in a zero-sum world. When someone else is generous, we can't help but wonder what that will cost us.

If we could have been the recipient of a generous gift, we would certainly value it more highly than the ne'er-do-well who received it. We would have been able to turn a pound of nard into an even better return than a pound of heroin. In our imagination, we can see all the good we would do with that resource. Of course, there would have to be just a little taken out for administrative costs. Then, certainly, there will be a consideration given for management of this fund. A laborer is due their due, so a little more may have to come out. Obviously, there are a few palms to grease to efficiently and effectively oversee the movement of these monies to the poor souls so in need of a hand-out. Yes, someone would certainly receive something if only we had the nard.

Here in this week called "Holy", we may need to question the capitalist model of charity. It does seem we have poor folk all around us. It is hard to make a maximal profit with them having so many needs. Surely we should be able to market Jesus Nard or Lazarus Wrappings—with some of the proceeds going to the poor. We wouldn't expect to do worse than the American Tract Society's administrative expenses of 68% of their take as reported by Charity Navigators. Well, we might do worse, but we would not expect to.

As a first reflection on life this week, we see that we don't see clearly. The way we measure importance and identify key values gets pretty messed up pretty quickly. Generous women have to go. People miraculously alive have to go. This is not to mention all the unmentionable folks we already dismiss as a matter of course by rendering them invisible. When honor comes up against profit, honor loses. When new life comes up against institutional survival, new life loses.

What is the half-life of generosity in your life? What is the distance between a reason to be generous and generosity itself?

John 12:12–16
False Dawn Sunday

When will stony hearts understand and sing truth to power? After there has been a resurrection.

Of course, this implies that things will get quite dead first.

No wonder these are difficult scenes. The palms will turn to ashes before the ashes can intentionally lead us toward resurrection that comes in its own time (3 days or years or generations or eras).

Here we see knee-jerk reactions to an immediate hope that someone else will take care of the issues of the day. Come "King" Jesus and make it all OK for us. Take us off the hook. Now there's a bandwagon we all want to jump on.

But there is no white charger here, only a grey donkey. What asses we were to think we could return to our mother's womb, re-enter Eden, and nevermore wrestle with what we know about good and evil in the world and these images of G*D we call ourselves.

Believe it; stones and stony hearts can change—do change. But not easily or immediately. In remembering past changes, we can anticipate the general theory of change without knowing the details of a particular change or trying to turn that into a technique.

John 12:20–33
Conviction [5]

G*D: "I have glorified; I will glorify. I have been who I have been; I will be who I will be." And so the bookends are in place.

Self: "I am beloved." And so the content is in place.

Now comes the living with new covenants, steadfast love, abundant mercy, clean hearts, joyful salvation, and a willing spirit. Thrown into these qualities that open us to an expansive future are those elements that narrow us down: strayless commandments, sinless statutes, reverent submission (with cries and tears), and learned obedience.

As we go along, there will be requests to bring folks to Jesus. What will you show these inquiring hearts and minds first, second, third, and finally? Will you start with something from an expanding list or a narrowing list, and why? Will it depend on the nature of the searcher and begin with where they are (if looking for more, start with the expansive), or begin with where they are not (if looking for more, start with the narrower)? Both have their appeal and effectiveness, but they are probably both equally incapable of being turned into a technology to be applied universally.

Will you start with where you are instead of where the questioner is? Here, the questions of application may be even more difficult.

Finally, will any of this impact the kind of life you are going to live (which may have an impact on what kind of death you will have)?

---

someone is coming to dinner
they wish to see what makes me tick
that of course cannot be seen
it must be planted and replanted
grow unseen and burst dark bonds
a fruit here and there and everywhere
may yet appear in miracle and mystery

fed and encouraged
some choose to dive
into the dark
of a miracle self
invested as fallow seed
until tears of pain
waken it to bloom

a boom of thunder
echoing from the past
awakening a future
with morning glories
twining upward
drawing beauty with them
here today gone tonight

John 12:20–36
Clarification Week Tuesday

From one side: Two days ago, we were so close to being in like Flynn. There was this parade happening the next street over, but we were just settling into the Inn. We missed it.

Now we're trying to get a belated autograph and have a lead through a Mr. Philip, who apparently knows someone who knows someone.

And just as quickly, there is no response; our contact didn't show up. We're left behind.

From another side: Jesus says, "We're full up. Disciples, stick closer than ever; no more taking bribes so someone can get their picture taken. Everyone, huddle up. The game's going to depend on this next play."

Well, believe it or not, this is a different time and place from these ancient stories. What are our criteria for helping someone come close to Jesus? What litmus test do they have to pass? What is the minimum ante? Will we take the time to introduce someone to the value source of our life ourselves or wait to see if someone else will blackball the idea? Is there still time available to slowly transform interest into involvement, or must we expect instant conversion?

Is the game plan still to huddle up? Does looking back on this story from post-Easter make a difference for how we are going to act in this, our next pre-Easter season?

John 13:1–17, 31b–35
Courage Thursday

Washed by Jesus and still unclean.

Jesus' actions are not unilateral. Jesus is constrained.
G*D's actions are not unilateral. G*D is constrained.
My actions are not unilateral. I am constrained.
Your actions are not unilateral. You are constrained.
Our actions are not unilateral. We are constrained.

It appears that not only are servants not greater than their master, but the master is not greater than the servants. Neither servants nor masters are unilateral. Both are constrained.

Where G*D is received, creation is also received.
Where Jesus is received, G*D is also received.
Where I am received, Jesus is also received.
Where you are received, I am also received.
Where we are received, all are also received.

It appears that we find our identity in our varying relationships. Each of our varying relationships with every other part of our life is based on having love for one another, recognizing and receiving each other's belovedness.

Washed and still unclean, but washed nonetheless. Washed and still containing every opportunity to express our having been loved, no matter what else also happened.

John 13:21–32
Clarification Week, Wednesday

Very truly, I tell you, each one of you will betray me.

And so it is. We all do it in our own way. Some larger. Some smaller.

- Betrayal of authority.
- Betrayal of self-avowed loyalty.
- Betrayal of others.
- Betrayal of witness by comrades.

During this last week, it is time to acknowledge our betrayals, whether of Jesus or the least of his sisters and brothers.

Given the time, energy, and resources available to us, choices have to be made, and in so doing, we betray one part of our desire to satisfy another part.

In the midst of this reality, what is left? "Glorifying" G*D?

Not even betrayal will keep transcendence at bay!

Not even betrayal will keep us from moving toward unity with G*D.

John 15:1–8
Assured [5]

Long, long ago and far, far away, there were two fruit trees in a garden. One was taken and one remained. Retribution, revenge, and punishment didn't seem to patch things up. After many adventures, we come to a vine growing from the same garden source. Finally, restoration came along—and victim and assailant talked together.

How is restoration of trust, hope, love, and the rest worked out? Well, from the taking of fruit to the giving of fruit, of course.

In this reversal, all concerned found life a much more renewable resource than previously thought. Instead of coming up against a flaming angel, a new angle became available—leading and being led toward G*D and thus moving behind the guardian of the trees to find a storyline of welcome rather than warning.

Bear fruit; restore losses of the past. Become a disciple; restore a focus on the future.

John 15:9–17
Assured [6]

Institutionally, United Methodists are called to "make disciples of Jesus Christ for the transformation of the world."

This passage from John clarifies that we are not to make servants of Jesus Christ. But if we are to "make" friends of Jesus Christ there are additional questions to be asked.

Can you "make" friends? What does that take?

If you have tried bringing your various friends together, intending that they would become friends of one another, you may remember how difficult that intention is to pull off.

This passage can fruitfully be read to be primarily about our motivation—what would you do for a friend, for Jesus? Lay down your life?

What difference would being a disciple or a friend bring to your motivation and consequence-in-living?

Would this be primarily about an expansion of Jesus' friends (as if Jesus were incapable of being someone's friend on his own), and so we become the proverbial and catalytic best friend who gets left behind when new connections are made between your best friend and another (sound like a familiar movie plot)?

How would it change a congregation to be made up of friends of Jesus rather than disciples of Jesus? On this question hangs the renewal of Church.

This friendship talk is supposedly to strengthen our love for one another. How's that working out for Jesus? Has this tactic worked?

We might profitably play with these intersections between servant-friend-lover. On which boundary are you finding your work these days?

John 15:26–27, 16:4b–15
Energy to Witness

Can't you just wait to be proved wrong about sin, righteousness, and judgment?

If you had to locate three key arenas of life that need to be revisited and revisioned, would they be these three or others? Sometimes our identification of the key issues of life can sharpen our responses.

Here is one way to look at these three.

> Sin: not believing in a journey of Jesus toward
> compassion, kindness.

> Righteous: being on a journey with Jesus toward
> compassion, kindness.

> Judgment: reflection on and course changes through a
> journey with Jesus toward compassion,
> kindness.

Having identified the issues, can we get on with a closer approximation of our lives with our view of G*D (The Compassionate One)?

[Note: This posting was stimulated by Karen Armstrong's book about an Axial Age and the Golden Rule—*The Great Transformation: The Beginning of Our Religious Traditions*.]

John 17:6–19
Assured [7]

Prayer is interesting as it can reveal our deep-seated fears and can pull us toward our best ideals. Sometimes it does both.

For the moment, I would point toward an ideal—praying for protection/community for others (verse 11).

What might this mean in the context of Memorial Day in the United States of America? Might we listen in on the prayers of the dead for the living instead of the other way around? Would those prayers be for the protection afforded by a community? Would it make a difference if that sentence were constructed the other way around: for the community within which issues of protection were no longer needed?

What might this mean in the context of a church that automatically sets aside the gifts of women or a racial/cultural group or a subset of one sort or another, such as sexual identity or orientation? Might we listen in on the prayer of the discriminated against instead of those prejudiced against them? How else might we hear this prayer for our current limitations, our being in the world without being one with the world?

John 18:1–19:42
Annihilation Friday

A long, long reading summarized:

Jesus gardened
Judas and soldiers bring broad-band herbicide
I AM me (are YOU you?)

Peter infected by intended violence
cuts off another's ear
Again, "get behind me, Tempter"

Jesus bound for trial (jury-rigged)
seen as scapegoat by priests
denied by Peter

Jesus from frying pan to fire
redefines fire
truth beyond fact

Jesus bartered for
Barabbas released
Jesus beaten

a "nonsuit" ruling given
but mob politics rule the day
negative campaigning comes to the fore

Jesus handed over to crucifixion
carried his own torture instrument
crucified naked

I AM your son
I AM your mother
enough

meat thermometer read "done"
cooled and put in the freezer
... to be continued

John 18:33–37
Evaluation Day / Proper 29 (34)

A most intriguing passage for a Sunday traditionally called Christ the King. This is a series of direct questions with slippery responses.

"Are you King of the Jews?" [In a context of Roman occupation, what would any response to this question mean?]

"Who's asking?", asks Jesus. This sends us on our first trip. The question is no longer that of hierarchy, but behavior—"What have you done?"

And Jesus spins around again. "My kingdom is not from this world." So does this respond to the first question about kingship, or is it a one-hand clapping statement? Kings are very much of this world. They can't be king without the world desiring and allowing it. What is this other world?

Pilate took the bait with a presumption that this was a response to his first question. "So...you are a king!"

"You keep harping on power when I'm talking about an authenticity or truth beyond political or religious privilege," clarifies Jesus.

Conveniently, the lection cuts Pilate's retort of "What is truth?" as he spins to leave the room. So Pilate doesn't have to hear Jesus mutter, "The truth is you are Governor of Nothing and never will be the King you desire to be."

Whether you call it "Christ the King" Sunday or the "Reign of Christ", Jesus says you got it wrong, and the church won't be a source of healing until it puts such arrogance away. This is especially the case when, next week, we claim the failure of kingdom talk with the beginning of a needed Advent or start on a different journey than the crazy-making one of repeating doctrines as if they were factual.

John 19:38–42
Absent Saturday

There is not much more that can be done than to bury or otherwise dispose of the body. Conveniently, the tradition for Jesus was one of burying (though there is a great question about this happening if Jesus was crucified in the usual course of events).

Imagine the metaphors of physically arising if the body was burned on a pyre or left for the birds to pick away the flesh. We might have ended up with a Phoenix or dry bones or a return to a Word as our way of signifying a life.

Whatever the mode of disposal, death is a way of metonymically marking a whole life. They died, and in that dying, we remember their life. We can do that on their birthday (remembering they also died). We can remember some special anniversary or place of significant encounter with them and bring to mind and heart that which preceded and proceeded from that time or place. We can remember their teaching on a cultural Day of the Dead or All Hallows, as well as a specific date of their death.

This is a day of despair when it settles in that our friend, mentor, family member, partner in mercy, is no more with us in a direct fashion.

This is a day of strange remembrance and a commitment to take our common journey that much further. In this, we also find a day of renewal through new creation and a freedom to go ahead.

Absence can make the heart grow fonder in the short-run, but over time it needs props to help us hearken again. Some 2,000+ years later, this is an artificial day forgotten by most, almost a missing day or missing link, which needs highlighting that we not skip too easily over the reality of loss and all the adjustment it takes to take on responsibility for what was previously shared.

John 20:1–18
Assured

Expectations are usually traps, set-ups for disappointment. In this case, a broken expectation becomes a release, a source of mystery upon mystery that joyfully engages our sense of meaning.

Having gone out with weeping, we return with a song on our lips.

It was bad enough to visit the tomb, but to find it empty meant an insult of thievery is added to the injury of loss by death. Mary sequentially trudges in sadness, runs in dismay, stands distraught, and went announcing what shepherds and magi before her reported—"I have seen creation at work."

An Easter of remembrance and familiarity is not an Easter. An Easter of turning resurrection over to G*D is not an Easter. Easter is only Easter insofar as we have an experience of holding and being held and then being released and releasing to be able to move on with an assurance and an announcement.

Interested in measuring Easter, whenever it should come this year? Relate your experience of turning from lost to found. If you actually tell that story, then Easter has arrived. If you have no story to tell, it didn't. A resurrection in a garden without a story being told is like unto a tree falling unheard in a forest—it is still a reality, but a lonely one.

May you and all be blessed through your catch-and-release story.

John 20:19–31
Assured [2]

"Now the whole group" – "when kindred live together" – "that you also will have fellowship with us". These phrases set a tone of what it means to be joined in joy.

A test comes when someone is not part of our gathering, and a very specific and significant event happens. Regardless of the reason they are not present, they are not present. Their absence from a revelation could very well drive a wedge between the "true" experiencers and those without that experience. And so Thomas' story is an important witness to continued openness. Thomas was still welcome even without a corroborating experience. Fortunately, he received one. That helps a lot in binding a community together. But, and this is significant, unanimity of experience is not foundational to community.

The downside of uniformity is that expectations are set up that folks will be required to come to believe in the same dramatic way as did those who experienced a risen Christ Jesus in a specific way. We, to this day, separate folks out according to their experience of faith and their differences from the majority or the powerful. If they measure up, they're welcome. So Thomas' story is used to convince people that they cannot be different (doubt) because that would bar them from fellowship in an already together group.

Thomas is laughed at rather than revealing how laughable are our restrictive standards.

Remember that Thomas was with those who had already experienced a resurrection. Use this as an inclusive evangelistic witness for inviting "others" to be present. This will offset the temptation to have the inexperienced set aside until they measure up. If a community is not focused on key words in the opening phrases—"whole", "live", and "also"—it has learned the smaller lesson and missed the larger.

---

revelation is not theory
it is experience-able
with eye and hand
with kindred and enemies
with ancestors and descendants
with light and dark
with male and female
with all orientations
with slave and free
with all economies
with self and others

revelation is not unique
revelation is not eternal
revelation is not owned

revelation is invitational
revelation is expansive
revelation is prophetic

Acts 1:1–11
Our Turn to Witness

Conversation about the presence of G*D is a good thing. We can huddle up and cuddle up a little closer for forty days and still not be assured that all is already well and all will be well again (no, it is not a contradiction to have them both going at once).

Having such an intense focus on our center spot is almost like worrying at a zit until we pop it. Jesus popped right on out of that embarrassing grave, exclaiming that healing power would soon be present.

Well, such a surprise. We were dumbfounded! What just happened?

Note to disciples: Move it. Live out the internal dialogue you've been having. The next stage of life will come just as quickly as did this one. Be so focused on becoming (beautifying and transforming into) the presence of G*D that you will be surprised when it actually shows up around you as well as in and through you.

The return of Jesus is not deserved judgment—it is our establishing the presence of G*D on earth as we have imagined it in heaven.

----

still standing around?
yep
git
start walking around!

still talking about?
yep
git
start living about!

still here?
yep
git
start here!

start here!
yep
git
still here?

Acts 1:15–17, 21–26
Assured [7]

So often we define ourselves against someone or someones. We are not as bad as they are, so we must be good.

At least Judas was still seen as one of the twelve, even as Thomas was after his desire for personal confirmation of the witness of the other 10. This leaves room for me and for you when we have done our own betrayal or evidenced our own deep questions of authority and life.

Back then, there was magic in numbers. There still is; ask any theoretical mathematician or physicist. And so, more magic was used to determine who would be added for the purpose of a desired number. Neither Justus nor Matthias seemed to have anything going for them other than having hung around for long enough. Sometimes that is all we have going for us, longevity.

So why would G*D shave the dice to favor Matthias, of whom we nevermore hear? No good reason. Why are you where you are, with the opportunities you have? No good reason, so go ahead and make the best of it.

And what of Justus? Was he humble enough to get back in line? Did he pack up and leave, as so many others had done over the years? Did he pick up a third alias?

These are probably the wrong questions to be asking, so let's return to numerology. Imagine a rule that no Christian Community should be larger than 12. This size can engage one another and fruitfully have both a Peter and a Judas in it. Larger gets into voting folks out or pressuring them to not be themselves. Imagine what limiting a congregation to 12 might mean for freeing up resources (no building needed); for engaging the world prophetically (what other option would there be); and for attending to the mystery of a community together (folks called together, not a social club).

Acts 2:1–21
Energy to Witness

Think you were scared for your life? Think again, for now you are scared to life.

Before, you were fearful of another taking your life. Now you are only afraid that you will not be giving your life across what used to be perceived as razor-wired boundaries.

Before, your coat of arms consisted of representations of hiding:

> *affright, awed, chill, daunt, dismay, freeze, given a fright, given a turn, intimidated, paralyzed, petrified, scared silly, scared the pants off, shaken up, struck terror in, terrified, terrorized, afraid, aghast, anxious, fearful, having cold feet, panic-stricken, panicked, panicky, shaken, startled, terror-stricken, abashed, aghast, alarmed, anxious, apprehensive, aroused, blanched, cowardly, cowed, daunted, discouraged, disheartened, dismayed, distressed, disturbed, faint-hearted, frightened, frozen, horrified, in awe, intimidated, nervous, perplexed, perturbed, rattled, run scared, scared, scared stiff, scared to death, shocked, spooked, startled, stunned, suspicious, terror-stricken, timid, timorous, trembling, upset, worried, amazed, astonished, chilled, dismayed, made jump, surprised, unnerved . . . .*

Now, you exemplify :

> *calm, comfort, reassurance, soothing, confidence, encouragement, boldness, braveness, composition, cool, courage, fearlessness, heroism, intrepidness, undauntedness, valiance, assurance, gladdening, repose . . . .*

That which stimulates a shift from some aspect of the first list to an extension of the second can be termed a Pentecost Experience.

May you be blessed with another Pentecost at this late date. Whether in time or out of time, vision and dream strongly enough that you will gladly follow where they lead.

Acts 3:12–19

Assured [3]

Bait and switch is an ancient tradition. Come for the miracle and stay for the doctrine.

To document this, read what just went before this pericope. Earlier, it sounds as if the man healed was the one with faith in Jesus. But remember that the lame man was only asking for alms, as he had done for all his life. It was Peter who entered Jesus into the conversation. It was Peter who started talk about faith in Christ into the scene. It was Peter who said, "I have no silver or gold, but -what I have- I give you; in the name of Jesus Christ of Nazareth, stand up and walk" [emphasis added].

Peter continues this switch as he turns to those observing this event and claims his, Peter's, faith is the only blessed one available. Believe with me, or you will be utterly rooted out. This is a precursor to Constantine enforcing one particular strand of Christianity as the only orthodoxy available.

The Message puts the dynamic at work here as, "When Peter saw he had a congregation, he addressed the people." Ahh, an audience. Were Peter simply to have dealt with a lame man, we would never have gotten this apology for orthodoxy that makes heretics out of equally faithful folks, just differently faithful. Without this apology, we might again pay attention to the wild variety of gifts and calls and miracles and signs and faith available at different times and stages of life and opportunities for experience.

Starting again from the top:

Who is not lame from limping around a variety of altars? Lameness, even from birth, as we deal with our cultural lameness, is a most unoriginal sin. There's not much to lameness; it's not like soul-searing thievery, murder, adultery. It's pretty lame to just be lame.

Here we are without a foot to stand on, still in the midst of community, being carried to our assigned spot. The only thing equal to the gift of being carried where one needs to go is the carrying of another—what a partnership!

Just live with the first 11 verses without breaking into blame and conversion at verse 12. Experience again the various shifts you have experienced of seeming to have no choice and then having a choice. It is astonishing. It is also astonishing that we so quickly forget those experiences. When it happens again, we are astonished all over again. See if you can sense the beginning of astonishment before its full-blown arrival and be ready to jump in with both feet.

Acts 4:5–12
Assured [4]

What an openness to life! Teaching (being led forth), Fellowship, Feasting, and Communicating within and beyond—these are still key elements in a healthy community—whether of one faith or another.

These four qualities bind a community closely enough together that trust of their most prized possessions (even survival) to one another can take place. Without this vital communitarian impetus, organic growth doesn't take place. Oh, there can be surface unity, but the lack of deep trust will eventually shine through, and fracture will show.

In today's untrusting environment, where winning and losing metaphors abound, what Teaching is most needed that would lead us toward trust? What Fellowship and Feasting? What Prayers? Note that teaching toward trust is different than teaching toward a particular doctrine.

There are undoubtedly many responses to these questions. Instead of waiting to come up with one grand theory of everything, you and I are encouraged to Teach, Fellowship, Feast, and Pray as best we can, leaving any later form of such to such a time.

---

called to endurance
is a strange gift
to receive
in a world valuing
this quarter's bottom line
only in light of the last

to pile value high
pack it down and heap it higher
is still a long-term strategy
with a proven track record
sustainability trumps a Vegas hit
enduring and guarding life

so our ancestors found
again and again and again
forgetting this teaching imperils life
hoarding goods and celebrations
for a privileged few
diminishes possibilities

and our descendants call out
again and again and again
to be included in the bounty of life
and so we endure today
with ancestral solidarity
received and passed on

Acts 4:32–35
Assured [2]

When we are together but fearful, we are not together.

When we are together under a word of "Peace" signed as "Mercy", we are of one heart and soul. Our possessions are each other's. Common good means both "common" and "good".

This is a sign of resurrection—that the last word to the disciples has become real—"Love one another as I have loved you."

Resurrection opens our eyes to need, beyond want, and addresses need directly. When resurrection is only a concept, but not a reality, we find all manner of means to cover "need" with "want", and it turns out that my want always trumps your need.

Acts 8:26–40
Assured [5]

Inquiring minds want to know what horsepower chariot Philip had to contend with. Had the chariot pulled into a fast-falafel joint and reading passed the time (1 horsepower)? Did the Ethiopian have a driver so he could read as they bounced along (several horsepower)? Whatever it was, apparently Philip had an angelic booster at his side or on his back. Please, no Jr. Hi. jokes about backside boosters. Apparently, Philip was in good enough shape that he could run and talk at the same time.

I often scratch my head about understanding what is understood. Said understanding always seems to come with a particular perspective, not an alternative one. When you hear Isaiah being pondered, I presume readers of these notes automatically think, "Jesus is what needs talking about here." But, with a head scratch, maybe they don't always go to that default?

Fortunately, Philip arrived just in time to hear this particular portion of Isaiah. Some other sections would have presented a bit more hermeneutic *alakazam* to connect Jesus in such a way that a request for Jesus-authorized baptism would be a logical response and request by this Ethiopian eunuch fellow-traveler of YHWH.

It is this at-just-a-right-moment phenomenon that is of the most interest today. Providence is a powerful, sometimes too powerful, perspective. Even though we don't hear of it, one might presume that an angel of the Lord was preveniently whispering in the Ethiopian's ear to set off at just the right time for Philip to intersect his reading at a particular point in Isaiah. There are many variables the angels had to attend to along the way: the speed of the horses, construction zones, thieves along the way, Dramamine's precursor, etc.

Providential moments can be seen as fated or as an opportunity to make the most of an opportunity. Around these parts, we tend toward the latter. This means our search for meaning can show up running alongside, and that we can strike up a conversation in the most unconventional of places and among the most unlikely of folk. The folks caught up overmuch in angels plotting ahead can miss an opportunity to engage an unaware angel hanging out right here and right now. Whether you see life through the lens of "the hand of G*D" or "a god-damn fluke", may you be open to receive and to proclaim good news, where'er ye be.

Acts 10:34–43
Beloved — Assured

In his baptism, Jesus joins us all in repenting of sins and experiencing the nearness of G*D's presence. It is this "all-ness" that Peter just experienced and is trying to put into language.

Jesus' baptism led him to go about doing good and healing all who were oppressed (whether you think of the devil as personal or structural doesn't make any difference here), for God was with him (Emmanuel was with Emmanuel—all are one and one, all).

Peter had his baptismal experience with a tablecloth coming from above, instead of a dove. Both Peter and Jesus are living out of an enlarged understanding that what G*D has made clean they are not to dismiss (regardless of what scriptural or traditional rules there are to the contrary). Non-kosher and non-saints are no longer nonsense, but the very venue within which they are to work.

So it is that Peter has gone about doing good and healing. And while trying to explain the basis of his experience and remembrance of Jesus' teaching, Spirit is at work again. When we are living out our baptismal experiences, good happens.

The end result is that those who had been religiously held at bay were now included in. I sure wish all those who are baptized by water these days would catch the fever for inclusion that Peter and Jesus did after their respective baptisms. Were that the case, the church would certainly be a different place with its confrontation of racism, heterosexism, and war (to mention only three of today's arenas of religious retrenchment).

Acts 10:44–48
Assured [6]

This Spirit dude is certainly disruptive (the ADHD aspect of G*D?). "While Peter was still speaking …"

In the midst of the hubbub, without any planning for it (such as everybody wearing red), Pentecost is revisited—the wonders of G*D are recognized and related in surprisingly different cultural contexts and languages.

Question: In what cultural/language group of today would it be most surprising to find this Spirit gal showing up?

Question: Given the track record of the surprising presence of Spirit, why, again, would we be surprised?

Question: Is there a minimum amount of work we need to put in (both amount and content) before Spirit will plunk its magic twanger? How much scripture, how much energetic interpretation of it and life, how much authority needs to be present to force the hand of Spirit?

Question: Is this baptism by Peter ineffective or illegitimate because only the Jesus Christ part of a later rubric was used? What is the minimum daily requirement amount of Baptism and how is it applied—in a monthly shot of B12 in the butt or doled out day-by-day in pill/liquid or natural food?

Question: Are four questions in a trinitarian system one too many? or just right because there are not only three unique components but a synergy of them together? And, then, what are we going to do about any fifth question tagging along?

Acts 19:1–7
Beloved

Amazing. They were disciples before they were baptized in Jesus' name. Apparently, repentance is enough to be a disciple.

This is not to suggest that disciples don't grow and deepen their understanding, but there is no indication that they were "better" disciples than before. They did have a new experience to fold into their understanding, but there is no dismissal of them as second-class disciples because they came late to Jesus' baptism. Presumably, over the next months, they learned even more than tongues and prophecy as they were invited by Paul to travel on with him (v. 9).

It will be helpful to focus on the issue of growth here, rather than the hierarchy of military rank and measuring ourselves against one another or setting baptism against baptism.

This is also a hint for us about the persistence of Pentecost. What does it mean to speak in tongues and to prophesy? This brings back images of speaking and hearing the wonders of G*D's presence (Acts 2) in differing languages.

Whenever we hear echoes of Pentecost, we need to remember that the power to be present to very different people is always with us. We can also remember that disciples come in all shapes and sizes and understandings and are placed all along the continuum we know as "spiritual living". We can experience Pentecost again today—and tomorrow—from both sides. Sometimes we will be the speakers and sometimes the spoken to. In both cases, we are to grow.

Don't let someone take your discipleship away because you don't yet measure up to their standards. Simply work at understanding and being understood in regard to experiences of G*D's wonderful way of including everyone in.

Again, imagine that—they were disciples before they were "really" baptized.

Romans 4:13–25
Conviction [2]

We all trust in a variety of mechanisms, processes, and theories. At question is whether these "promises" reveal grace or not. If so they will grow over time. If not, they will eventually falter and fail altogether.

If we are interested in participating in a story of creation-long development bearing witness to great fecundity, we will be asking whether or not the basic storyline we are trusting in has room for surprising twists, turns, and reorientations. This openness to mutation is trustworthy and turns out to be our grace, our righteousness.

Lent is an opportunity to remind ourselves where it is we want to be headed—into boring grace, standard grace, everyday grace—far deeper than being amazed at such.

Abraham hoped against all expectation regarding what he understood was G*D's promise to him (a promise that energized his travel and his aging)—descendants.

A question I am still wrestling with is what promise has so captured me that it will energize my living and aging? So far it is a picture of being able to participate in beckoning to earth and heaven to draw near to one another that they might be joined to bring forth a new heaven and a new earth—now there's a descendant.

This is distinguishable from earth using heaven to justify its wars and from heaven belittling earth as impure, both of which keep them from joining together.

What is the promise that energizes you? That keeps you hoping against all expectation?

Romans 6:3–11
Hopeless Hope Vigil

Vigiling is a strange practice. It implies some foreknowledge of what is being waited for. So we use sleep deprivation and repetitive chant to move us into an altered state to bring us as close as possible to a prior emotionally charged event.

How does one of our transformative events get passed through the generations without keeping later folks from being present to their own wonders because they are attending to ours? Religious rites hold power for a while as they expect some repeatable experience, but, eventually, they become only a vaccine against transformation until, finally, a new experience can't be denied, and it breaks through ritual barriers.

Baptism is seldom experienced as a death and resurrection. Even if talked about that way and symbolized with ghostly white baptismal garb of one fashion or another, this being baptized into death has lost its focus. Today, at best, it is an individualized event, not communal. There is no mourning the absence of the dead to prepare for a new way of being in the world. Baptism becomes an easy, "Whoop!", rather than a deep and slow, "Wow."

Turning our vigiling for a next call or gift runs up against a marketing ploy of one-and-done. Appreciating a once-baptized/always-baptized approach signifying a basic prevenient grace does not keep away the radical nature of subsequent experience, gift, or call. Our vigiling needs components both steadfast and ever new.

What will this vigil lead to if not a living with a Living G*D that will make all previous vigils obsolete? Will we recognize our limits in order to find a next step beyond them? How does this vigil not repeat tradition, but extend it past the very traditions that provide a springboard for a new tradition to arise?

Romans 8:12–17
Live Together

The choice of feeling tone is that of assurance/witness or fear. These manifest themselves in issues of adoption or slavery.

When we are assured of our relationship with G*D, we are open to affirming our own adoption and willingness to aid others in being adopted. When we are fearful, we become slaves to a zero-sum game of life, always on the lookout for not losing.

The difference is focusing on offense or defense. In sports, the emphasis is upon defense, for that is where championships are won. However, we are in a never-ending series of seasons, and so Jesus' way puts an emphasis upon offense, simply putting forth the best one has without defending one's self to the last where it doesn't matter if there is another season or not for this one was so well lived (Resurrection trumps Crucifixion).

Consider the image of Trinity. Are you adopted into a family to make it four and more? Are you bought as a slave to serve and praise the three and only three?

Rejoice; you are adopted. Spirit touches spirit, and we breathe deeply and persistently.

Romans 8:22–27
Energy to Witness

With birthing images galore, we might hear verse 26 as: "...Spirit helps us in our gestation periods."

In the midst of all the busy-ness of life, it is sometimes difficult to see ourselves as still gestating, not yet ready for birthing. Our innate narcissism and sense of privilege don't know when we are out of our league, inarticulate, waiting, growing. And so a sense of preveniency is good to have to wrap around and remind ourselves that we are being interceded for by many friends, ancestors, descendants, and all of a still-laboring creation.

Pentecost is another name for yet another birth opportunity flooded with the blood of birthing and one last great push and whoosh of breath exhaled. Let's see if this next birthing can have us rebuilding alongside one another and call it G*D at work or, more simply, expectant hope.

There are many things yet to be learned, but they are beyond our current bearing of them. Until we come to grips with a basic understanding of more-to-be-learned, bones remain dry; labor pains continue; and we remain trapped in our current-sized room repeating ourselves in a single language to one another.

A breath of new creation, a new spirit, is needed as a catalyst to transform what we don't yet know into an important category of life and renewal for us. Without this, we are dusty dust, groaning groaners, sorrowing sorrowers.

Continuing the oneness image of I in you and you in them, the new comes to the old, unbidden. Consider this as a definition of Glory as well as an expression of Grace.

---

step out in faith with fear and trembling
a new vision comes beyond what we know
cast a new vision beyond what is yet known
fear and trembling become solid enough to stand on

Romans 12:9–16b
Elizabeth and Mary Meet

Magnifying something means being able to see more details.

Spend some time with each of the details mentioned in this passage to see how your life is growing and encouraging growth in others. This passage presents us with a chart design that can be used at the beginning of a day to anticipate our response to usual opportunities or at the close of day to evaluate the day so better responses will be available tomorrow.

Reflect on	☑
Be sincere in avoiding harm and choosing a better way.	
Deepen your relationship with others to encourage one another in your choices.	
Honor those gifted beyond your own gifts and those who provide a context within which your gifts might add their part.	
Be ready to add to the common good by actually investing in it, not just intending to do so.	
Understand and investigate again faint signs of hope that you never lose touch with a sense of "Joy to the World" poking its head out to wink as if to say and ask, "I'm still here; are you?"	
Become OK with time that keeps everything from happening immediately and simultaneously, so even difficulties become loci to practice being steadfast.	
Expand your generosity, day-by-day, to and beyond those deemed worthy of being shared with.	
Listen for how folks desire to be treated and treat them thusly, remembering that their desire might not be conscious in their life and only recognized when you gently honor it.	

In summary: Bless; Rejoice; Be peace.

Romans 16:25–27
Needed Change [4]

Are you still remembering the first line of Romans: "Paul, a servant of Jesus Christ, called to be an apostle, set apart for the gospel of God...."

Now we come to the end of that beginning: "...to the only wise God, through Jesus Christ, to whom be the glory forever! Amen."

The movement starts with one (Paul) to those whom he served (all). At the end, the lens through which we work is first and last Jesus (though not necessarily the only lens), and the focus is not on one or all or Jesus, but G*D.

This patterning leads us to the center of Romans, the last of Chapter 8 and the first of Chapter 9.

> ...absolutely nothing can get between us and God's
> love because of the way that Jesus, our Friend, has
> embraced us. At the same time, you need to know
> that I carry with me at all times a huge sorrow.

Isn't that an interesting juxtaposition that usually gets overlooked because of the power of chaptering and our propensity to break things into meaningful segments that, once so divided, can never be put together in another way.

Loved and sorrow-filled. That's us.

Because we are loved, we are bold to do what we can about our sorrow. This is a call to action that can be directed by our experience.

You are loved. You have a sorrow. Now smash those together and you have your vocation, your way of focusing on G*D.

1 Corinthians 1:3–9
Needed Change [1]

What might it mean to be called by G*D into companionship with Jesus?

If Jesus was about coming to oneness with G*D, we join him on such a quest. We journey toward oneness with G*D.

If Jesus was not about this, then what was Jesus about? Was Jesus about making new rules? Was Jesus about forming an exclusive community? Was Jesus about being worshiped?

The NRSV says our fellowship with Jesus is a reflection on G*D's faithfulness.

The NJB reflects in a note, "Because Jesus is our partner in human nature, we are his in the divine nature."

If we back up just one verse to #2, we find we are also called to be holy or saints or God-filled (depending on translation).

All of this is wonderfully circular. *The Community Christian Bible* reflects, "You have to become holy, but you are already. Holy, in the biblical sense, is the person or thing that belongs to God."

There never is a time when we are not companions or partners with Jesus. There never is a time when anyone else is not a companion or partner with Jesus. [Admittedly, sometimes the companionship and partnership are tighter and looser.] When looked at through the lens of holiness and oneness, what is said about Jesus might be said of Abraham and Moses and Mohammed and Buddha. A holy one is free to surpass all these limits—even those of one's own companions.

Whew, I have every spiritual gift.
Oh, I am strengthened to use each in its time.
Ahh, fellowship shines in remembering, in anticipating, in medias res.

Whew, I am blessed.
Oh, I am blessing.
Ahh, simply Ahh.

1 Corinthians 1:18–24
Relic Day

The language of a symbol is nonsense, whether to those who don't speak it or to those who do.

Those who don't get your symbol have no experience to tie it to.

Those who appreciate your symbol take much of it for granted and narrow it down to its lowest common denominator.

Simply wearing a cross doesn't honor it. It becomes a stereotype for folks to think they know more about you than can be known from such a multivalent sign. Those who don't get it will peg you as being more unlike them than is probably true. Those who appreciate the symbol will assume your understanding of it is in line with theirs and make an unwarranted assumption about your value system.

Whether seen as nonsense or as scandalous by gatekeepers who would deny your claim on their tradition, it is worth the trouble of again evaluating how a symbol engages your everyday life. In some sense, a cross is a prayer best present in your closet and not used on the street corner. Mostly, this implement of torture and death is a meditational device and ill-suited to be a self-explanatory billboard.

"Use with caution" should be prominently stamped on a religious use of the cross, as it is the far easier metaphor than a non-representational empty tomb. Its very ease is its danger. It is far too easy to stop with a cross that divides than start anew with an empty anticipation.

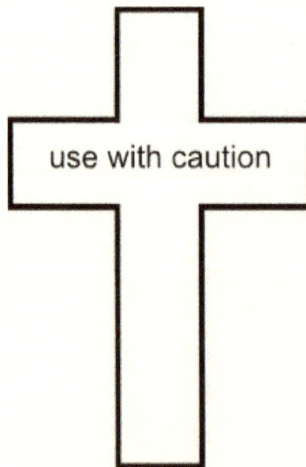

use with caution

1 Corinthians 1:18–25
Conviction [3]

The message about the cross is foolishness.

The message about the 10-to-613 commandments is foolishness.

The message about loving G*D, self, neighbor, enemy is foolishness.

The message about negotiating from strength is foolishness.

The message about preemptive violence is foolishness.

The message about tax relief for the rich is foolishness.

Foolishness, like beauty, seems to be in the eye of the beholder.

So, what foolishness are you intentionally participating in these days, and what foolishness are you illuminating as long-term stupidity?

By our foolishnesses are we known.

1 Corinthians 1:18–31
Clarification Week Tuesday

When was the last time you talked about G*D's foolishness? This puts a new light on being "a fool for Christ."

When was the last time you talked about G*D's weakness?

Are these character flaws? Do we so desire unchanging solidity that we insist that G*D be immutable, unchanging, omnipotent, omnipresent, etc., even when G*D's own witness about repentance and mind-changing and bringing a new heaven and earth just don't compute with us?

Might these be exactly the character virtues needed for creation? Without them, we wait for some static perfection that will last and last and be devoid of growth in meaning. Here we are open to not only considering the foolishness and weakness of G*D, but reveling in it. When we hear we are made in the image of G*D, this begins to make sense to us. The humility this takes stands us in good stead. We don't need to make up things about the future, speculate on G*D's judgment and what heaven/hell looks like, or even imagine there is a heaven or a hell.

Now it is before us. Do we pay attention to G*D's foolishness, or will we show our denseness by denying it? Do we pay attention to G*D's weakness, or will we show how out of touch we are by denying it?

It takes a great deal of wisdom and strength to attend to fools and weaklings, whether that of G*D or Neighb*r. It takes a great deal of foolishness and weakness to attend to such as you and me.

1 Corinthians 5:6b–8
Opened Heart Evening

A united, faithful community will only be divided and destroyed from within. So no more boasting—either by word or effect, such as a widening gap between rich and poor.

This insight is fine enough, but it only goes so far in its analysis. When it tries to pull Jesus into a Passover tradition, it begins to sound like the very popular game of blaming the victim.

If only the Israelites had policed their own better, getting rid of any who could not lead exemplary lives, they would never have been constrained to stay in Egypt and could have walked out at any time. What is never acknowledged in internal purity schemes is the reality of multiple covenants, variability in people's experience and interpretation of same, and principalities and powers.

The point of this passage is to set up a procedure to serially divest a community of any growth edge, as if constructing a fortress is the best mode of hospitality. Little-by-little, those in charge of religious rules isolate an ever more homogenous body from a need to transform their own lives, much less the lives of those not a part of the elect.

The motivation that begins this process of remonstrance, shunning, and exile may well be to make a group more consistent in their messaging/marketing/missioning but eventually an official decision to give up on one group infects the whole body with a fear that silos and isolates real lives from official-line lives and sets up the accurate charge of hypocrisy, literalism, and being out-of-touch.

Purity and sincerity are valuable qualities, but they need assistance to escape discriminatory venues set up to limit the spiritual to individual behaviors and outlaw any plague of direct action.

Be pure and Act Up!

1 Corinthians 6:12–20
Guiding Gift [2]

Licentiousness is in the eye of the beholder. There are so many ways rules about behavior hinder healthy expressions of life. We start with sexuality being a good gift from G*D and end up ruling only one sexual position as acceptable, that sex is basically about procreation, or is limited to cross-gender relationships. Each of these, and more, is patently false to anyone able to think about their *a priori*-ness.

Arguments from natural law about natural experiences seem to always fail at the same point—nature. Gift and creation are not only always more expansive than our ability to codify them, but also more independent. Limiting gifts and creation is an exercise in herding cats.

Eventually, we come to recognize a larger pattern that frees us from our artificial constraints. We have moved outward from a tribal center to a regional center to a planetary center to a solar center to a galaxy center to a currently known universe center. Who knows where we have yet to go to be centered?

The same goes with sexuality moving into larger arenas when we remove fertility and other barriers through birth control and affectional experiences beyond a limited model of genital plug-and-play.

Defining Spirit helps us set and break our understanding of our body's relationship to G*D and any particular gift of sexuality we do or don't participate in. This passage needs much more work done on the, "… but I say to you . . ." work of Spirit continuing and breaking previous ground rules. It is far too easy to see sexuality as something to be controlled and not about the state of our being and our welcoming a larger-picture spirit.

1 Corinthians 7:29–31
Guiding Gift [3]

There is no time to waste. This means time cannot be saved (as in storing it away, saving it for a rainy day). I highly recommend reading *Momo* by Michael Ende. Here is a review by a reader at Amazon.com that I agree with and it brought back memories of our reading *Momo* to our children in a chapter-a-day fashion.

***** [five stars out of five]
I could never forget this book..., December 11, 2002
Reviewer: Kenia from New Jersey, USA

> I read this book when I was very young. I was twelve years old, and I was still back in my country. I remember this story and the impact it had on me, even as a young teen. I remember not being able to put it down. Not the first, second or even the third time I read it. Although I read this masterpiece in Spanish, it still carried the same message. A message about life and how important it is to make the most of it. A message about time, about how we often misuse it, applying it to things that are wasteful and don't have much meaning. It really shows how we can get wrapped up in society and its needs, forgetting what's really important. I loved the characters, the metaphors and analogies, the narrative, the set up. I remember reading chapters over just to be able to absolutely comprehend what something meant. Although many think this book is for children, I disagree. Adults should be familiar with this story, for we are the ones that forget what's really essential. I am ready to purchase it and re-read it. Ready to get sucked in it all over again. Ready to cry my eyes out at the end one more time... It is an unforgettable experience... I read it more then 10 years ago... and never forgot.

1 Corinthians 8:1–13
Guiding Gift 4

It would be so loverly to have Paul think with us after we sent a letter to him instead of listening in on a conversation between others. If we wrote about issues of our day (the obscene/obese use of food as an idol of our culture?), we would be able to know what Paul said that was in reference to our letter, and where Paul was adding things we hadn't asked about. As it is, we get confused about process and tend to claim it all by Paul.

Given these difficulties, how can we read the first verse aloud?

The NIV has it, "Now about food sacrificed to idols: We know that we all possess knowledge.* Knowledge puffs up, but love builds up."

Their *footnote indicates, "Or, 'We all possess knowledge,' as you say."

This would put them more in tune with the NRSV which reads, "Now concerning food sacrificed to idols: we know that 'all of us possess knowledge.' Knowledge puffs up, but love builds up."

Some commentators indicate that this is an example of call-and-response, all in one verse.

If this comes close to what is going on, we need to be careful about voice and cadence in our reading to make that distinction. It would also be helpful to start a new paragraph halfway through the verse (another way in which versification narrows our reading rather than opening it).

Can you hear Paul slightly mocking the line from the Corinthians (just to get their attention, of course) as he quotes from their letter "all of us possess knowledge" and then more seriously stating where that perception begins to break down—when knowledge begins to be used as a club against another—"You can't eat that because I don't like it." or "Here, put on this sweater; I'm cold." or "I'm heterosexual and you're not, so you change." or "I know you got weapons even if I can't find them, so I'll bomb you, anyway." or "etc."

So Paul makes the distinction, "Knowledge puffs up, but love builds up", and in that we have the rest of the story. If the church could again hear this distinction, we might get out of the doctrinal battles and express the love we are called to have for one another and thus make our little witness effective.

1 Corinthians 9:16–23
Guiding Gift [5]

Martin Buber echoes verse 19 in his book, *Good and Evil*.

"I am free" follows one in a whirlpool, letting go and catching on to event after event or seeming security after seeming security. Without an anchoring spot, the winds of doctrine sweep one away. One form of evil—freedom.

"I made myself a slave" follows another in that same whirlpool, hanging on for dear life to the first support one finds and never letting loose. Without a graceful hand that knows when to hold 'em and when to fold 'em, doctrine turns into a club. Another form of evil—slavery.

An older version of a charge to parents at an infant baptism puts before them the challenge that their life "become" the gospel. That wonderful word, "become", works in both maturing and beautifying ways.

To play with these pairs, when we are both free to leave and bound by loyalty, we find comeliness (the beauty of a glorious weakness). And, a thing of beauty is a joy—however long it lasts.

---

haven't you heard
has your heart not known
it is not what gets stored up that counts
but what passes through

hearts get attacked
with storage blockages
they faint and fail
in need of new flow

as we pass through
we store or loose
set your heart on this choice
that others might also hear

1 Corinthians 9:24–27
Guiding Gift 6

Do you not know that in a race the runners all compete, and everyone receives a prize?

Our competitive environment leads us to think there is only one winner per race. If everyone, then, is going to win (good old universal salvation) then there will be a whole series of races until one race has only one runner. Actually, it is this last race that exemplifies all the others. Everyone competes against their own limitations and dreams of what might yet be.

I can still remember being a 440-yard record setter in my high school, and conference champion. That qualified me for the state tournament, where I came in last. Believe it or not, I learned more in that last race than I had in all the previous ones, and it held me in good stead when I went on to a university track team.

I didn't get the perishable gold medal, but the imperishable one of clarity on what goal I was really running for—running to be the best runner I could be and the best learner I could be.

I wonder what Paul would think of the Special Olympics and how that would inform his imagery of faith journeys.

We sometimes set very high goals for everyone, which forces everyone to fudge to make themselves seem better than they are. Our religious language actually gets in the way of our spiritual maturity.

In today's world, what does it mean to "run to win"? Are spiritual steroids appropriate? Can one hire a mercenary Prayer Warrior to cover your back? Are there limits to using perishable means to arrive at an imperishable end?

While there is much to be said for Type-A, workaholic, intentional, and disciplined people, the other side of the coin is good old grace. Paul, so into grace, not law, comes pretty close here to relying on the law when it came to evaluating himself.

Give yourself a break, Paul; relax your hyperbole; just do your best. Jesus will reach out and hug you, paunch and all; a leper told me so.

1 Corinthians 11:23–26
Courage Thursday

Paul passed on what he received. The same is incumbent upon each of us. As generation is added to generation and experience to experience, what have you received? What have you passed on?

Are you proclaiming the building of community through common meals and common good? Are you threatening judgment on any who does so through an "unworthy" manner (meaning not approved by the received knowledge of those in power)?

Yes, examine yourself. Are you still connecting creedal purity with physical health? Are you still using portions of the scripture to shun baptized and communing members for whatever reason?

A common meal is not a formal ritual; it is a multi-valent experience of common life with all the messiness such brings. Feast well. Gather strength to helpfully deal with weakness, including your own.

1 Corinthians 15:1–11
Assured

How do we get beyond what has been handed on to us?

Here, the business of tradition keeps alive the sacrificial motif as basic to faith. What else have we come to "believe" because it has simply been around and we find ourselves in its midst?

Conversion mania of being more faithful than the faithful is a phenomenon that deepens hearsay into eye-witness reports. You can almost bet that the ever-more-righteous, who show it by being even more righteous than the current most-righteous, will devolve the gift of life into a reward for themselves. No matter how slyly Paul protests that it is just the grace of god that has enlightened him, his passing on what he had been taught as a good sacrificial Pharisee is not helpful or excusable. In terms of counter-espionage, Paul might be considered a double-agent or mole as well as by his current sobriquet of saint.

Easter pushes us beyond what has been handed on to us. There is a new reality afoot. Follow the clues of Jesus' faithfulness, and you will not find a sacrificial utilitarianism, but a decision for a radical hospitality with those traditionally left out.

2 Corinthians 1:18–22
Guiding Gift [7]

To stay in the realm of "Yes and No" is to put blinders on, to veil ourselves. This is not our desired veiling of Moses, Jesus, or G*D to protect ourselves from their direct and challenging input to our life, but a veiling to restrict what can be seen going out from us. As long as we can stay between "Yes" and "No", we think ourselves safe.

It is true that there is always more information coming, and our very decision to say either "Yes" or "No" changes the situation. This reality gives us plenty of excuses to stay stuck because of all the extra work of adjusting to a new situation after we have engaged it.

Nonetheless, our call is to let loose the "Yes" and "No" living within us. A clear "Yes" will brighten the darkness of a veiled "Yes/No" and clarify a "No". A "Yes" will shine on nearby paths to identify the darkest way and not go down it. For generations, we have tasted the knowledge of "Good" and "Not-good". It is time to take that knowledge and put it to work with good energy in affirmations.

Of course, we will need to be gentle with those who get a "Yes" mixed up with a "No" and stick their head where the sun shines not. Likewise, our compassion will be with those yet unable to leave the comfort of confusion or who enjoy the speculative play of forever pitting a "Yes" against a "No". Sometimes that gentle compassion will need to be directed toward our own misuse of "Yes".

Through whatever fits and starts your practice brings, let your light, your "Yes", shine out of darkness. For my sake, please, shine. I'll do my best to return the favor.

2 Corinthians 3:1–6
Guiding Gift [8] —Proper 3 (8)

Our relationship with G*D and one another might be imagined as written in stone or an Etch A Sketch®. Both have their place. Remember here that steadfast love manifests itself in a great variety of circumstances and thus of manners.

The record of our life is not written in an archival quality ink on acid-free paper or carved ever so lightly or deeply into granite. Even when it comes to some epitaph on a gravestone, our life never was, is, or will be static.

Our responses to circumstances change. What we once could put up with has now become an insult to our soul, and up with such we will no longer put.

Circumstances simply change, regardless of our desire for control, and affect all those around us. We encase the current flower of our life in polyester resin, set it in our trophy case, and use it to discern the worthiness of others by their response to the relic we have become.

A new possibility awakens and bubbles up from within. A different future beckons, and we drop all to follow its promise. We finally practice what we preach and our modeling is changed, our relationships transformed.

Sometimes we can fool ourselves by packaging old bloody atonement in a more polite guise with a time-delay fuse attached, but it is still law, not grace. Static thinking of up and down and back and forth doesn't usually beautify an Etch A Sketch®. When a spirit is active, everything in life works at the same time into new angles to find new angels.

So, what new covenant needs to be invited to play among all the old established covenants you have? This will reveal the law/spirit relationship you have been living out and offer an opportunity to adjust it.

2 Corinthians 4:3–6
Mountain Top to Valley

Good news is veiled, burka-ed. What it shall yet become is un-known. There may be a sweet perfume emanating, but it is like catching a mere glimpse of beauty—looking around for more—and wondering what triggered that sense of "more" for everything still seems everyday-ish.

This is true for all of us, whether we want to claim any particular one is on a track to perishing or flourishing. Our own beauty seems pale, not transfigured at all, very ordinary. What beauty is present in us and will last beyond us? Inquiring minds want to know.

Our current circumstance (mores, taboos, economies, powers, and authorities) blinds us to the gifts available to and through ourselves and our neighbors.

While it is momentarily comforting to be humble and claim our unimportance in relationship to mighty prayer-warrior Jesus or judge-and-sender-off-to-hell Jesus, we really cannot deny the good news that is inside us and is ours alone to reveal.

If light is going to shine out of darkness, it cannot be a slave-light. It will be our own knowing that we, too, are a light of the world, and sin is our hiding of that under whatever cultural basket is convenient at the time. This is a week to practice shining forth.

2 Corinthians 4:5–12
Guiding Gift [9] —Proper 4 (9)

What might it mean to "preach ourselves"? If we are partnered with Jesus, we do have permission to represent ourself as well as the partnership, to represent our own needs as well as yours.

This business of partnership, contrasted with servanthood, does bring with it more room for confusion—both that which will dissolve into sides, breaking any relationship we had, and that which will dissolve us into laughter at one more of those moments when all goes astray, strengthening our relationship through the mystery of humor and humanity. The common clay of confusion reveals both our G*D and ourself. Whether this is a burden or a joy is yours to decide.

For those for whom difference is death—there is going to be a lot of death to come to terms with. Differences within one's self, from stage to stage of life, can be upsetting. Differences that come from the world around, sometimes called trials, discouragements, perplexities, despairs, persecutions, and abandonments are more common than those we see as complements and enhancements (the ice cream sprinkles of life).

When we hand ourselves over, even to a seeming good of helping another, we are handing ourselves over to death. This does not suggest becoming an independent Lone Ranger. Rather, it recognizes that the death of one is a diminishment of all. Our quest is not to avoid a fear of death but risk the delight of light—available to and from each and all. If light and life are not at work in each part, the whole is slowed in its growth.

Facets of a larger light are gifted to each of us. It is exactly my wavelength that is needed to shine from my living; it is exactly your wavelength that is needed to shine from your living. Now, whatever the trial, joy will always be the larger and brighter.

Affirmation
Light Shines from Me
Light Shines from You
Light Shines from even You
Light Shines from especially You
Light Shines from Me and You and You
Light shines forth
Choose Light

2 Corinthians 4:13–5:1
Proper 5 (10)

The spirit of faith that moves one from "belief" to "speech" is universal. It is the same whether it is a political right or left party or religion. In and of itself, there is basic sound and fury signifying only intensity of felt belief.

This faith-to-speech-to-faith process is a wonderfully circular business. Around and around it goes; where it stops, nobody knows. Here it is believed that G*D raised Jesus (rather than Jesus using his own bootstraps, unless, of course, G*D is Jesus, as so many affirm) and will, of course, raise us (and you, if you join "us").

So we don't lose heart or think a second thought. Everything is lined up, and we are not willing to stretch past the limits of this purity of process and purpose. In fact, everything that happens to us is a reflection back of what it is we experience. If it should bring persecution, which is how we interpret any resistance (it being Dalekian futile), this is but a temporary setback—we never lose the war, only a battle.

Faith, thus exercised, is a wonderfully comfortable restraint that we will not give up without considerable cognitive dissonance first.

2 Corinthians 5:6–10, (11–13), 14–17
Proper 6 (11)

When we talk judgment, we are talking negatives. That is what holds power over us.

Imagine a movie theater where every person's life is being shown in front of everyone else. Now pan the crowd and focus in on the next person to have their life revealed to them and all. Do you see them alert with anticipation to see how things were connected and where some editing would have helped? Or, is this just a set-up for laughter at their expense and an excuse to say that at least your life wasn't as inane as theirs?

Where we are tempted to claim judgment is in the hands of the Director, we might find a new great judgment choice: slink down in your seat or sit up and pay attention.

[Note: we were not able to get permission to print a cartoon that is pertinent here. You can view it at: http://www.reverendfun.com/add_toon_info.php?date=20060510]

Now, presume the story of your life is not yet over. Why not look forward to what is going to happen next instead of shying away from what has already occurred?

For a moment, consider your own usual image of a judgment seat. Is it something to be avoided as long as possible or something to hustle along to get a front row seat on what might yet be done? It is time to enjoy judgment as a learning opportunity, not fear it.

2 Corinthians 5:20b–6:10
Self-Recognition Day

Paul claims to put no obstacles in anyone's way. Except, of course, pride that comes about by coming through difficulties. It seems Paul's hardships were not temptations to stop what Paul was doing but dynamic tensions supporting his run for "victory". I wonder what Paul would acknowledge as an obstacle and whether he would be a good judge of what others experienced as such.

In some sense, we do put obstacles in each other's ways. Sometimes we call them temptations, and sometimes they are simply a desire to be ultra-meaningful, to have a corner on meaning.

Proceeding two more verses, all this overcoming ends up with an appeal to have an open heart. It is that characteristic of Jesus that we are continually being tempted away from. We will put up with almost any difficulty but the difficulty of vulnerability. Almost anything can tempt us away from open-heartedness.

We would rather focus on alms and charity than living with the current poor in such a manner that they won't remain poor. We focus on praying for folks without ever thinking of living with them to challenge oppressive structures. We focus on formal seasons of fasting, whether for a meal a week or a lunar month of Ramadan or 40 days of Lent, rather than fasting for justice every day.

Instead of being able to brag about our fantastic overcoming of dire obstacles, we might pay attention to little fasts that not so much avoid chocolate as fast in order to purchase and distribute Fair Trade Chocolate.

2 Corinthians 6:1–13
Proper 7 (12)

Here is quite a list of afflictions. If one took the time, I expect we could each come up with examples in our own lives that would illustrate the difficulty listed. Go ahead, give it a try.

affliction _____
hardship _____
calamity _____
beating _____
imprisonment _____
riot _____
labor _____
sleeplessness _____
hunger _____
dishonor _____
ill repute _____
treated as impostor _____
seen as unknown _____
being of no more account than one who is dying _____
punished _____
poor _____
having nothing _____

What holds these from being defining realities and allows an alternative action in their midst is having an open heart for others.

For Paul, this openness is not passivity, but an active voice of speaking frankly, honestly, openly. How open is your heart in this regard?

2 Corinthians 8:7–15
Proper 8 (13)

We just completed a successful Capital Fund Campaign. Our scripture theme was 8:12—"It doesn't matter how much you have. What matters is how much you are willing to give from what you have." (CEV)

The practical use of this passage is thus validated. A part of every encounter with the holy includes, but goes beyond, the practical. For instance, the very folks who responded well to verse 12 would have a most difficult time with verses 13-15. Their individual/personal concept of fair stops short of a communal vision of fair. If it should come to actually sharing their surplus and having their deficit covered by others, there would be great grumbling about "socialism". Corporate welfare seems to be alright, but not sharing with the poor. A capital campaign to benefit themselves seems to be alright, but a straight-up equivalent campaign for the poor is out of the question, and these are good and generous people. Without lessening our tendency to greed, part of the difficulty is the inability of the whole system to adequately frame the issue.

This is a difficult concept for disciples of any era—from perceptions of Cain regarding Abel, to responses to a woman anointing Jesus, to commitments by Ananias and Sapphira, to any who are hearers but not doers, to the Laodiceans, to prosperity preachers, to profit-first economists, to you and me.

It is so difficult to see what we can do and so easy to see what we cannot do. From here, it is no stretch at all to cocoon ourselves. Come quickly disaster. Come strongly enough that we will learn.

2 Corinthians 12:2–10
Proper 9 (14)

To keep us from being too inflated or elated we are given a thorn, a hometown. Here, people changed our diapers. Here, people saw the bad haircut we gave ourself. Here, errors in judgment as we moved through the stages of life are laughed about every holiday. Here, people join in expecting to honor a conquering hero returned home.

Out of his own experience at Nazareth, Jesus sends out the twelve, and ourselves. They and we find places as humbling as a hometown and new places that become our hometown.

Whether needing refuge and defense or providing such (opportunity for repentance), we stretch our walk with G*D to include folks for whom we are a thorn and folks who are a thorn for ourselves. Mutuality is not just support, but also correction.

---

teaching is in order
in season or out

caught on a thorn or
caught up to seventh heaven

no surprise here
both are unrealistic

hometown rejection
along with

hometown adulation
we will receive

without surprises
learning to live

in season or out
learning is in order

Galatians 4:4–7
Naming Day

Ahh, fullness of time. It's about time. Do you sense time's fullness in your life?

We might also talk about the birthing of time. A whole new continuum has been birthed with the choices we make. These choices begin to set up a whole new set of relationships with the rest of creation. Want to adopt a new future? . . . Adopt a new choice.

The Jewish Annotated New Testament, edited by Amy-Jill Levine and Marc Zvi Brettler, offers another approach in their reflection on verse 6.

> 6: *Spirit of his son*, Paul distinguishes between Christ and God but not between the Spirit and Christ. In the fourth century the Nicene Creed distinguished God the Father, God the Son (Christ), and God the Spirit. This Trinitarian conception is unknown to Paul and is barely attested in the NT. *Abba! Father.* Rabbinic theology, following biblical precedent, often conceived of God as father and Israel as son or sons. Still, although rabbinic prayers were sometimes directed to "our father in heaven" or "our father our king", no rabbinic prayers invoke God as *Abba*, which affects a level of intimacy with the divine that made the rabbis uncomfortable. [references to rabbinic works and scripture deleted]

Can you read the New Testament without foisting later conceptual models on it, including your own? While helpful to see how others have dealt with the imponderables of life, there is a freshness available when we have to deal with source material itself.

I was also intrigued with their observation that the first verses of chapter 4 suggest we are moving on to adulthood, maturity, and in but a few verses the metaphor shifts to being adopted. Try playing with verses 1-2 in comparison with verses 4-5 and see what fits your experience of yourself and your setting.

Ephesians 1:3–14
Blessed Body 2 — Proper 10 (15)

What does it mean to be chosen, whole, and blameless since before whenever and before we might come to claim these qualities?

The nature of a Living G*D goes beyond these desired states of being. That which is chosen must be chosen again and again for it to keep evolving from its experiences and reflections on same. Even steadfast love needs to be confirmed again and again. That which was whole holds the hope of a wider wholeness that receives and rejoices in what it wasn't until now. Blameless in one context becomes actual guilt in another. The only way around this is the way of death that cuts off change at a particular time and place. Fortunately, guilt revisited can receive mercy and move on.

All predestined plans are phooey. There are only plans made and initiated. Beyond that, we are in the phase of plans revised. To paraphrase a comment about Sabbath time, "Plans are made for people, not people for plans."

This business of life is underway, and we are building it as we go, never giving up at a needed rest or detour. We are tinkering with the plans as we get feedback about the plan to this point. Note that plans are much more detailed than goals and hopes.

It would be more helpful to claim G*D had hopes and dreams for us since some earlier whenever. To get as specific as a plan limited by a particular time- and place-bound incarnation is stretching things too far. Even with a Jesus model, we keep forgetting Jesus' hope and dream for the work of a spirit after him.

How is your hope and dream of doing even better than Jesus coming along? Any plan you develop on a hope or a dream will have to adapt to the bumps and shifts that are present or can be expected in the course of everyday everydayness.

Ephesians 1:15–23
Our Turn to Witness

"...as you come to know G*D."

What! This is a process?

Wisdom and Revelation are still coming clear?

Hope will be further clarified?

Would that we would take this journey seriously enough to honor the stages of one's own life and the differing stages of the lives of others. We are still coming to know, to understand, to live with the presence of a Living G*D and a Living S*lf and a Living Neighb*r.

May we continue to "come to know" as we return to everyday life with all its bumps and bruises, its overcoming and coming through.

Ephesians 2:1–10
Conviction [4]

To be rich in mercy is to look around, see what's down, and raise it up.

Mercy has been shown to us, and we have grown.

Mercy has been shown by us, and we have grown.

This pairing is something to be boasted about. Seeing ourselves as worthy of mercy and able to do works of mercy is no small thing.

Ephesians 2:11–22
Proper 11 (16)

We are always dealing with idolatry—external evidence of a spiritual presence. Then it was circumcision. Now it is a particular economic system, theological surety, narcissism, etc.

Compassion for the un-whatever is being Christlike. It is by this process that we offer peace to those far off (the un's) and those nearby (the un-un's).

This process of compassion is a key keystone of our being. Place your keystone where your wobbly sides need someone to press against you to bolster your ability to bridge any competing sides.

This process of compassion compresses and restrains us so we hold back an angry word or a fast slap. Our Neighb*rs are pressing so hard among us that we receive their difference as support. Talk about your mystery!

This process of compassion compresses our spirit until it cannot help but welcome the tension of those near and those far as they meet right here.

Ephesians 3:1–12
Guiding Gift

There is still a passion to save souls that makes a huge difference in the energy of a congregation. While admitting that such energy has gone astray by emphasizing a passing on of accumulated cultural norms, the power that is available in the phrase, "for the sake of . . ." is amazing. A trick here is to have that desire be in relationship and a willingness to be as changed as one is looking for change in another. A one-way "for the sake of" becomes tyranny.

I'm not holding my breath for a congregation to claim the name of *For the Sake of . . . Church*, but I would hope that such a sentiment would be more imaginatively held by congregations than automatically forcing "Jesus" to be the ". . .". Usually we would say, for the sake of Christ we do . . . . Here we can say that for the sake of lesbians we will . . . , for the sake of immigrants we will . . . , for the sake of those uncovered by health insurance we will . . . , and find this specificity to lead us to a larger community that receives and offers prevenient justice and redeems violence already committed.

There can be real and artificial humility in seeing oneself as "the least". A measure of our humility is how adamant we are about imposing guilt on another when they don't respond to what-I-have-done-for-their-sake. To simply be persistent in living/loving for another's sake is a worthy humility. To demand they act on our timeline turns that humility sour.

Paul reminds the Ephesians that they have access to G*D in boldness and confidence through faith in Jesus. That is one pole of the double great commandment—to boldly and confidently love G*D with all of one's heart, soul, mind, and strength.

The line about "for the sake of . . ." is our entry into the other pole–to boldly and confidently love our neighbor as we love ourself. If we need to, we can also ground this in having faith in Jesus.

Here, Jesus again acts as a catalyst in binding our life to that of G*D and Neighbor. It may be that faith is best seen as a catalyst that enters and leaves situations trust-full.

Ephesians 3:14–21
Proper 12 (17)

St. Teresa, not satisfied with thinking about or talking about G*D as if about an object, says, "I carry the heart of my God and the God of my heart everywhere."

What would that be like for you?

One way to get at this is through the matryoshka nested doll, a symbol of motherhood and fertility. Our heart within G*D's heart and our neighbor's heart within our heart and our heart within our neighbor's heart and our neighbor's heart within G*D's heart. Through such multiple nestings is the gift of community solidified. Through such mysterious nestings is the gift of Messiah/Christ evidenced.

Pray for Christ to be within hearts. It makes a difference to the prayer and the prayee. The matryoshka nested doll—a symbol of a spiritual artisan. Try it out. Herein lies the fullness of G*D.

Ephesians 4:1–16
Proper 13 (18)

"Make captivity a captive." This reversal of fortune is key in every story worth the telling and hearing. It is the journey we are on toward some larger wholeness or maturity. It is a changed relationship to ourselves and the world around us that reveals a loyal opposition to our desires and social discrimination.

When we wrestle with that which holds us captive, we discover gifts aplenty within that had been tamped down through self-censorship and peer pressure. Gifts here reveal our part in building up a context that will be healthy for others as well as ourselves.

It is these various gifts that we yearn for and eventually allow to come forth. Until they begin to bloom and blossom, we find our desires running away from our own better judgment and behaviors subject to all manner of crafty, deceitful scheming of others.

Without our gifts being engaged, we continue to fall apart. With our gifts engaged in growing and maturing, we are bound together, stronger.

Claim your gift and simply engage its implementation. In this, we live our version of Jesus and other heroines and heroes.

Ephesians 4:25–5:2
Proper 14 (19)

Puns are fun. A pun in any other language is still a pun. This is nothing to quibble about. Let's wrap our tongue around some geeky Greek. It turns out the Greek word we translate into English as "kind" in verse 32 sounds like "Christ" in Greek. I hope this isn't Greek to you. Through punnish parallelism, we end up with an encouragement to "be Christ to one another...."

Therefore, imitate the meaning of Christ—focus on the steadfast kindness of G*D. Imitate the kindness of Christ, the Christ of kindness. Keep at this until, in years to come, your name, also, will be used as a substitute for "kindness". It won't be Tom, Dick, or Harry; it will be Kindness, Kindness, or Kindness. It won't be Bob and Carol and Ted and Alice; it will be Kindness and Kindness and Kindness and Kindness.

How would our religious life be different if we were known as Kind-ians instead of Christ-ians?

Ephesians 5:15–20
Proper 15 (20)

In a season of Pentecost, it is important to pay attention to how we behave.

One way is the way of fear—we hide ourselves away and refuse contact with any who may be different from ourselves. This takes some spiritual dynamite to shake us loose from a dark place.

Another way is that of intentional contact with those who are so different from ourselves that we have no reasonable chance of conversing with them. Yet, every time we do so, there is a surprise of unexpected connection and a sense of participating in a larger scope of life.

This passage reminds us that the wise way is that of taking advantage of present opportunities. To hide behind an appeal to religious purity is not an opportunity.

Remember how folks went out on Pentecost to tell the wonders of G*D and Jesus and Spirit Windy Fire and their own coming out? This is the same story here. Gather, pray, and sing until your very celebration sends you forth. Image here Brownian Movement. The more energetic your attestation to a wonder beyond our differences, the sooner you will be sent beyond any current boundary into the near and far reaches of the universe.

Lucretius' poem on the nature of things says,

> Observe what happens when sunbeams are admitted into a building and shed light on its shadowy places. You will see a multitude of tiny particles mingling in a multitude of ways...their dancing is an actual indication of underlying movements of matter that are hidden from our sight... It originates with the atoms which move of themselves [i.e., spontaneously].... So the movement mounts up from the atoms and gradually emerges to the level of our senses, so that those bodies are in motion that we see in sunbeams, moved by blows that remain invisible.

Now observe and pay attention to your experiences that cannon you into new relationships. Bless them. They will reveal the Presence of G*D in your life. Your current song of wonders will be added to— sing a new song!

Ephesians 6:10–20
Proper 16 (21)

Finally, be beautiful, not strongly armored. Remember: you are an image of beauty. Remember: others are also images of beauty.

Our struggle is not against others as much as it is against those messages planted within ourselves that we are less than beautiful. That which negates beauty is a principality and power. Therefore, take up Libby Roderick's song "How Could Anyone"[1] and put down all that other armor, for those who put on armor will die in armor, and that's no way to live.

Pray that we may boldly declare—"It gets better."

Not only can beauty be substituted for strength, so can time. Listen to Utah Phillips:

> The big system can be pretty overwhelming. We know that we can't beat them by competing with them. What we can do is build small systems where we live and work that serve our needs as we define us and not as they're defined for us. The big boys in their shining armor are up there on castle walls hurling their thunderbolts. We're the ants patiently carrying sand a grain at a time from under the castle wall. We work from the bottom up. The knights up there don't see the ants and don't know what we're doing. They'll figure it out only when the wall begins to fall. It takes time and quiet persistence. Always remember this: They fight with money and we resist with time, and they're going to run out of money before we run out of time.

[1] Recommended—http://youtu.be/oBG5c8V0wVU

Philippians 2:5–11
Naming Day — Premature Fear Sunday

How does intentional humility work? Is it humility or practice toward humility? Is it humility or the appearance of humility? Is it humility taking advantage of humility? Is it simply humility?

To humble oneself in anticipation of a later benefit seems just a touch proud.

These same questions come about the privilege of not claiming one's privilege.

Perhaps what is being driven at here is some transparency of motive.

Just before this text, we hear of Paul's joy in loving accord through a mechanism of looking out for others' interests. This will probably have a helpful effect on oneself, but there is certainly no guarantee that those with other interests will reciprocate and have our interest in mind.

Just after this text, we hear the injunction to work out our communal health together—always a dicey matter. Look at the comments on nearly any blog, and you won't have to scroll far to find flamers whose good pleasure seems to be in displeasing others.

Somehow, humility is not just a personal virtue, but a communal one. Living in a culture of humility would be transformative. So far, our track record has been poor. It is difficult to be humble when you are a "city on a hill". We have caused more fear and trembling than actual healing.

1 Thessalonians 5:16–24
Needed Change [3]

Rejoice; Anticipate; Give—these are ways G*D is revealed and drawn near to.

These qualities of relating keep one grounded and flying high.

Rejoice in opportunities available, even in the most dire of situations. Even Uncle Sol[1] was able to start a worm farm in his demise.

Anticipate an unceasing flow of time. Regardless of how erratic time is, our engagement with it continues. We cast an eye ahead and translate what we see into our work of this day.

Give. Yes, thanks, but ever so much more as well. Give energy where you sense spirit is loosening the grip of the past. Give heed to questions of a current system thinking it is the culmination of creation, and claiming there is only fear and chaos beyond the current limits of our thinking. A G*D of peace is also a G*D moving ahead, for the violence of today is not a good place to rest.

Test everything. Particularly test the tried and true.

Advent is practice time for breathing in (keeping a gleam in your eye), engaging processes of change, and breathing out (participating in the potlatch jubilee of life).

What equation are you using these days to keep progressing toward wholeness/soundness for self and others? Try this one:

$$R+P+GT-QS-DP+TE+HFTG-E=S/S/B(KS)$$

+ rejoice
+ pray
+ give thanks

    - quench spirit
    - despise prophets

+ test everything
+ hold fast to good

    - evil

        = spirit/soul/body kept sound

[1] http://cummingslove.tumblr.com/post/12892798672/

1 Timothy 2:1–7
Thanksgiving

Pray for everyone. Paul goes on to specifically include praying for people in high places, people who otherwise might not get prayed for. This might be considered to be a prayer for an enemy, someone whose dishonest wealth/power has led to a dishonest spirituality and keeps the one who is praying poorer and poorer.

The emphasis upon "people in high places" is an appropriate reminder that the prayer behind the prayer is to be revolutionary. It is hard to live a quiet and peaceable life in all godliness and dignity with all the division and inequality of resources that are required to keep people in high places. The lifestyle they have grown accustomed to and want more of requires some to be physically, psychologically, or socially enslaved—hardly a quiet and peaceable life.

While traditionally read as "leaders are more sons of God than anyone else and so support them with prayer and praise just like you would a God", we can still hear echoes of a more radical call from G*D and Jesus to break down the dishonesty, the hypocrisy of wealth, and all that supports it.

If Thanksgiving is a universal, we need to be careful about the ease with which we are thankful for our benefits without mourning the reality of those whose lives have so few.

When leaders give their lives, wealth, and power to ransom the poor, we might have a clearer way to engage the multitude of ways in which "salvation" becomes manifest.

Titus 2:11–14
Blessed Body, Proper I

Where did the gift of surprise and choice go so quickly? The gospel lessons are poetry and story. By the time we get to the epistles, we are confronted with the didactic and doctrinaire. Christmas moves from a particular to the general only with a great deal of danger to its own integrity.

We hear about incarnation being a source of atonement: "God has appeared, bringing salvation to all".

This act of G*D soon gets shifted to the crucifixion: "[Jesus] gave himself for us that he might redeem us from all iniquity".

What begins with the fulfillment of a promise to our ancestors, becomes, all too quickly, angels not announcing G*D's work but "worshiping" some idolatry of an eternity beyond flesh and blood birth and life.

Be careful what gets ingested along with all the sweet carols of Christmas. Is Christmas just a setup for a later Good Friday atonement, or is it a sufficient grace in its particularity?

Titus 3:4–7
Blessed Body, Proper II

While we often talk about Jesus as Savior, this is really just a shortcut way of talking about the wholeness Jesus committed his life to: G*D.

Spend your next meditational time with "G*D our Savior" and see if you get a new picture of incarnation. Where we often see "Christ Jesus our Savior" lying in the manger, we might see the whole manger scene as lying within creation.

Taking just the Jesus route to salvation without attending to the G*D route of salvation tends to make our religious experience rather small. It is about the rituals that make sense to us, that warm our heart, or that we offer to others.

When we see G*D as Savior we will also pay attention to the variety of incarnations (reincarnations) of G*D we might find that increase our ability to make sense or meaning in the world, that toss another resource into our heart to warm it further than anything we had already burned up, and more deeply connect us with the salvation of all, not just ourselves.

For those who come to Christmas (and Easter) services, thank you. But for those who come to Christmas service without anticipating a rebirth through baptismal renewal and an ongoing teaching Spirit, so sorry.

As verse 7 might have said it, "By the grace of G*D we are holy and lay claim to an inheritance of eternal life in this moment." Do note that "eternal life in this moment" is not about some "first day of the rest of your life". We are claiming it for this moment, and we will reclaim it anew in a next moment.

We can enter into "G*D our Savior" in many ways, including that of "Christ Jesus our Savior", but it is always a larger space than a narrow entry place.

It is so easy to dispute and split over details. How many different Christ Jesuses do we appeal to for our entry into G*D? How easy it is to set all of these against other entry spots. To make it more difficult to move toward a schism, use "G*D our Savior" on a regular basis and periodically substitute it for "Christ Jesus our Savior". It promises renewal for yourself, the church, and all.

Hebrews 1:1–4, (5–12)
Blessed Body, Proper III

To leave nature out of revelation, doesn't work. To leave a reflection of G*D out of our experience, doesn't work. To leave ourselves out of Christmas or any other thin-time, doesn't work.

Imagine you are a reflection of G*D's presence. This will bring Christmas to many all through the year.

Imagine you are an exact imprint of G*D's very being or might become such. This will give courage and strength to train well that it might be so.

———————————

O Child of G*D—Yes, you!

Your call is to transform
   wickedness to wholeness.
For this you have been anointed with
   oils of gladness and compassion
   beyond your comprehension.

Can you still feel that anointing?
   Good.

Can you still feel that good anointing?

Isn't it good to still feel that anointing!

Hebrews 2:14–18
Old Welcomes New

What does it mean to be made perfect through "suffering"?

Try this – The word translated as "suffering" here is "pathema", a presumed derivative of "pathos" from a root, "pascho".

Pushing through the various definitions, we can hear "suffering" as a negative (bad, depraved, sick), a positive (to be well off), or descriptively (whatever, to simply feel or experience).

Here we might say that Jesus was made whole through his experiences, his feeling the realities around him and beyond him.

This sense of wholeness, healed-ness, or salvation is experience-based, not doctrine-based. Jesus, and those who draw near to G*D by reflecting on his experience, appreciate his appreciation of his experience of what befalls everyone in the process of living. Therefore, mercy is a key response to life. It is experienced life that draws us together (atonement, if you will).

"Suffering" has gotten a bad rap when it is only seen in a negative light. I'm not sure the word can be redeemed from centuries of one-sided use. This might mean that we need to refrain from its use, or find a longer descriptor to say what we really mean, because it can only be heard negatively, regardless of how we intend it.

To demonstrate this, can you read this passage in terms of "passionate deeds" rather than through purgation?

Another approach to this is to look at the Indo-European root of the word "suffer"—"bher" which means to carry or to bear children. Here, too, we might put it this way, "Jesus was made whole through birthing in others an ability to bear G*D". Might this be difficult/suffering? Yes. Might this be simply-the-way-life-is/suffering? Yes. Might this be participating-in-mercy/suffering? Yes.

Blessings upon you in this time of introducing Jesus, who will introduce you to bearing on your own tongue better descriptors of salvation—difficult, simply-the-way-life-is, merciful—rather than falling back on the inadequacy of using "suffering" language.

Hebrews 4:12–16
Proper 23 (28)

Ah, to arrive at the spot of receiving or taking mercy upon ourselves and to be filled or to find the grace to accept the help needed to move into living as though G*D's presence dwelt among us.

What a wonderful end spot. Here is the community we have been dreaming of. When each knows mercy and is supported, we are able to extend mercy to one another and to be of assistance in one another's growth.

Now, how do we get there? At least one beginning spot is to experience a living voice of G*D shooing away all our excuses and resistances to living mercifully with one another and creation. We can no longer live under the illusion of being self-sufficient or in control.

A second beginning spot is like unto it—it's the grace of help that binds us together. Mercy for ourselves and help for others. Mercy for others and help for ourselves. Around and around we go with support and correction and confession and pardon and grief and joy—all out in the open.

Hebrews 4:14–16; 5:7–9
Annihilation Friday

What is this "once made perfect" in verse 9? It is such a static image, not suited for much other than obedience.

There must be a jump that is made in the elided section to move from the affirmation of Jesus as Merciful to Jesus as Perfect Master.

We begin here affirming that Jesus is able to sympathize with our weaknesses, and so we can confidently approach the grace known as mercy for this and every time of need.

By the time we come to the end of this reading, it is not a matter of Jesus' empathy, but our response. Somehow, grace has gotten tied into our behaviors rather than the nature of G*D.

After looking again at 5:1-6, it is difficult to discern just where the narrowing and hardening of mercy went on. Is it in the repeated work a priest has to do on their own life? Is it some magical appeal to the unknown Melchizedek that gives a free pass from growing in grace because, somehow or other, he is simply grace personified?

We may have to leave it that our temptation to have more order than G*D desires enters in here. It is a recapitulation of the Garden of Eden fruit choice all over again. We will have a strict knowledge of good and evil and insist on obeying the surface of good without understanding the long-term consequences of any given short-term good.

However it came to be that in the days of Jesus' earthly life he offered up prayers and supplications with tears and loud cries (not just for his own state of being, but out of connectedness with all of creation) and after having been made "perfect" through the suffering of a crucifixion there is now only obeisance to be made, consider whether it is time to return to a focus on our mutual care of each other.

In this way, Good Friday may still be redeemed from doctrine to mercy.

Hebrews 5:1–10
Proper 24 (29)

Priests take folks to God through their gifts and sacrifices—intermediary after intermediary.

Imagining Jesus as a priest, high or low, turns Jesus into a functionary.

Hebrews does us the great injustice of turning Prophet Jesus with a word from G*D into merely a sacrificing priest. This has sown seeds of a hierarchical church, orthodoxy, and creedal standards that keep us tied to the past and oh so slow to repent of each of these methods that ask for continued sacrifice of minorities within and without the church walls.

Want to get your faith energized again? Throw out the priestly imagery of Hebrews and return to Prophet Jesus. We don't need a perpetual priest, but a present prophet.

Hebrews 5:5–10
Conviction [5]

Here is a handy mnemonic device: Melchizedek can be sung to the Mickey Mouse Club theme song. Try it, you won't soon forget how to spell it. And . . . forever hold His banner high!

It seems true that "Christ did not glorify himself in becoming...." Can we leave it there without going on to the High Priest stuff?

How soon we forget that High Priests have one function and lowly prophets another. My sense is that we need to reclaim Jesus as a lowly prophet, remembering the Priestly function is part of what he lived against. To be hung on our walls as a Great High Priest, with all the rest of us being pale imitations, doesn't seem in keeping with the Jesus I hang out with.

As a lowly prophet, Jesus engages our brokenness to shift our focus toward wholeness. This is different than the distance of Priestly perfection that magically, *ipso facto* and *quid pro quo*, slips us into the eternal realm and bars others.

Hebrews 7:23–28
Proper 25 (30)

And why is a permanent high priest needed? In most ways, Jesus is anti-king and anti-priest. This whole priesthood thing seems to be more in keeping with our desire, Adam-old and Saul-deep, to avoid responsibility and set up someone to blame. When this eternal high priest is established, we have taken our desire to the nth degree. Jesus is not only a perfect man and a perfect god but a perfect out for our maturing. "Go Jesus! Speak up for us, save us!"

It would be helpful to hear the author of the Letter to the Hebrews respond to Jesus' question, "What do you want from me?" This section would seem to say that we want a buffer between humanity and G*D, that we don't want to see any further change to our heritage.

Until this restrictive view of participating with G*D shifts, we won't hear those challenging words from Jesus, "Go on your way!"

May you be well on your way today.

Hebrews 9:11–14
Proper 26 (31)

William Loader has commented:

> There are many ways of helping people to this confidence [that they are a people loved and forgiven by God]. Hebrews offers one very complicated way. The idea that a sacrifice or a symbolic reminder of blood kept God in touch with the validity of love might strike us as odd if not bizarre, but it must have worked for some. We are not committed to using the same methods, but we are committed to the same message—if that is our faith. We are today more sensitive to different religious traditions than our author, but we also need to come to terms critically with our own. We might even seek to emulate the level of creativity our author has shown when we face the challenge of speaking this same message to people in our day who live in a different symbolic world but face substantially the same needs.

I appreciate the challenge for us to speak of love and forgiveness in a creative manner in our context. For the physicists among us, we might speak of Jesus giving up his Higgs boson. For others of us, this brings a big, "Huh?"

When it comes to the blood sacrifice imagery, I am in the "Huh?" category. If Jesus can bypass the sacrifice of goats and bulls, why limit him to a simple blood substitution as though Jesus were religiously type O-negative? In today's world, we might also wonder about hematopoietic stem cells being a new image regarding Jesus' ongoing experimentation and creativity rather than repeating a past out of touch with today's and tomorrow's realities.

Perhaps it is enough to ask what a "new covenant" is and how it might be symbolized. If it is redemption from the past, then we may need to find images that will walk into a new future rather than repeat past patterns.

Hebrews 9:11–15
Clarification Week, Monday

I don't know that I will ever get my head around sacrificial atonement. How about you?

This whole section posits an interpretation of a radical break with a sacrificial model by doubling down on the sacrificial model. I'll see your substituted blood by my own blood.

If we might remember the Annunciation of a Spirit coming over Mary that would bring forth a Jesus, it becomes difficult to line up with a Jesus now moved by Spirit to bow his head and be killed. Modeling life is nowhere near such an acquiescent action. Jesus is not Isaac or Ishmael.

If Jesus' life reveals anything, it is that cleaning out our lives opens us to better partner with a Living G*D. Simply serving G*D neither serves G*D's intent for creation nor honors the life of an image of G*D.

Is this week going to clarify our relationship with G*D, or is it going to reinforce our place in the lower hierarchy of principalities and powers that raise us up just to show us our place and send us back to it.

---

this week is before us as a test
may you bring your best
and rely on mercy for the rest

Hebrews 9:24–28
Proper 27 (32)

No Plato here—no copies.

No Sisyphus here—no again and againing.

Still a little Aaron here—one last, extra-strong, sacrifice.

Here, a two-stage rocket to heavenland is proposed. First stage, "sin-bearing"; second stage, "salvation-bringing".

As you consider the implications of this division of labor, remember where you are in this model that has yet to convince many: your sins have been borne; you are awaiting salvation.

This could be an enviable position to be in. So, what are you going to do while you wait?

- Pull a Vladimir and Estragon?

- Engage your eagerness by encouraging the end to come more quickly?

- Planting a tree?

- Forgive others preemptively?

There are many choices regarding your wait time. You could complain about the kind of music being played while you are on hold. You could learn some new music or join a choir to learn how to harmonize. You could compose an anti-opera (much like the vaunted reverse country song by Rascal Flatts) that would move us back to creation to find paradise right where we are.

Lots of choices in this waiting time. Pick one. Make it up, if necessary. Be proactive in your waiting.

Hebrews 10:4–10
Creation's Conception

The impetus here is worthy enough; it is just that the larger context keeps coming back to sympathetic magic: As to Jesus, so to me.

Since we are nine months away from Christmas and this is an ancient Birth Day of Creation, let's look at a before and after shot of the angelic announcement of no fear and bearing the future (and why is it that "pro-lifers" don't do more honoring of this day of conception?).

Before:

G*D didn't want sacrifices and offerings.

G*D created/prepared life to be lived bodily.

Somehow, these came to the fore through either an errant word or interpretation of same.

Somehow, a veil has been placed over our experience of G*D, and we can only approach through intermediaries.

After:

Here I-AM connected to that which reveals I-AMness that is.

Here I-AM, an assurance of G*D Being-Here.

Somehow, we are continuing to step into a future without preparation (sacrifice) that all will be alright.

Somehow, we are moving beyond the provisional into the providential.

It is in the process of living that this shift goes on. The announcement was for a traditional Messiah who would conquer. The result was one who lived so mercifully that mercy lived on after their death.

This shift is still going on in your life and mine. Our question is about how stuck we are in our before stage that we never go through the difficult work of transformation that results in the after. It is almost that we are vaccinated against change.

Having had another opportunity to reflect on what a before and after would look like in our life, we are yet able to hear at least the first part of the announcement of this day, "Fear not", and then see where that much takes us.

Hebrews 10:11–14, (15–18), 19–25
Proper 28 (33)

It is verse 18 that offers a better approach to sacrifice than a mega- or meta-sacrifice. If forgiveness operates, sacrifice becomes moot.

Using this approach, we might then work toward a priesthood of all based on forgiveness. In this way, we would affirm that every priest, day after day, offers, again and again, forgiveness of both form and content. It is not that forgiveness takes away sin, but it does obviate the need to continue repeating it or substitute sacrifice (formalized forgiveness without its presence) for it.

If forgiveness applies to the privileged of G*D, the predestined, who's to say that G*D has not privileged or predestined everyone? For the moment, presume Arminius did better in this particular than other followers of Calvin. Now we can jump to the Wesleyan renewal movement with its practices and social structures that would help individuals attend to preparing to greet "the Day" as an occasion of joy, rather than sorrow. [This last sentence modifies a comment from *The Wesley Study Bible*.]

Good news—forgiveness is available. We don't have to go through some sacrificial system, but can jump right to being proactive in being a forgiver who thus provokes love and good deeds. This is evangelistic enough to spend time together—encouraging and being encouraged. Hmmm, forgiveness as a church growth (root-deepening) principle. Is this possibility intriguing enough to lead you to actually experiment with forgiveness on a congregational level?

Hebrews 10:16–25
Annihilation Friday

Another interesting choice: How are we to view today's crucifixion (either Jesus' long ago or the latest one in the news)? If the cross is a metaphor for entering a next stage of life, how might we most constructively view this sign?

The author of Hebrews here suggests we have the confidence to enter the Presence of G*D by either:

> A) The nature of G*D as described by a Spirit Real. G*D coaxes, cajoles, beckons us onward with compassionate responses and merciful thoughts. G*D further welcomes us by resolving the past in such a way that we are able to enter today with joy and tomorrow with hope.

> or

> B) The blood of Jesus, who was sacrificed and now, alchemically, uses blood against blood to open a way forward.

In the first, we are partners, in the second, we are disciples, servants, who are sometimes called friends.

When push comes to shove in this particular, all the pat religious responses that "Jesus" is always the right-answer come to naught in verses 23-25.

Our task is always wrapped up in relationships (A), not mechanisms (B). Finally, we remember the source of promise—creation. We spur one another to love and good works—encouragement, nudging, complement, and correction. We do this through inquiring of another how it goes with them, to practice a next step, and hold one another accountable—gathering.

Whenever there is a question of a choice, choose (A); Jesus did.

Hebrews 12:1–3
Clarification Week, Wednesday

Yes, think of Jesus and his faithfulness to his perceived relationship with G*D and the rest of creation. Remember, there were disciples who never did seem to note where Jesus was looking, only at what he was doing, and so both during his time with them and afterward they kept refocusing from G*D to Jesus. There were temptations that came out of the blue and from a Syrophoenician woman, betraying followers, misremembering traditionalists, and an intolerable social setting. There was his own spiritual journey of retreats and reengagements. There was more.

Remembering Jesus' faithfulness to a picture larger than himself or even the tradition within which he matured helps us consider a larger picture than ourselves and our particular set of experiences. In so considering, we are helped to not put all our eggs in our own handmade basket and not be trapped by the fatigue engendered by protecting what doesn't need protecting. There is no religious tradition that has come down to us that must be defended, only lived.

When we keep an eye on Jesus, we will note that he did not wiggle his fingers toward himself as if to say, "More applause". Rather, we see Jesus gazing onward to his "Abba". He kept pointing and saying, "Look!", and we would look at him, not where he was looking. It is as if we hear someone say, "Duck!" and we look up to get clobbered in the eye by a foul ball. Perversity, thou art us.

Do you think Jesus saw Joy ahead of him? No matter what the frustration of the moment, did he see Joy?

How about yourself? Joy ahead, and so keep on trucking? A Joy large enough to risk any short-term difficulty, such as misunderstanding or death? If so, you are already present in the Presence of G*D. So giggle and go ahead.

Giggle because the Presence of G*D brings with it all that has led us along the way. From every stumble we learned. From every completed task, we moved on. From every gift received and call responded to, every hope enlarged and fear faced, every mentor and mentoree, every friend and lover (even every enemy), our own weaknesses are re-valued. Chuckle that you once thought life a veil of tears to slog through. Finally laugh aloud that the deal is not "hard work and perseverance, grim determination of the soul!" (Do listen to Lou and Peter Berryman, who have a song by this title.)

As you read this comment, did you note it worked its way backward from verse 3 to verse 2 to verse 1. This is a helpful technique to see where assumptions begin to fall apart.

James 1:17–27
Proper 17 (22)

ABCC'B'A' — a wonderful pattern in verses 26-27.

> A - think and use religion
> B - unbridle tongue against others
> C - worthless religion
> C' - pure religion
> B' - care for widows and orphans
> A' - care for spiritual disciplines

Here we have an example of the great reversal ever needed.

Another way of looking at this is with the pattern of quick to listen, slow to speak, slower to anger. An implication is that our usual pattern of quickly angered, rapid to speak, slow to listen needs to be retrained, not retained (what a difference an "r" makes).

Set aside 5 uninterrupted minutes; listen to this passage as you read it aloud three times, slowly. How did it change from the first to the last reading? Did some words begin to echo? What interconnections became clearer—interconnections not just internally, between the words, but with your life?

Were you able to actually do the above exercise, or did you only read it—and not act on it?

James 2:1–10, (11–13), 14–17
Proper 18 (23)

Ahh, the old joke (or not) about a boss who gets an invisible finger from a demigod of the marketplace and bawls out an employee, who bawls out a partner, who bawls out a kid, who kicks a dog.

"Can't you track things" asks James, and in so doing asks, "Can't you break the pattern you are in?"

While appreciating that faith by itself is "dead" if it has no "works", this does lead us to a new legalism, keeping every jot and tittle of a work ethic and setting all laws as equally valid in all situations. This passage was shaped to lead us to this conclusion. An important antidote to a Protestant Work Ethic and literalistic doctrine is found in the missing section—mercy triumphs over judgment. While James is talking about specific rules in a negative fashion—whoever keeps the whole law but fails in one point has become accountable for all of it—we do also need the positive spin of mercy that brings the freedom to intentionally break some rules when they lead to a reduction in love of neighbor.

It is this mercy that will rebalance the world, not equalizing income, but, amazingly, the equalizing of resources does open up new possibilities for mercy to become an organizing principle for human interaction. And around and around we go. A helpful focus here is connecting "loving Neighb*r" with Mercy. This helps us deal with those we would otherwise make invisible. And so a restatement might be, "You shall be merciful with your Neighb*r as you are merciful with yourself." This reestablishes a relationship rather than a rule that is too easily based on whether or not I like my Neighb*r.

James 3:1–12
Proper 19 (24)

Check your eyesight; it may just clean up your mouth.

To see G*D or a likeness of G*D sets loose a blessing.

Now, go ahead; look around. See a likeness of G*D? Feel a blessing moving back and forth, to and from you?

Or did you notice a lackness of G*D? Go ahead; let loose a curse.

Now comes a diagnostic tool for the refrigerator door—a scale with "G*D's Likeness" on one end and "G*D's Lackness" on the other. Note your day's location with a dot and a date. After a week, see if you've clustered more toward "Likeness" or "Lackness". After a month or year of recording, your location should be more definable. After a lifetime, may you find blessing after blessing.

Likeness   Lackness

Day 1 ——————————————————————————————

Day 2 ——————————————————————————————

Day 3 ——————————————————————————————

Day 4 ——————————————————————————————

Day 5 ——————————————————————————————

Day 6 ——————————————————————————————

Day 7 ——————————————————————————————

James 3:13–4:3, 7–8a
Proper 20 (25)

Confession/Assurance
[based on *The Message*]

Where do you think all these appalling wars and quarrels come from?
    Do you think they just happen?
        Think again.

They come about because we want our own way
    and fight for it deep inside ourselves.
We lust for what we don't have
    and are willing to kill to get it.
We want what isn't ours
    and will risk violence to get our hands on it.

You wouldn't think of just asking G*D for it; would you?
    And why not?

Because we know we'd be asking for
    what we have no right to.
We're spoiled children,
    each wanting our own way.

So let G*D's intention work in you.
Yell a loud "No" to the Devil
    and watch the scampering.
Say a quiet "Yes" to God
    and in no time you'll live together.

James 5:13–20
Proper 21 (26)

This passage makes it easy to confuse what it attempts to clarify.

What is not clear is the distinction between "suffering" and "sick". Our tendency is to equate these.

Suffering is affliction from the outside, and this falls into the great prophetic tradition of dealing with evil as a systemic reality that has fallen away from best community practices. Prayer, here, is not a quietism. Note the example given of Elijah and the elements. Why was either drought or rain seen as a result of prayer? It was to address systemic injustice arising as a result of breaking communal care (think Ahab and Jezebel). Prayer is an open-eyed engagement with the principalities and powers. We do prayer an injustice in making it a solitary appeal for a *deus ex machina* to be engaged. Prayer is bold and confrontative. Prayer is not head-bowed petition as much as an in-your-face claim or affirmation.

While being sick can be too easily equated with a lack of faith, it is in contrast to suffering by its internal orientation—something we do to ourselves (even if expressed as hurting another), and its source is from the inside out. Here, we look to models of community that elders and shamans from every culture engage to reset a person's relationships toward meaning and strength. Here, too, prayer is active, is anointing, dancing, purging, etc.

A grand model responding to both suffering and sickness is restorative justice. That which harms others, be it systemic or personal, can be redeemed, restored. It is this restoration that measures prayer.

If we had these two better paralleled, we might better see their connections and distinctions.

A difficulty or possibility in making this connection lies with how we engage blessings. How does song parallel prayer?

Were I advising James on this letter, I would ask for another word or two about prayer and singing. This expansion might unpack deeds entrusted to reset broken relationships/covenants. This extension might clarify faithful work that engages not only past contracts but new potentials arising out of subsequent experiences.

As we continue to learn more about insides and outsides, prayers and psalms, hopes and dreams—lift up your voice.

1 Peter 3:18–22
Conviction [1]

This passage would benefit from an earlier start—either verse 8 or 13; take your pick.

Starting earlier gives a much better context for talking about suffering. This sets suffering in the context of a blessing opportunity when mean and nasty things occur (intended and unintended). Otherwise, we tend to get into theological and Christological debates with much sound and fury. It is to this blessing business we are called, and suffering is, at best, a sub-point under that.

It is the blessing opportunity rather than the opportunity to suffer that allows us to engage with gentleness and reverence rather than grouchy retribution.

Start earlier—the lection committee will never know, and if they do find out, they may change their plan.

With the contextual matter now cared for, we continue to look at the extended passage itself. Who will harm you when you are about doing good?

Well, more than you would think. Everyone with a conscious or unconscious investment in things staying the way they are will do harm, because doing good means changing a situation in which "not good" has been operating.

What, then, makes it worthwhile to proceed apace and against a hurtful status quo? Is an understanding of blessedness sufficient? This is a baptismal, transfigurational blessing that brings repentance for our participation in whatever hurt is happening and a commitment to see a reconciliation, a "trip to Jerusalem", through to its end.

There are apparently two different ways of moving ahead. One way is that of non-violence, proceeding with "gentleness and reverence". The other way is not. This choice is implied in the need to make such an instruction in the first place. Our usual go-to position is to project ourselves as good, rather than to see ourselves as part of the problem. What is needed is deciding to do what we can where we have the power to make a difference.

Imagine spending a whole Lent in a quest for a conscience that recognizes and responds to "good". It will probably take that long, at a minimum, to make a shift that can be seen on your outside and not just felt as an intention on the inside. A blessed Lent to you.

1 Peter 4:1–8
Absent Saturday

It really isn't because Jesus suffered that we pay attention to drawing near to G*D and living appropriately to that relationship. Jesus' suffering points out the importance of so living, come what may. The suffering draws attention to living with G*D, not to the suffering itself, real as it is.

For the sake of our prayers not to give in to temptation (as instructed by Jesus in Gethsemane), we do lead examined lives that are disciplined by that prayer. When so living, we will not do everything that is possible or attractive. Rather, our keys will be loving one another (Mandate Thursday) and, if we can extend to verse 9, being hospitable (Jesus forming a new family while on the cross).

Now that we are a day away from all the emotion, it is possible to look beyond the surface of the cross and the suffering to the fullness of life issues before us. This is a day of evaluation—just sitting with memories of our experiences and reflecting on deeper meanings than spin-doctor, short-cut, religious phrases. It is not all about the suffering; it is all about the living.

2 Peter 3:8–15a
Needed Change [2]

How do you measure waiting? What connection does it have to time? The dictionary says "waiting" comes from older words of "watching" and "awake". Waiting is a directional focus rather than a moment-by-moment experience which, after a while, wears us out to the point when we falter in our waiting.

Waiting, old-school, awakens us to that which is being watched for. It is not a question of how long until it is here, full-blown, but whether we are paying attention to catch a glimpse of it. In this regard, waiting is very similar to hoping for things yet unseen.

It takes a great deal of hope to wait creatively, to wait peacefully.

So, what are you hoping for, waiting for? A new heaven and new earth? For righteousness to be lived, to be at home, rather than wandering as a potential? Either of these will have an effect of closing off, dissolving, our current situation. And either of these will shift our perspective and affect, assisting us to see a new heaven in an old earth and a present righteousness yet able to be drawn from current injustice.

1 John 1:1–2:2
Assured [2]

If we say we have no sin, we deceive ourselves.

If we say
>they are greedy and we are honest,
>they are lazy and we are hard-working, or
>they are alienated and we are authentic,
>>we deceive ourselves.

We are all of this and more.

If we say we don't make distinctions that make us look good and someone else look bad, we deceive ourselves.

The opportunity for deception of self and another is ever-present. Participation in deception is all too tempting.

There used to be a list of different ways of phrasing behavior that said one way would put one in a good light and if phrased differently would cast grave doubts upon another's motivation and action ["I'm careful with money; you're a tightwad"].

At this point, I asked if any readers still had such a list. Two responses came forward:

>I am assertive; you are aggressive.
>I am rigorous (or demanding); you are unreasonable.
>I am flexible; you are lax and undisciplined.
>I am sensitive; you are overly-emotional.
>I am in control of my emotions; you are unfeeling and cold.

>1st person: I am assertive.
>2nd person: You are aggressive.
>3rd person: He/She/It is an asshole.

Ai yay yay—
What is to be done with silly old folk such as ourselves?

1 John 3:1–7
Assured [3]

Definitions are like assumptions in that they set up results. If you can set the definition of sin, you can separate sheep from goats, holiness from profanity. Blame can be found and applied.

Setting definitions of sin also allows you to determine the loopholes and escape to still be a twinkle in G*D's eye. In so doing, a definition can also contain a derivation, so there becomes a circular interior logic that the Bible says "this" and so it is not me kicking you out; it is this external authority that doesn't like the way you "that" in life.

A difficulty with definitions of sin comes when the Bible says, "everyone is loved by G*D and is G*D's child" AND "no one who abides in G*D sins" AND "no one who sins has either seen G*D or known G*D". It becomes necessary to parse out how "being loved" is not the same as "abiding in". Good luck in working your way through this ecclesiological precision drill team without dropping your bayoneted definition.

Just how far have you been able to walk in someone else's definition of sin? Soon you will find where it pinches because your call, gifts, and experiences of G*D are different.

Even more difficult is listening to others report on how your definition pinches them. If they've been walking in your definition of sin and found it wanting, might you not also find it is a bit too tight? To reevaluate our definition of sin is transformative work and thus takes a community to help each of us through our particular stuck places.

We need several definitions of sin that can be applied as needed, rather than one size fits all. Sin is ultimately as mysterious as love or forgiveness.

1 John 3:16–24
Assured [4]

What power does it take to lay down one's life? Does it make a difference if you lay down your life for one of the in-group or for an enemy?

A key question for our capitalistic consumer-oriented culture—can you lay down your life more easily than you can lay down your goods? Or will they have to pry your goods out of your cold, dead hand?

I am always heartened when belief is paired with love. Too often, we separate the two. Do both your belief and your love lead you to multiple versions of laying down your life, laying down your goods, laying down your belief, laying down your preferred worship style, laying down your experience of life, laying down your in-with-G*D?

If you are laying down these important matters, what are you picking up? In some sense, it is the old addiction issue that if you shoo one devil away and do not fill in its place, it will return with seven more addictions, and you'll be worse off than before. What are you adding to the pool of life when you lay your life down?

At the United Methodist 2012 General Conference there was to be a time of "Holy Conferencing". Debate over Rules caused this time to begin late. Gil Rendle prefaced this time with some helpful words about changes in church and culture in the last years that could and should lead us to look again at what it means to be in mission in a world that is asking similar questions but coming up with a whole variety of different responses than our church answers. Time constraints and poor leadership caused the "holy" conferencing opportunities to generally be horrible experiences for LGBTQQIAA people, hearing all manner of lies about their lives.

This passage would have been helpful to review before an intentionally deeper conversation than usual. What does it mean to lay down one's life for another? If Jesus could do it, why can't his followers? It is difficult to integrate truth and action into situations where we feel threatened and compelled to defend our truth against all others. How do we get beyond our feelings that have tied us to G*D in such dogmatic ways? We keep confusing loving another with desiring everyone else to reflect our self-identity.

Without a serious attempt to abide in another and to have that reciprocated, there is no conferencing—whether supposedly "holy" or not.

1 John 4:7–21
Assured [5]

Want G*D to be recognizable within your life?

"Love" another, each other, one another, others.

G*D's love lives in us, and our love lives in G*D.

Now, if only we could figure out what this "love" is.

Is it "bearing fruit"?

Is it "shared understanding"?

Is it "happy, happy, joy, joy"?

Is it "participation in a great congregation"?

Is it "confession"?

Is it "response to being *loved*"?

All of the above and more?
None of the above?

1 John 5:1–6
Assured [6]

> "...whatever is born of God conquers the world.
> And this is the victory that conquers the world, our faith." (NRSV)

John Wesley emphasized that the God in whose image we are created is love. Thus humanity "was what God is"—love....

In Wesley's vision, this love, though properly directed toward God, includes and integrates the love of self, fellow human beings, and all other creatures. As Daniel Day Williams notes, however, the human being is a 'battlefield upon which many loves clash.' Our constitution in love (and, therefore, in the image of God) becomes disintegrated as we become preoccupied with some loves to the exclusion of others and as we turn in on ourselves, or as we love creation more than God. This disintegration of love is what we mean when we use the word 'sin.' So it is that, for Wesley (and, as we shall see, for process theology), sin is ultimately a failure to love. Conversely, what Wesley spoke of as a 'perfection' of love may be understood as the reintegration of love and, in that sense, a vanquishing of sin.

["Process and Sanctification" by Bryan P. Stone in *Thy Nature & Thy Name is Love: Wesleyan and Process Theologies in Dialogue*, p. 71]

Now, what would happen if we were to substitute growth in perfection for conquering? It feels as though conquering tends to "preoccupation with some loves to the exclusion of others." It feels as though the author of 1 John slipped here (preoccupied with getting correct doctrine in somewhere?) and might have more helpfully said, "And this is the victory that perfects the world: our maturing in love."

1 John 5:9–13
Assured [7]

Here is the testimony: God gave us eternal life.

Do you remember the flaming angel guarding the tree of life? All our attempts to return and grab that gift went to naught. We were first intended to live with the gifts of life and knowledge. Then we grabbed for all the gusto we could get and ended up with a portion of the fruit of knowledge.

Not able to live "with" but needing our very own, the little we had was taken from us and well defended.

There is a weak spot in every defense, even a defense of a Tree of Life by an angelic flaming sword. In this case, it was an internal flaw. G*D really did want us to live with eternity and wisdom. Since we weren't able to find a way back in (knowledge is never enough in such situations), G*D, from the inside and behind the angel's back, stole, prometheus-like, the gift and did an end run to continue offering eternity.

It might almost seem that this is enough of a twist on a tale until we figure out this gift of eternity was and is manifest in human lives already; we just didn't get it (it takes more than knowledge to catch eternity in the present).

Enjoy the gift of life. Pass it on. From this experience—believe.

Oops, the official line is believe first.

Might this be a diagnostic tool for identifying which religious/political pole one is on? In a list of equals, does belief (right) or experience (left) come first? Is G*D/Eternity with us right now (left) or is that something for later (right)? Yes, a crude tool. What refinement would you make?

Revelation 1:4b–8
Evaluation Day / Proper 29 (34)

What else can one do in the presence of "is and was and about to arrive" than grin all over yourself? And here we were so preoccupied with our entitlements . . . what is, was, or will be that about?

And then, adding in seven spirits to the recipe, the grin turns to a guffaw.

Now our imagination is freed from the fear of the moment. It sets a larger scene—peace to be transformed into freedom and *vice versa*.

Now you try—understand you are Alpha and Omega. This will help focus you on your gift for this time. See them become your parentheses. All that you have been working on and all that has been working toward you surround you to work together as a lens () clarifying today's task that will complete a partial past and set the groundwork for a better future.

It would be so easy to have this just be about G*D, but this expansive view of G*D is intended to have an effect of expanding you and me. If it is just about glorifying Jesus and G*D, we are most to be pitied.

On a culmination day when thanksgiving in the present might be the case, we are still looking forward. We are instructed to look to the clouds that are notorious for their changeability, and everyone will see a cloud that looks like Jesus, even those who are against him. Good luck with that. Claiming Jesus is like catching a cloud formation and freezing it into place. Even then, take three steps to the left, and it's gone.

More to the point, incarnationally, G*D is with us, already. Any waiting on our part is an excuse to not make the changes available to us to join the healthy of every tradition. With time up for this year, we will give it one more try to see if we can live in the present without a diploma. We have been *in medias res,* and we continue to be in the middle of a story. No artificial final Sunday will change that. Onward to our most realistic of seasons—Advent.

Revelation 21:1–6a
New Year's Day — Honoring Day

Saints are those who see beyond the literalness of this and other passages to be able to translate our various fears and visions of everything good being ours and others getting everything bad we can possibly think of into a new relationship between the hurtful and the hurting.

This is not a time to seek revenge and recompense where the tortured now torture their previous torturers.

---

look and look again
G*D and humans
belong together
one for all
and all toward one
from now onward

how disappointing
each has been to the other
tears have flowed aplenty
tears continue flowing
neither gives up
to call in death

always our disappointments
showed us our distance
mourning and wailing
have become normal
passing away moments
revealing a new fountain

Appendix — Sunday Designations

Past Designation	New Look
Advent	Needed Change
Christmas	Blessed Body
Holy Name of Jesus	Naming Day
New Year's Day	New Year's Day
Epiphany	Guiding Gift
Baptism of the Lord	Beloved
Presentation of the Lord	Old Welcomes New
Transfiguration of the Lord	Mountain Top to Valley
Lent	Conviction
Annunciation of the Lord	Creation's Conception
Ash Wednesday	Self-Recognition Day
Liturgy of the Palms	False Dawn Sunday
Liturgy of the Passion	Premature Fear Sunday
Holy Week	Clarification Week
Maundy Thursday	Courage Thursday
Good Friday	Annihilation Friday
Holy Saturday	Absent Saturday
Easter Vigil	Hopeless Hope Vigil
Easter/ Resurrection of the Lord	Assured
Easter Evening	Opened Heart Evening
Ascension of the Lord	Our Turn to Witness

Pentecost	Energy to Witness
Trinity Sunday	Live Together
Season after Pentecost	Community Practice Propers 3–29
Visitation of Mary to Elizabeth	Elizabeth and Mary Meet
Holy Cross	Relic Day
Thanksgiving	Thanksgiving
All Saints Day	Honoring Day
Reign of Christ/ Christ the King	Evaluation Day

Abbreviations

The following are abbreviations of Bibles referred to and used:

CCB—Christian Community Bible: Catholic Pastoral Edition
CEB—Common English Bible
CEV—Contemporary English Version
IB—The Inclusive Bible: The First Egalitarian Translation
JANT—The Jewish Annotated New Testament
JB—The Jerusalem Bible
JSB—The Jewish Study Bible
KJB—The King James Bible
MSG—The Message
NCB—The New Community Bible
NIB— The New Interpreter's Bible
NJB—The New Jerusalem Bible
NISB—The New Interpreter's Study Bible
NRSV—New Revised Standard Version
REB—The Revised English Bible
SB—The Schocken Bible, Volume 1
SFB—The Spiritual Formation Bible
WSB—The Wesley Study Bible

Unattributed—indicates paraphrase/translation by the author.

About the Author

Wesley White has been partnered/married with Brenda Smith White since 1972. He is father to two: Shai, daughter; Brandon, son; and grandfather to Nathan and Nicholas.

Wesley grew up outside a small town in southern Wisconsin, went to a one-room country school, and graduated from the University of Wisconsin—Whitewater with a degree in Sociology. He served for 2 years in the Peace Corps in the Philippines. After returning to the United States, Wesley graduated with an M.Div. from Garrett-Evangelical Theological Seminary in 1971 and served in ordained ministry for 38 years before retiring. He is also a trained and registered Transitional Intentional Interim Ministry Specialist and has served three congregations in that role.

Wesley has received recognition for work on inclusion from the Wisconsin Commission on the Status and Role of Women and other justice issues through the Perry Saito Award of the Wisconsin United Methodist Federation for Social Action.

His most recent work has been with LovePrevailsUMC.com to remove a false testimony within the church about the incompatibility of LGBTQQIAA persons and Christian teaching.

Production Details

Manuscript: formatted in Apple Pages

Cover: *Abstract Blue Backgrounds Photo*, Silvertiger
     Image Credit: © Silvertiger | Dreamstime.com -
          Abstract Blue Backgrounds Photo
     Design Consultant: Amy DeLong
     Typography: Title is Trebuchet MS

Book Typography: Headings: Helvetica, 11 and 12 points
          Text: Optima, 10.5 point

Book Graphics:
     Page 17: *Love Prevails Logo*
          © Love Prevails | LovePrevailsUMC.com

     Page 125: *Never place a period where God has placed a comma*. Slogan of The United Church of Christ. This presentation designed by Emily of Atlanta on the blog of "My Mom Made That" and available on Pinterest,
     http://www.pinterest.com/pin/403987029044589485/

     Page 390: *Matryoshka Photo*,
     Patruschka Hetterschij – Meppel, Netherlands
     © Patruschka | Dreamstime.com - Matryoshka Photo

     Publisher Logo: designed by Susan Eaton Mendenhall of www.JazzArt.biz for use as a logo for *in medias res*. It represents being in middle of things as a way of life—lifting the past to make way for the future.

     Other illustrations and charts: Wesley White

www.ingramcontent.com/pod-product-compliance
Lightning Source LLC
Chambersburg PA
CBHW031041110426
42740CB00047B/768